RECONSTRUCTING AFRICAN CULTURE HISTORY

BOSTON UNIVERSITY
AFRICAN RESEARCH STUDIES
NUMBER 8

DT
19
.R4

Reconstructing African Culture History

EDITED BY

Creighton Gabel and Norman R. Bennett

BOSTON UNIVERSITY PRESS
Boston, Massachusetts
1967

© Copyright 1967 by the Trustees of Boston University
All rights reserved
Library of Congress Catalog Card Number: 67–25932

Printed in the United States of America

PREFACE

With one exception, the following essays on African culture history represent the results of a symposium held at Northwestern University in November 1962, for the purpose of surveying some of the basic techniques that can be used for exploring Africa's past. Those invited to attend were asked to submit papers far enough in advance to be distributed among the participants. The two-day conference subsequently provided a forum where everyone had an opportunity to further air his views, clarify his impression of the other disciplines, compare outlooks on the subject as a whole, and—hopefully—suggest means of attacking it with maximum effectiveness. A majority of the contributions were later revised for publication with the results of the discussions in mind.

One additional paper, that by Professor Marvin Miracle, was not presented at the symposium but has been included here because of its clear relevance to material discussed in several of the original contributions.

The question posed to each of these specialists was essentially this: What techniques in your field can be applied to the reconstruction of African culture history? Each participant was asked not only to outline the historical possibilities provided by his discipline but also to at least briefly describe its inherent (or practical) shortcomings. The emphasis, therefore, was placed upon techniques of observation and description and upon analytical methods. That some of those present might disagree about specific interpretation of existing facts was taken for granted. In spite of this, there appeared to be remarkable accord concerning general principles. We can always expect differences of opinion, and these do not prohibit us from pausing to examine the methods by which the whole problem of culture-historical reconstruction can be most profitably pursued in an integrated manner; the cardinal premise is that any reliable approach must be an interdisciplinary, or at least multidisciplinary, one. A few of the papers which follow do deal with specific historical questions, but the primary intent nonetheless is to demonstrate the application of certain historical techniques. In most of the papers, methodological considerations constitute the preeminent theme.

One of the facts made clear by the symposium, at least to the editors, was that specialization, essential as it is, has a tendency to foster ignorance; one's own point of view or grasp of any complex problem is tempered by one's misapprehensions or lack of understanding of other disciplines. This ignorance includes not only a lack of comprehension of their techniques but also attitudes about their reliability and scope. This situation is damaging to an area of inquiry, such as African culture history, that demands interdisciplinary investigation; it must be rectified as far as possible if research along these lines it to be significantly improved. One of the major contributions of this symposium was the impetus given the breakdown of these barriers of mutual ignorance and misunderstanding. These hurdles cannot be surmounted without continual interplay between all specialists with a common interest in Africa's past.

There seems little need to stress the importance of Africa's history at this time when most territories on the continent have achieved self-rule. Greater understanding of the indigenous peoples of Africa is no longer purely a matter of academic interest; and to understand them fully is to be aware of past currents and patterns which have set the stage for today. The general bewilderment evoked by African political systems in Europe or America, for example, might be alleviated by some knowledge of African political history, much of which has no direct reference to European colonial rule as it antedates the contact period.

African history has yet to be written for the most part, and it has become perfectly obvious that traditional historical investigation, based on written documents, cannot accomplish the task alone. There are two reasons for this. First, written history in

Africa is severely limited in chronological depth, especially in the interior where history, in the limited sense of the term, covers only the past century or so. In order to extend our time perspective, we must employ methods drawn from other disciplines, such as archaeology, linguistics, ethnology, and the natural sciences. Secondly, written histories and archival materials, although abundant, do not yield fully adequate data for cultural-historical reconstruction. Too many details are ignored, slighted, or treated from a biased viewpoint. These, of course, are shortcomings inherent in historiography, not reasons for discarding the large and important bodies of information it has to offer. But improvement can be obtained through the complementary use of other methods of inquiry which serve to broaden the base line of description and explanation, and this is just as true of disciplines other than history. No single approach to culture history is capable of answering our questions adequately, for none is either reliable enough or all-encompassing. The solution lies in the co-ordinated application of as many of these methods as possible. The use of written documents, therefore, is not displaced but rather augmented by other techniques, and it is these which are emphasized here. Some of them, such as archaeology, linguistics, and oral tradition, have received serious and detailed attention elsewhere. The potential of others, such as botany, physical anthropology, ecology, art, ethnology, and music remains relatively untapped. The last four in particular are often treated from strictly non-historical viewpoints, which may account in part for the lack of well-developed ethnohistorical research in Africa.

In our review of the problems of African culture history, we did not attempt to deal with all the subjects which might have substantial value in this light. Historiography was left out of our considerations, not because we failed to recognize the extent of its worth and applicability but because more has been done along this line already in various history conferences and published African histories and because we felt that a resumé of current anthropological and natural science techniques would be useful to all those concerned with African history. One might add that this survey should be of interest to historians as an adjunct, or series of adjuncts, to their own methodology. Other fields have also been excluded in spite of the real or theoretical contribution they can make in terms of data and concepts. We might well have included a human ecologist, epidemiologist, physical anthropologist (other than a geneticist), zoologist, palynologist, or folklorist, but it was felt that a better-than-average cross section of specialists was represented and that more was to be accomplished by keeping the symposium small. For some of the omitted disciplines, there were no readily available specialists anyway, and our resources permitted us to bring no one from abroad. So we offer our apologies to those whose fields are given little or no attention, assuring them that by so doing we are not overlooking their significance.

We wish to express our appreciation to Professor Paul J. Bohannan, formerly director of Northwestern University's Center for Social Science Research, who supported the idea for a symposium of this kind without reservation and provided financial support for it through the center. The late Melville J. Herskovits, in 1962 director of the Northwestern Program of African Studies, contributed much to our program through his participation as a discussant. We also benefited immensely from the presence and participation of Professor George P. Murdock, whose own ideas on African culture history did much to stimulate the formation of this symposium.

Creighton Gabel
Norman R. Bennett

Boston, Massachusetts
June 1966

CONTENTS

I   **J. D. Clark:** A Record of Early Agriculture and Metallurgy in Africa from Archaeological Sources   1

II   **Herbert S. Lewis:** Ethnology and African Culture History   25

III   **Roger W. Wescott:** African Languages and African Prehistory   45

IV   **Jan Vansina:** The Use of Oral Tradition in African Culture History   55

V   **Alan P. Merriam:** The Use of Music as a Technique of Reconstructing Culture History in Africa   83

VI   **Roy Sieber:** African Art and Culture History   115

VII   **Frank B. Livingstone:** The Origin of the Sickle-Cell Gene   139

VIII   **Edgar Anderson:** The Bearings of Botanical Evidence on African Culture History   167

IX   **Jack R. Harlan:** Biosystematics of Cultivated Plants   181

X   **Marvin P. Miracle:** Murdock's Classification of Tropical African Food Economies   199

Coda   **Creighton Gabel:** Toward an Interdisciplinary Method for African Culture History   227

MAPS

Agricultural Areas and Archaeological Sites	12
Peoples and Languages of the Lower Kasai Area	74
Distribution of African Sorghums	170

TABLES

Chapter IV

Table 1. Population movements of clan sections within the Kuba kingdom, 1600–1965.   65

Chapter X

Table 1. Comparison of the relative importance of major foodstuffs in the diet of selected areas of Nigeria, according to Murdock.   210

Table 2. Comparison of the relative importance of major foodstuffs in the diet of selected areas of Nigeria, according to Nicol's data, 1947–1957.   212

Table 3. Comparison of the relative importance of major foodstuffs in the diets of selected areas of former French Equatorial Africa, according to Murdock.   214

Table 4. Comparison of the relative importance of major foodstuffs in the diets of selected areas of former French Equatorial Africa, according to Bascoulergue and Bergot, 1956–1958.   214

Table 5. Relative contribution of major foods to the diet of five rural families in Ruanda-Urundi, 1956.   216

Table 6. Relative production of the major foodstuffs in circunscrições in the districts of Lourenço Marques and Gaza, Mozambique, 1954–1955.   218

Table 7. Acreages of selected food crops in Uganda, 1917–1959.   220

I

A Record of Early Agriculture
and Metallurgy in Africa
from Archaeological Sources

J. D. Clark
Professor of Anthropology
University of California
Berkeley

The chronology and spread of food production and metallurgy in Africa have been summarized recently in two papers; the little new evidence that should now be added to this information strengthens rather than amends the conclusions previously reached.[1] It is therefore proposed to review here the main sources of evidence on which any reconstruction must be made, to bring up to date the factual information these sources provide, and to indicate where and how further archaeological investigation could best be directed to solve the problem of the origins of food production and metallurgy in sub-Saharan Africa.

It is with essentially archaeological sources that we shall be concerned here, although, of course, when it comes to reconstruction, the modern prehistorian employs a host of other evidence mostly provided by his colleagues in the anthropological and natural sciences.

The Sources and the Problems

The prehistorian is concerned, in the first instance, with the dating of his finds. Therefore he needs to recover them in stratified positions which will indicate the relative relationship of an assemblage of artifacts from any single horizon to both earlier and

1. J. D. Clark, "Africa South of the Sahara," in R. J. Braidwood and G. Willey, *Courses toward Urban Life* (New York: Viking Fund Publ. No. 32, 1962), 1–33; J. D. Clark, "The Spread of Food Production in Sub-Saharan Africa," *Journal of African History*, III:211–228 (1962).

later cultural manifestations. If he is fortunate he may be able to construct an absolute chronology through radiocarbon or other means. Today, therefore, the professional worker is not greatly impressed by the large quantities of surface material collected over the past fifty years and more, which is fairly certain to contain artifacts of more than one cultural stage. Although the prehistorian has various aids to assist him in distinguishing associations in mixed assemblages of this kind, any reconstruction from this type of evidence must remain uncertain until it is supported by systematic excavation.

In Africa, the Pleistocene cultures are more satisfactorily dated and better known than those of later times, mainly because energies have been more systematically directed to recovering and interpreting the evidence from this remarkably rich storehouse of man's biological and early cultural development. The long time scale involved has also made interpretation relatively easier where the material is sealed in stratified units. The student of Neolithic and Metal Age times has all too often had to work with surface material that has to be fitted much more accurately into a considerably shorter time scale. Not infrequently it is impossible to be certain whether an assemblage recovered from, for example, field clearings in a West African rain forest or from the eroded beach of an East African freshwater lake, should be dated 5000 B.C. or 500 A.D. It is true that sites such as those in Aouker and Hodh, where stone hoe blades occur in profusion in country which today is desert, although they imply environmental conditions suitable for agriculture, also postulate an appreciable antiquity.[2] But even such postulations are not the direct evidence that only excavation can produce; indeed, the lack of absolute dating is still the main problem the prehistorian faces, for until it is available correlations remain uncertain.

It seems that some of the earliest manifestations of food production appear in the Sahara, the Sudan and the West African forest zone. It is all the more regrettable, therefore, that most of the material from these areas consists of surface collections. Much

2. R. Vaufrey, "Le néolithique paratumbien: une civilisation agricole primitive du Soudan," *La Revue Scientifique*, III:205–232 (1947).

of it is of extreme interest, but it is impossible to date it accurately or in many cases even approximately. A few key excavations have, however, been carried out in these regions, and they can sometimes be used to provide a relative sequence into which it proves possible occasionally to fit the surface finds.

In tropical Africa, the protohistorian has been much more concerned with excavation, with the result that the relative succession of cultures in post-Pleistocene times in East, Central, and South Africa is fairly well established. However, many of these excavations are in cave sites, which are not the most reliable or likely places in which to find evidence of food-producing cultures which generally imply a regular pattern of open settlements. Cave sites are more easily located, however, especially in a moist tropical environment where the vegetation cover is thick and erosion is at a minimum. Unless there are substantial earthworks or middens, the kind of open settlement associated with slash-and-burn cultivation stands small chance of being discovered. While caves and rock shelters are often attractive sites for hunter-gatherers, they are much less so for peaceful settlements of agriculturalists or stock herders. Where caves have continued in use until later times they may be an indication of unsettled political relations or may have been used for some special technological or ritual activity.[3] Cave sequences do, however, show that in some cases the change from a stone to a metal technology was an abrupt one, suggesting replacement of one population by another. Sometimes a gradual change can be seen, indicating a slow economic transition on the part of the aboriginal population.[4] But, although the relative age is established, few sites can as yet be fitted into an absolute time scale.

The establishment of radiocarbon laboratories should bring this state of affairs to an end. One at least of the three recently opened

3. C. T. Shaw, "Report on Excavations Carried Out in the Cave Known as 'Bosumpra' at Abetifi, Gold Coast Colony," *Proceedings of the Prehistoric Society*, X:1–67 (1944); F. Willett, "The Microlithic Industry from Old Oyo, Western Nigeria," *Actes du IVe Congrès panafricain de Préhistoire et de l'Etude du Quaternaire* (Tervuren, 1962), 261–272.

4. J. Hiernaux, "Le debut de l'Age des Metaux dans la région des grands lacs africains," *ibid.*, 381–390.

—at Dakar, Leopoldville and Salisbury—has started to produce results. Until now it has been by no means easy to have African samples dated at European or American laboratories; but we may expect from here on a regular flow of results for Africa which will revolutionize correlation work. But, although the problem of chronology will be considerably eased in the immediate future, the work of identifying centers of origin and determining rate and direction of spread of populations still has to overcome the problem of sparse regional coverage and the lacunae that exist in the knowledge of some areas. For example, virtually nothing is known of the post-Pleistocene archaeology of the formerly French territories south of the Sahara (other than Chad) of Angola, Mozambique; of large parts of South Africa and Rhodesia, or of the interior of Tanzania. Until work is carried out in these areas to fill in the gaps, we shall be able to learn no more about the origins and distribution of such interesting Metal Age cultures as the Kisalian of the Katanga, the Leopoldian of the Stanley-Pool region or even of the Channelled and Dimple-Based Ware complex. Unfortunately, it seems likely that facilities for working in some of these archaeologically unknown regions will become more difficult rather than easier in the immediate future because of the uncertainty of the political adjustment from colonial to independent rule which is taking place.

Besides the actual imperishable cultural remains preserved on a site, there is information about past populations available from analysis of the prehistoric art that is found in certain parts of the continent. The chief problem here is, of course, that of the association of the drawings on the wall with one or more of the stages of cultural remains in the floor. Such associations and attempts to date the art have been made with varying success, and, generally, although precision is lacking, relative accuracy can be obtained and the information from the artifacts alone can be supplemented by a study of drawings and paintings in the northern Sahara, the Horn, Rhodesia, and South Africa.

Human skeletal remains are an important means of determining the physical ancestors of a prehistoric population. As yet they have been used definitively in Africa in only a few instances.

A Record of Early Agriculture and Metallurgy • 7

The inadequacy of the prehistoric sample and the lack of somatic information about the present-day populations are the chief reasons skeletal remains have been so little used. The identification of Negro, Bush-Hottentot, or Afro-Mediterranean characteristics may often present no difficulty but, when it comes to interpreting the hybridization of these physical stocks, or to determining what represents a "pure" type, the trouble begins. However, some extremely important associations have been established between physical types and culture in certain regions—notably in the Sudan, the Rhodesias, and in the Transvaal and Cape provinces of South Africa.

In cases where middens or at least some depth of occupation materials exist, the archaeologist will sometimes have bone and carbonized vegetable remains preserved that can be analyzed and used to interpret dietary preferences and the subsistence activities of the group. As yet, however, little analysis of this kind has been attempted for protohistoric African cultures. In most cases, a bare list of identified species and genera is given and no attempt made to estimate the relative numbers of the species connected with the different cultural stages, of the proportions of juvenile to adult creatures, or of wild to domesticated forms. All too often not even a faunal list is given—as, for example, at Zimbabwe or Mapungubwe.

Again, there have been but few attempts to reconstruct technological processes from the waste products or to identify sources of origin of stone or metal objects by spectrographic or other means. Knowledge of mining and metallurgical practices is probably the furthest advanced in this respect, but it is based largely upon observed ethnographic practices.

The main field of study and deduction has been centered around the artifacts themselves which, in some cases, are sufficiently specialized or functionally distinct to be used as zone fossils and for correlation purposes. Certain forms of winged arrowheads, axe or adze blades, and pottery wares have been used to good advantage in this way. While they can provide the basis for reconstruction of economic ability and cultural relationships, they yield no evidence of the social grouping. The different Iron Age and Neolithic pottery traditions, for example, can be clearly distinguished; but practically nothing is known of the settlement patterns of the groups who practiced these traditions. Where there are definitely visible boundaries to the settlement this does not usually apply, but even at the Zimbabwe/Monomatapa Culture stone-ruin sites, practically nothing is known of the density or duration of the occupation, of the size and grouping of the family units, or of the organization behind the construction of the buildings. The task of excavating complete settlements is a large one and till now has been beyond the means of the prehistorian in Africa. It is hoped that this difficulty may be largely overcome by the judicious use of the proton magnetometer, which has proved invaluable on later sites in Europe and should now be given a trial in Africa.

So much for the sources and the problems—of which one can see that there are a goodly number. We will now discuss the reconstruction that can be built up legitimately on the basis of the technology and typology of artifact assemblages, using a few radiocarbon dates, a little economic information deduced from midden waste, and, for the earlier part of the post-Pleistocene, some knowledge of the extent of climatic and environmental fluctuations.

The Reconstruction

By the end of the Pleistocene, or shortly after (8000 B.C.), specialized hunter-gather populations are to be found living in more permanent settlements in three kinds of particularly favorable environments. These are the fringes of the equatorial moist forest of the Congo basin (Tshitolian and Lupembo/Tshitolian cultures) and, one may presume, also in West Africa; around the lakes of the Gregory and Albertine Rifts (the Ishango and Kenya Capsian cultures); and on or adjacent to the sea coasts (Matjes River, Taforalt). In the case of the Congo cultures, the staples provided by the plant foods, particularly the oil palm and wild yam, must have gone far toward making the populations independent of the seasonal scarcity of wild foods which always occurred in the savanna. But here, as in the other two habitats, the most important staples were undoubtedly fish and shellfish or, in the case of the strandlooping groups, seafood generally. Until the end of the terminal Pleistocene in Africa, as also in Southwest Asia, fish and seafoods do not appear to have been used to any great extent; only then the advantages of this food source became apparent. It was these Mesolithic populations, now largely sedentary and combining fishing with hunting, who made a Neolithic food-producing culture possible. The favorable climatic conditions that pertained during the Makalian Wet Phase (= Atlantic Alti-Thermal Period, 5500–2500 B.C.), particularly in the Sahara and Mediterranean basin, made possible the spread of this intensified Mesolithic culture in Africa and prepared the way for domestication. During this period the Ethiopian fauna and the Negro peoples spread westwards into the southern Atlas and the Fezzan; Afro-Mediterranean peoples spread southwards to mix in the central Sahara. The site of Early Khartoum shows what these Mesolithic waterside settlements must have been like.[5]

While the environment of the Sahara during the earlier part of the Makalian certainly must have been a favorable one for this Mesolithic form of life, even there the advantages of domestication must have been readily apparent and quickly adopted. The evidence of the spread of crop cultivation and stock raising forms an as yet incomplete but consistent pattern and shows that the earliest signs we have of both practices come from North Africa. South of the Sahara, the earliest dated evidence of food production is considerably later (*ca.* 1000 B.C.).

It should be borne in mind, however, that three separate processes are involved: (1) the cultivation of cereal crops, (2) the cultivation of plant crops, and (3) stockbreeding. While (3) provides the most substantial material evidence for domestication by virtue of the bone debris, (1) only rarely leaves direct evidence in the form of carbonized grains or impressions, or more usually, indirect evidence in the shape of grinding equipment; and (2) may not leave any permanent archaeological evidence at all. Allowing for this, however, direct archaeological interpretation based on equipment and the nature of the settlement points to the replace-

5. A. J. Arkell, *Early Khartoum* (Oxford, 1949).

ment in sub-Saharan Africa of Mesolithic food collecting by food producing only after the breakdown of Neolithic culture in the Sahara, sometime after 2500 B.C.

The reason for this is to be found in the extreme richness of the tropical environment. Nowhere else in the world is there evidence of an abundance of fauna as great as that which existed in Africa. This abundance provided the Mesolithic hunter with an unlimited source of meat; indeed even the Neolithic herdsman of the Sahara made considerable use of wild game to supplement his domesticated meat supply, as can be seen in the rock art. Vegetable foods also, especially in the higher rainfall zones, provided a regular source of food all year around. On the whole, therefore, it was much easier to live off these unlimited resources and to move camp as the seasons demanded than to rely on the uncertain yields a tropical environment held out to the Neolithic farmer. Moreover, it is time and again borne out, both by historical record and direct observation, that early Iron Age populations, whose equipment was a good deal more efficient than that of the Neolithic peoples, also continued to make extensive use of wild food sources. They continued to practice regular transhumance, and an abundance of wild as well as domesticated animal remains are found in the middens of their settlements. In my opinion, these factors are the clue to the spread of food production in sub-Saharan Africa.

The earliest dated evidence of the cultivation of cereals is from the Fayum A Neolithic culture at about 4500 B.C. These populations lived in open villages of flimsy dwellings, grew wheat and barley, and probably had domestic sheep, goats, and cattle. Certain artifact forms suggest cultural connections with Southwest Asia, implying that domestication came from that region, wheat and barley had already been cultivated there for some 2,000 years before their first known appearance in Africa. The Fayum dates are considered by some prehistorians—notably Caton Thompson and Arkell—to be too late, and 5500 B.C. is thought to be a more likely date for the first appearance of agriculture in northern Africa. The samples dated for Fayum A had been lying in a museum for several years and may well have been contaminated; the same may also be true of the Merimde samples. Indeed a date of 5050 B.C. for the earliest Neolithic stage at Haua Fteah in Cyrenaica also suggests that the Fayum A date is too young.[6] Fayum A and B (a derivative of the A stage) influences and tool forms made themselves felt in the eastern oases, in Cyrenaica, and in the Sirtican Gulf at the same time as they appeared in Egypt;[7] the circumstantial evidence for incipient pastoralism in North Africa by the middle of the fifth millennium B.C. and for the full pastoral life by the fourth millennium B.C. is good.[8]

Fayum B forms probably made their appearance in the southern Sahara during the fourth millennium B.C., at about the same time as they appeared at the Neolithic sites of Shaheinab and Khartoum (ca. 3200 B.C.).[9] Here again, Arkell believes that the shallow depth of the deposit has resulted in contamination of the carbon sample and that the site is in fact appreciably older. No direct evidence for crop cultivation exists at any of these sites, but quernstones and the distribution of the bifacial and serrated sickle blade may be indicative of the cultivation of wheat and barley in the Sahara oases and northern Africa generally where the environment was favorable. The early Neolithic people of the Upper Nile and Sahara were certainly pastoralists, however, breeding goats and sheep, judging by the Shaheinab and rock art evidence. It may, in fact, be considered that, except in some of the oases, the Sahara generally favored the pastoral rather than the agricultural way of life.

Some further substantiation for the earlier dating of the Fayum Neolithic comes also from two carbon dates for earlier Neolithic stages of culture in the northern Sahara which give dates in the

6. J. C. Vogel and H. T. Waterbolk, "Groningen Radiocarbon Dates IV," *Radiocarbon*, V:171 (1963).
7. C. B. M. McBurney, *The Stone Age of Northern Africa* (Harmondsworth, 1960), 237.
8. H. J. Hugot, "Radiocarbon Dates for the Sahara Neolithic," *Missions Berliet-Ténéré-Tchad* (Paris, 1961).
9. A. J. Arkell, *Es Shaheinab* (Oxford, 1953).

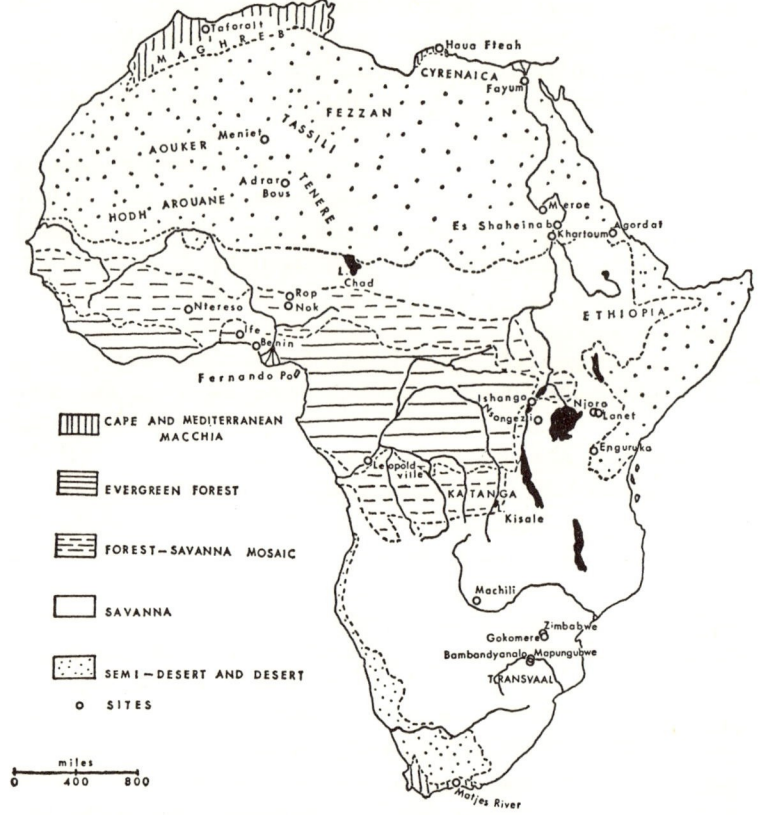

Agricultural Areas and Archaeological Sites

middle of the sixth millenium B.C. One of these was associated with the interment of a Negro child.[10] Dates for the later stages of the Sahara Neolithic, considered contemporary with the art of the pastoral people in Hoggar and Tassili, fall between the middle and the end of the fourth millennium B.C. These dates come from the Sefar Shelter (Tassili Neolithic)—3079 B.C. ± 150 years; the Adrar Bous Site 3 (Ténéré Neolithic)—3180 B.C. ±

10. F. Mori and A. Ascenzi, "La mummia infantile di Uan Muhaggiag: osservazioni antropologiche," *Revista di Antropologia*, XLVI:125–148 (1959).

300 years; and Meniet (Neolithic of Sudanese tradition)—3450 B.C. ± 150 years.[11]

The domestic sheep or goat was certainly established in Cyrenaica (Haua Fteah) about 4800 B.C., but there is no evidence that this was an indigenous domesticate. Neither does the Haua Fteah evidence support the possibility of cattle domestication from one of the North African indigenous forms (*Bos primigenius; B. ibericus*); the dates from the Sahara sites with cattle paintings do suggest that domestic cattle were present in northern Africa by the beginning of the fourth millennium B.C.[12]

As one proceeds farther west and south from the Nile, the Neolithic cultures of northern Africa retain more and more of their Mesolithic character, though incorporating numerous Neolithic projectile points and axe forms. While this does not necessarily mean that these peoples had not reached a fully pastoral stage, their equipment emphasizes the continued and major importance of hunting to the community, just as the importance of fishing is indicated by the presence of bone harpoons and spear points in association with the remains of fish, hippo, and crocodile around now dry lakes, pans, and river courses in the central and southern Sahara. The available radio-carbon dates suggest that the Sahara Neolithic reached its peak in both the northern and southern regions between 3500 and 3000 B.C. One of the significant features of Saharan Neolithic culture was its mobility and general cohesion. When statistical analysis of the assemblages is undertaken this will become even more apparent. We can broadly distinguish an eastern and a western variant with, perhaps, a Maghrebian one also; but the homogeneity of the complex from one end of the Sahara to the other is apparent. This can be seen, for example, in the vast distance over which the Dotted Wavy Line and Cardial pottery are distributed.[13]

11. H. J. Hugot, *Recherches préhistoriques dans l'Ahaggar nordoccidental, 1950–1957* (Paris: Institut français des Sciences humaines en Algerie, 1963).
12. E. S. Higgs, "A Metrical Analysis of Some Prehistoric Domesticated Animal Bones from Cyrenaican Libya," *Man*, LXII:119–122 (1962).
13. A. J. Arkell, "The Distribution in Central Africa of an Early Neolithic Ware." *Actes du IVe Congrès panafricain de Préhistoire et de l'Etude du Quaternaire*, 283–285.

Pastoralism was of great economic importance in the northern Sahara, though possibly less so the farther south one goes. The increasing dessication of the land after the middle of the third millennium, hastened no doubt by overgrazing and indiscriminate cutting of bush, caused a migration of pastoralists out of the desert to the north and south. It would seem most likely that it was sometime after 2000 B.C. that cattle herders entered the Horn. The rock art clearly indicates that the movement was from the north or northeast southwards and not the other way around; the content of the lithic industries shows unquestionable connections with the Sahara rather than with southern Arabia.[14]

Regular contact between the Saharan populations and peoples living in the Sudan and, later, with those in the rain forest zones, must have encouraged experimentation with potential cereal and plant domesticates in these regions, perhaps from the beginning of the sixth millennium onwards, though no dated finds are known before the first millennium B.C.

The cultivated cereal crops of the Sahara oases were wheat, barley, sorghum, millet, and maize. Wheat and barley were the staples mostly north of the tropic while sorghum and millet became increasingly common to the south. The first two crops are associated with the early Neolithic cultures of northeast Africa, and it is certain that they were cultivated in the Sahara where the habitat was favorable during the Neolithic. Since, however, they are winter rainfall crops they do not do well in summer rainfall areas unless under irrigation or in the temperate high grasslands of Ethiopia. Effective cultivation in the Sudanic belt south of the Sahara must, therefore, have been dependent upon local domesticates; and it is necessary to suppose a period of experimentation with local species before productively efficient local cereals were evolved. It is possible, indeed probable, that sorghum and millet occurred wild in the southern Saharan oases and so would have come under observation earlier than some other species. By 2000 B.C., therefore, when the increasing dessication of the Sahara brought some of the population south, these may

14. J. D. Clark, *The Prehistoric Cultures of the Horn of Africa* (Cambridge, 1954), 242, 254–259, 277–282.

already have been serving as a subsidiary crop for some of the eastern groups in West Africa. When or how this experimental period began is unknown. In view of the distribution of the crops themselves it would at present seem very probable that such indigenous sub-Saharan domesticates as guinea rice, fonio, tef, and ensete were successfully cultivated only after intensive experiment. These crops are very restricted as to the regions where they are grown and occur wild; and the dispersal of the southern Sahara populations no doubt resulted in the necessity for some of them to look for summer rainfall substitutes for their traditional crops of barley and wheat.

The Nok Figurine Culture north of the Niger-Benue confluence was thought to date to the period from *ca.* 500 B.C. to *ca.* 200 A.D. with an absolute beginning date of 900 B.C.[15] The first settlement site has now been found at Taruga. Here characteristic pottery figurine fragments are associated with iron slag, shards, quartz hammerstones, and red ochre. The site has given a date of 2230 B.P. ± 120 years or 266 B.C.[16] The further association, in the alluvial sites, of such items with polished stone axes and adzes as well as smelted tin objects, shows that stone tools continued for a time to be used for the same purposes contemporaneously with metal ones. The fluted pumpkin, the oil palm, and *Canarium schweinfurthii* were food sources, and it may be assumed that other crops were grown, including perhaps sorghum. This culture may be considered primarily autochthonous though it made good use of outside contacts, and it must have formed an integral part of the later hoe culture complex that occupied the Sudan zone and portions of what is now the Sahel zone of West Africa. This West African complex, as it may be called, is known to stretch from Guinea as far as western Ethiopa and to include much of the high plateau west of the Abyssinian Rift. Its northern and southern limits are as yet unknown.

The association of this complex with the Negro physical stock

15. B. Fagg, "The Nok Terra-cottas in West African Art History," *Actes du IVe Congrès panafricain de Préhistoire et de l'Etude du Quaternaire*, 445–450.
16. Personal communication from Bernard Fagg.

is attested to in sites in the southern Sahara and at Nok. Ife and Benin have been shown to derive significant features of their art from Nok, and it is generally assumed that the classic style at Ife began somewhat before the late fourteenth century A.D. It is presumed that this West African complex flourished sometime between 2000 B.C. and 500 A.D. The earlier stages may well have been fully Neolithic, but the later era belongs in the early Iron Age even though in some places stone was used along with metal until very late. Effective cultivation in the rain forest zone itself, however, is unlikely on any large scale before the invention of iron tools and would only have become really efficient after the distribution of the Asian and American food plants. These forest cultures present a number of local variations.[17] An earlier Neolithic stage without pottery has been recognized in Ghana and Nigeria also (Rop), though it is more likely that the latter culture should be classified as Mesolithic rather than Neolithic. Late Mesolithic cultures of this kind were fairly widespread in Guinea, Ghana, and Nigeria, and their contemporaneity with the Neolithic until well into the present era is probable. Of particular interest is the site of Ntereso on the White Volta. Here a local Mesolithic/Neolithic fishing community, living in permanent dwellings, was later introduced to iron by immigrants, perhaps from Arouane in the Sahara.[18]

The East African Neolithic complex is completely distinct from what we have just been considering, and it would seem to be derived more directly from the Nile Valley. It is very imperfectly known but will probably be found to cover much of the northern and eastern high plateau in Abyssinia, Eritrea, and the East African highlands. Its introduction somewhere in the third millennium B.C. and its spread may similarly be associated with the same general movement which followed the dessication of the Sahara. The Jebel Korkan site near Agordat in Eritrea contains

17. O. Davies, "Neolithic Cultures of Ghana," *Actes du IVe Congrès panafricain de Préhistoire et de l'Etude du Quaternaire*, 291–302.
18. O. Davies, "Archaeological Exploration in the Volta Basin," *Bulletin of the Ghana Geographical Society*, Volta Basin Research Project Publication No. 8., 28–33 (1964).

shards similar to late C-group pottery in Lower Nubia as well as two-lugged stone axes reminiscent of seventeenth dynasty metal axes, suggesting a date near the beginning of the third millennium.[19] The Deir el Bahari bas reliefs show that Afro-Mediterranean and Negroid farming peoples with cattle were present in the Horn by the second millennium B.C. That the East African Neolithic complex was established in Kenya by 1000 B.C. is shown by the date from the Njoro River Cave; that it continued until much later times (sixteenth century A.D.) is indicated by the Lanet site.[20] This eastern complex appears to have been confined more to the high grassland country east of the Gregory Rift and while it remained dependent upon lithic equipment to have stretched no father south than northern Tanganyika (Ngorongoro).

The only other regions laying claim to a Neolithic food-producing way of life are the northeastern and western parts of the Congo Basin. As yet, however, no settlement has been excavated so that it is uncertain whether, although the way of life may have been that of Neolithic farmers, these people were also conversant (as were the Nok population) with the manufacture of iron tools, even if they did not themselves possess the ability to make them. The middle occupation layer of a Neolithic site on Fernando Po has recently been dated 550 A.D., thus confirming the overlap of Neolithic and metal-using economies.[21]

In the rest of sub-Saharan Africa, the spread of food production was the direct result of population migration into the subcontinent near the beginning of the Christian era. The history of domestication and metallurgy are here inextricably linked, and there can be little doubt that the superiority of the new economy in a tropical environment was due to the possession of efficient weapons and tools of iron, in particular the spear and the axe. There is no evidence for a true Bronze Age in Africa

19. A. J. Arkell, "Four Occupation Sites at Agordat," *Kush*, II:33–62 (1954).
20. M. Posnansky, "The Neolithic Cultures of East Africa," *Actes du IVᵉ Congrès panafricain de Préhistoire et de l'Etude du Quaternaire*, 273–282.
21. Personal communication from J. Sabater Pí.

outside the Nile Valley and perhaps Morocco and, when metallurgy was introduced south of the Sahara, the techniques employed in the manufacture of copper objects were those adapted from ironworking. This knowledge is believed to have spread either from Meroë sometime between 700 B.C. and 300 A.D. or across the Sahara from the north along the trade routes marked by the chariot pictographs, or, more likely, from both directions.[22] It may have reached Nok by 500 B.C. The initial movements of food producers into southern Africa that began to take place sometime shortly after that date in the first few centuries of the present era may well have been the result of this vastly superior technology. It was also, however, the time of greatest activity in the Indian Ocean, and the movements that are postulated as having taken place from Malaysia to Madagascar and the East African coast may well have been another contributory cause, through the introduction of Asiatic forest food plants.[23]

It is not known how many distinct and migrating ethnic groups moved into the subcontinent from the north at this time. One of the main ones would, however, seem to have been the bearers of the Dimple-Based/Channelled-Ware tradition who were present in the Zambezi Basin in 100 A.D. (Machili).[24] A closely associated culture (Gokomere Culture) had ceased to occupy the Zimbabwe Acropolis by 300 A.D.[25] These people lived in open villages, worked iron, and obtained a very few imported glass trade beads.[26] Ironworking Channelled-Ware people were in occupation of the Kalambo Basin at the southwestern end of Lake

22. R. Mauny, "Histoire des metaux en Afrique occidentale," *Bulletin de l'Institut français d'Afrique noire*, XIV:546–595 (1952).
23. W. Kirk, "The Northwest Monsoon and Some Aspects of African History," *Journal of African History*, III:263–268 (1962).
24. J. D. Clark and B. Fagan, "Charcoals, Sands and Channel Decorated Pottery from Northern Rhodesia," *American Anthropologist*, 67:354–371 (1965).
25. K. R. Robinson, "Excavations on the Acropolis Hill," in R. Summers, K. R. Robinson, and A. Whitty, *Zimbabwe Excavations, 1958* (Occasional Papers of the National Museums of Southern Rhodesia, 3, no. 32A, Bulawayo, 1961), 159–192.
26. K. R. Robinson, "An Early Iron Age Site from the Chibi District, Southern Rhodesia," *South African Archaeological Bulletin*, XVI:75–102 (1961).

Tanganyika by 550 A.D. but there is no evidence for any imported trade goods. Evidence for metallurgy is firmly established also for the Dimple-Based pottery complex in Rwanda, Burundi, and Uganda where a date of *ca.* 1000 A.D. was obtained for this ware at Nsongezi. The distribution of this complex points to a migration route down the western section of the Rift Valley ridge country. These high grasslands bordering the montane forests would seem to have been populated by cultivators and stockbreeders fairly soon after 1 A.D. whereas other regions, such as the Kenya and northern Tanganyikan highlands, were bypassed and retained their Neolithic way of life for nearly a millennium longer. It is probable that the Iron Age immigrants who destroyed the late Gumban Lanet settlement were Bantu. However, the persistence of a modified form of Stone Bowl Culture in northern Tanganyika, where it is associated with dams, wells, and rain ponds in a metal using context, may perhaps be related to the pastoral economy of the so-called half-Hamites preserved there today.[27] The initial movements by cultivators of the western complex into the eastern sphere may also have been indirectly responsible for the Afro-Mediterranean elements in South-West Africa and the introduction there of historic Hottentot culture.[28]

Therefore, it would seem to be, on the one hand, the woodland savanna and the fringes of the moist and montane forests and, on the other, the dry as well as the high grasslands that were first occupied by the early Iron Age peoples. Almost certainly the latter habitats would have been those favored by cattle owners since they are mostly tsetse free, while at the same time providing adequate grazing and water. The distribution of tsetse must have been one of the main factors influencing the distribution of the predominantly pastoral populations. The possibility should, therefore, be considered that a contraction of the fly belts in northern equatoria could have been one of the main factors contributing to the dispersal of the early Iron Age (Bantu-speaking?) peoples

27. N. Chittick, in discussion on Posnansky, "Neolithic Cultures of East Africa."
28. J. D. Clark, "Stone Vessels from Northern Rhodesia," *Man,* LXIV: 69–73 (1964).

from the Sudanic zone into the subcontinent in the early years of the Christian era. A drier climate is inferred for the period 1–400 A.D., which would encourage movement into previously unfavorable country.[29] The only cattle that appear to be resistant to *nagana* are the pygmy *Brachyceros* cattle of the West African rain forest region. If the tentative chronology is approximately correct it would, therefore, seem as if this immunity may have been acquired over a period of some 2500 years after ±500 B.C. Moreover, the wetter climate of the Nakuran Wet Phase, (±500–1 B.C.) when the tsetse belts would have expanded, may have been another factor restricting the spread of pastoral groups into the subcontinent.

The fact that the dates of the Channelled-Ware Culture in the south are earlier than those for the Dimple-Based pottery in East Africa may or may not be significant. We know from the Rhodesian sites that this complex had a very long history (from about 1 to 1100 A.D.), and it is probable that the Nsongezi date represents one of the closing stages of this culture in Uganda. However, the possibility must be considered that ironworking may also have been introduced into southeast Africa independently as a result of the Malaysian migrations across the Indian ocean. Early Arab accounts[30] of this part of the African coast make reference to iron as well as gold being among the chief exports, and it is also not impossible—as similarities in material culture between the later Indus civilization sites and the Iron Age A and B cultures of Rhodesia show—that there may have been contacts also with the west coast of India at this time.[31]

Quite unconnected with the Dimple-Based/Channelled-Ware complex was another that may have moved down into the Congo basin from the Cameroons or perhaps Ubangi. The earlier stages of the complex are as yet unknown but the pre-Luba Kisalian

29. Clark and Fagan, "Charcoal, Sands and Channel Decorated Pottery," 354–371.
30. R. Dozy and M. J. de Goeje, *Description de l'Afrique et de l'Espagne par Edrisi* (Leyden, 1866).
31. S. R. Rao, "Maturity and Decline of the Indus Valley Civilization: Religion and Industry Revealed in Excavation at Lothal, Part II," *Illustrated London News*, March 11, 1961, Archaeological Section No. 2047, 387–389.

culture of the eighth and ninth centuries in the eastern Katanga must have been derived from such a source, and the Leopoldian pottery ware from Stanley-Pool probably represents another expression of the same ancestry.[32] That these people were Bantu-speaking there can also be no doubt. The Congo Basin, outside the rain forest proper, must have been especially attractive to village cultivators and, although it was impossible to keep cattle in much of it because of the tsetse fly, any possible protein deficiency was more than compensated for by the supply of fish. Recent dates from sites in Angola indicate that village farming communities were settled here also by the eighth century A.D.[33] and, as we have seen, it would seem that earlier Bantu- and Semi-Bantu-speaking populations were already present in much of the savanna and forest zone of tropical Africa by the end of the first millennium A.D.

That village farming and metallurgy were first introduced into sub-Saharan Africa as a result of diffusion and population movement seems fairly certain. The indigenous cereal crops under cultivation in southern Africa today—sorghum, bulrush and finger millet—are derived from the eastern Sudan zone, so it is probable that this area made the greatest contribution to the spread of food production in the south. It must, however, be remembered that there is good reason for suggesting, as I have done elsewhere, that the indigenous Mesolithic populations were sometimes quick to effect the change from a collecting to a producing economy. This changeover took place as a result either of culture contact or direct coercion, but which was the more important is not yet known. It seems certain, however, that at least some of the present populations of the savanna zone of sub-Saharan Africa are, in varying degrees, the direct descendants of the Mesolithic populations of these regions.[34]

32. J. Nenquin, "Notes on Some Early Pottery Cultures in Northern Katanga," *Journal of African History,* IV:19–32 (1963).
33. M. Stuiver, E. S. Deevey and I. Rouse, "Yale Natural Radiocarbon Measurements III," *Radiocarbon,* V:337 (1963); R. Berger, G. J. Fergusson and W. F. Libby, "U.C.L.A. Radiocarbon dates IV," *Radiocarbon,* VI (forthcoming).
34. J. D. Clark, "Prehistoric Origins of African Culture," *Journal of African History,* V:161–183 (1964).

Some indication of where and to what extent the indigenous populations were able to become successful stockbreeders and cultivators may be learned from a study of the skeletal remains, though as yet significant examples exist in only a very few cases. In Southern Rhodesia, the earlier Iron Age cultures, whose traditions are sometimes preserved in present-day tribal affinities, were associated with peoples who were physically predominantly of Bush-Hottentot stock. The inhabitants of Bambandyanalo in the northern Transvaal are the best example of a Bush-Hottentot or Khoisan stock which had made a successful adaptation from hunting to farming by the twelfth century.[35] The makers of the Gokomere and Channelled-Ware cultures in Zambia and Rhodesia are as yet unknown though a child's burial at Gokomere is reported as "non-Bantu."[36] In Zambia and northern Tanzania it would seem that the same physical type belongs with some at least of the earlier cultures, but in Zambia there is certainly an increasing proportion of Negroid characteristics. So far as southern Africa as a whole is concerned, therefore, the evidence suggests that true immigrant populations are likely in the first instance to have been small. There is skeletal evidence that both the Negro and Afro-Mediterranean stocks were represented in these immigrant groups. Negroid traits are likely to have been present in equatoria from the terminal Pleistocene but they do not appear to have become dominant in the populations of southeastern Africa or of East Africa east of the Gregory Rift until the fifteenth or sixteenth centuries. The record of these later movements is much better known and can be found in the works of Posnansky, Hiernaux and Maquet, Vansina, Mortelmans, Summers, Robinson, Mason, and others.[37] Usually associated with these later movements were im-

35. A. Galloway, *The Skeletal Remains of Bambandyanalo* (Johannesburg, 1959); G. A. Gardner, *Mapungubwe*, Vol. II (Pretoria, 1963); B. Fagan, "The Greefswald Sequence," *Journal of African History*, V:337–361 (1965).
36. *Ibid.*, 351.
37. M. Posnansky, "Pottery Types from Archaeological Sites in East Africa," *Journal of African History*, II:177–198 (1961); M. Posnansky, "Some Archaeological Aspects of the Ethnohistory of Uganda," *Actes du IV⁰ Congrès panafricain de Préhistoire et de l'Etude du Quaternaire*, 375–380; J. Hiernaux and E. Maquet, "Cultures préhistoriques de l'âge des

proved metalworking techniques and strong cultural, political, and religious organization which, as Zimbabwe, Mapungubwe, and Enguruka illustrate, came as near to urban communities as village farming and subsistence patterns permitted.

It is apparent from this brief review that there are many lacunae and many uncertainties in the record; but these could be greatly reduced by a comparatively few systematic investigations. Other settlements of Fayum A type need to be excavated and precisely dated, and further excavations should be carried out at Early Khartoum and Es Shaheinab essentially for the purpose of verifying the dates. There are many occupation sites in the northern Sahara associated with rock art but up to now only four or five of these have been excavated and published.[38] One or more of the lakeside occupation sites in the southern Sahara in Ténéré or Chad, that at Adrar Bous for example where much charcoal exists for dating, should be systematically excavated. While we have fairly satisfactory stratigraphic records and excavations for the West African rain forest and Guinea forest zones, we have as yet no satisfactory absolute dates (other than for Nok) and neither can we date the hoe cultivation sites in the Sahel zone. Virtually nothing is known of the prehistory of the southern Sudan, which is likely to be most critical for an understanding of the origin and development of sub-Saharan food production and metallurgy. The same is true of Abyssinia and Eritrea and, in view of the importance attached to the high plateau country by Vavilov for the origin of barley and pea crops in Africa, it is essential that proper investigations be made there also. Sites of the eastern complex are already known, and it is certain that others suitable for

---

metaux au Ruanda Urundi et au Kivu, Congo Belge," *Academie royal des sciences d'outre mer* (New Series), LX:1–102 (1960); J. Vansina, "Recovering the Oral History of the Bakuba, II: Results," *Journal of African History*, I:257–270 (1960); G. Mortelmans, "Archéologie des grottes Dimba et Ngovo (région de Thysville, Bas-Congo)," *Actes du IVe Congrès panafricain de Préhistoire et de l'Etude du Quaternaire*, 407–426; R. F. H. Summers, "The Southern Rhodesian Iron Age," *Journal of African History*, II:1–13 (1961); K. R. Robinson, *Khami Ruins* (Cambridge, 1959); R. J. Mason, *Prehistory of the Transvaal* (Johannesburg, 1962), 372–438.

38. Hugot, *Recherches préhistoriques dans l'Ahaggar;* Mori and Ascenzi, "La mummia infantile di Uan Muhaggiag."

excavation must exist in the western or hoe complex zone of the Abyssinian plateau.

This record of the lacunae could be continued almost indefinitely but those mentioned are among the most important in the interior of the continent. Attention should also be given, however, to the coastal sites which may no more than middens along the shore of some natural harbor or landing which, like the "markets" referred to in the *Periplus of the Erythraean Sea* were the meeting places of Black African, Mediterranean, and Indian Ocean cultures. Neolithic and Iron Age studies in sub-Saharan Africa are now being pushed forward in a most encouraging manner, and we may hope that the next ten years will solve many of the problems that are still with us at the time of writing this review.

II

Ethnology and Culture History

Herbert S. Lewis
Assistant Professor of Anthropology
University of Wisconsin

This paper is not an attempt to present a series of methodological principles to be used in the reconstruction of African culture history. The fullest exposition of ethnohistorical techniques acceptable to American-trained anthropologists, those of Edward Sapir, is readily available.[1] Kroeber, Wissler, Steward, Dixon, and others have dealt at length with the possibilities and methods of reconstructing culture history through the analysis of cultural distributions.[2] Although they were not often concerned with African history, their discussions are as applicable to Africa as to the New World and Eurasia. Rather than a recapitulation of the principles and arguments of these men, this paper is intended primarily as a critical review of a number of assumptions and propositions common in African historical writing which, in the author's opinion, ignore several important lessons ethnology has learned in the past hundred years. More positively, it is hoped that some of the critiques presented will also suggest alternate interpretations and possibilities. In particular, we wish to emphasize the idea that comparative ethnology has an important role to play in suggesting

1. E. Sapir, *Time Perspective in Aboriginal American Culture: A Study in Method* (Ottawa, Geological Survey, Dept. of Mines, Memoir 90, 1916).
2. A. L. Kroeber, "The Culture-area and Age-area Concepts of Clark Wissler," in S. A. Rice (ed.), *Methods in Social Science* (Chicago, 1931); A. L. Kroeber, *Anthropology* (New York, 1948), 538–571; A. L. Kroeber, *The Nature of Culture* (Chicago, 1952); C. Wissler, *The American Indian* (New York, 1917); J. Steward, "Diffusion and Independent Invention," *American Anthropologist*, XXXI:491–495 (1929); R. B. Dixon, *The Building of Cultures* (New York, 1928).

which cultural processes are most likely or unlikely to have occurred in the past.

Historical Inferences from Cultural Distributions

The geographical distribution of culture traits and complexes is probably the most important basis for classifying peoples and regions, and it forms the foundation for much historical interpretation. Distributional data have been basic to the speculations of historically oriented anthropologists in the United States, Germany, Austria, and elsewhere. All-important as these data are, however, there are as yet few methods for dealing with them which, in the absence of other types of evidence, can be certain to yield trustworthy answers to basic problems. Without corroboration from other lines of investigation, there are no sure ways of telling whether an item of culture shared by two groups is shared because of diffusion, common origin and subsequent migration, or parallel and independent development. If there are no indications from other sources, it may be impossible to determine the direction of transmission of a trait or to get any indication of time depth.

The writers of the German and Austrian Kulturhistorische Schule have long maintained that there exist clear-cut methods for unraveling historical relations, cultural origins, and even chronological sequences by ethnographic distributions alone.[3] American-trained anthropologists have generally rejected both their specific reconstructions of culture history and their methodological claims. While agreeing with Graebner's principles of "quality" (the probability that two traits found in different areas are historically related if they show resemblances in both form and function that are not simply in the nature of the phenomenon) and "quantity" (that the greater the number of such qualitative resemblances between two areas, the higher the probability of a historical connection), most Americans do not agree with the conceptions about the processes of culture and history which underlie the rest of the Kulturkreislehre methodology and its application.

3. F. Graebner, *Methode der Ethnologie* (Heidelberg, 1911); W. Schmidt, *The Culture Historical Method of Ethnology* (New York, 1939).

The attitude of such Americanists as Sapir, Kroeber, and Spier (applied to Africa by Murdock[4]) has been that distributional data can be of great value when used with caution, an awareness of the hazards involved, and an eye to ethnographically-observed cultural processes. Inferences as to relative age and the direction and nature of cultural transmission may be drawn from investigation of the geographical dispersal of traits and complexes. Sapir has suggested ways to introduce time depth into the study of culture by studying traits in their larger cultural and geographical settings.[5] The probability of a reconstruction can be increased by consideration of lines of communication and geographical barriers. Age-area principles and inferences from split distributions may also be applied with care. But these are only rules of thumb; none are based on relatively stable and irreversible principles as are stratigraphic or chemical dating methods in archaeology or glottochronology and phonological reconstruction in linguistics. If reservation is always required in the acceptance of a radiocarbon date, the problem is just that much greater with respect to inferences derived from distributions alone. (Of course, when distributional data are combined with archaeological and linguistic evidence, they give us much stronger bases for our reconstructions.) Each situation, each distribution, must be worked out as a problem in its own right—not as part of a scheme.

A great deal of historical reconstruction done in Africa to date, while ostensibly resting upon distributional data, has ignored the implications of those data in order to mold them to preconceived formulations. For example, whereas "divine monarchies" are found in Africa across a five-thousand-mile band west to east and three thousand miles north to south, and although few, if any, of the characteristic traits of African sacral kingship are found in the Near East, writers such as Irstam, Schilde, and Baumann, and many others, do not hesitate to derive this complex from Southwest Asia.[6] The canons of distributional analysis certainly de-

---

4. G. P. Murdock, *Africa: Its Peoples and their Culture History* (New York, 1959).
5. Sapir, *Time Perspective*, 13–25.
6. Cited in T. Irstam, *The King of Ganda* (Stockholm, 1944), 191–193.

mand that such a wide distribution of a distinctive complex be seen as indicative of great age and elaboration *in situ* (within Africa). A distributional analysis must consider the "total record of occurrence of a trait" or complex, neither ignoring some occurrences nor a priori weighting others more heavily.[7]

Ethnology and Linguistics

Although ethnographic data alone are limited in the extent to which they can answer vital questions about the direction or manner of transmission of a culture trait or complex, a combination of both ethnographic and linguistic evidence can greatly increase the probability of a given reconstruction. On the one hand, we may focus our attention upon individual words connected with particular traits. On the other, we can get important evidence from the analysis of linguistic relationships between whole languages.

Since culture elements are all named, it is frequently possible, when confronted with a trait found in two societies, to determine whether borrowing has occurred and in which direction the trait traveled. Greenberg, in a study of Hausa and Kanuri culture words, has demonstrated the usefulness of this approach.[8] By comparing the sound systems and grammars of the two languages, and comparing them still further with related languages, Greenberg was able to demonstrate with reasonable certainty the direction of borrowing of such words as *writing, reading, market, gun,* and *saddle*. Evidence of the linguistic influence (in this case primarily of Kanuri upon Hausa) must also be presumptive evidence of cultural influence in these particular spheres.[9] At the very least, the fact that two peoples share cognate words for the same trait is an indication of some historical relation as against the possibility of independent invention.

Perhaps the most useful contribution of linguistics to ethnology and culture history is in the classification of languages into geneti-

7. Kroeber, *Anthropology*, 570.
8. J. H. Greenberg, "Linguistic Evidence for the Influence of the Kanuri on the Hausa," *Journal of African History*, I:205–212 (1960).
9. Sapir, *Time Perspective*, 51–75.

cally related families and subgroups. The importance of this type of classification cannot be overestimated, for it gives us what neither cultural nor physical taxonomies can: all-or-none categories which indicate formerly interacting communities whose origins must have been in an area common to all members of the group. "The concept of a linguistic stock . . . implies the former existence of a comparatively undifferentiated language which, by gradual phonetic and morphologic changes, has diverged into distinct forms of speech." [10]

If genetic relationship among a number of languages can be demonstrated, it constitutes prima facie evidence that the ancestors of the speakers of those languages shared a common location at some time in the past. In order for the speakers of those languages to have become dispersed there must have been some population movements. The distribution of those languages and the differentiation between them suggests both a probable point of ultimate origin and, consequently, routes of migration.[11] For example, Greenberg's demonstration of the close relationship between the Bantu languages and the Semi-Bantu languages of eastern Nigeria and the Cameroons indicates that the origin of the Bantu languages must have been in that region and that their subsequent movements had to be to the west and south.[12] Similar linguistic evidence indicates that the Galla and Somali originated in southern Ethiopia rather than in the northern Somalilands or Arabia.[13]

The knowledge that two societies speak related languages strengthens the supposition that cultural similarities between two geographically separated peoples may be due to common origin rather than to diffusion. Conversely, the absence of evidence of common linguistic origin must argue against the case for a hy-

10. *Ibid.*, 76.
11. *Ibid.*, 76–82; I. Dyen, "Language Distribution and Migration Theory," *Language*, XXXII:611–626 (1956).
12. J. H. Greenberg, *The Languages of Africa* (Bloomington, 1963), 36–37.
13. H. S. Lewis, "Historical Problems in Ethiopia and the Horn of Africa," *Annals of the New York Academy of Sciences*, XCVI:504–511 (1962).

pothetical migration. Migrations are so readily traced through linguistic evidence that in such an instance we must insist on very strong evidence from other lines of analysis before accepting a supposed migration.

Migration and Culture History

The idea that migration is the great motive force in the spread and development of culture underlies the work of the Kulturhistorische Schule and is a theme which characterizes much writing on African history. Some writers tend to view every cultural change as an indication that some movement of peoples has occurred.[14] Many have at least assumed that most kingdoms were the result of conquest by migrant groups.[15] Diffusion, stimulus diffusion, convergence, and independent development all tend to be ignored. Credence is frequently given to unlikely myths, and evidence of the influence of outsiders is passionately sought. There are myriad reconstructions which postulate the coming of a small group of migrants (usually from north North Africa, or the Nile region, or Ethiopia) who were then completely assimilated—in language, physical type, and culture—thus leaving no trace.[16] We are told that the intruders conquered and forced their political ideas on the populace yet lost all the rest of their own culture and identity.

Migrations have held a high place in romantic and literary historical speculation. Americanists (archaeologists, linguists, and ethnologists), however, have come to suspect not only the frequency of large-scale population movements but also the extent of the influence small groups of migrants may have on established cultures.[17] In a symposium on migrations and American culture history, Rouse, evidently expressing the consensus of most par-

14. K. H. Honea, *A Contribution to the History of the Hamitic Peoples* (Vienna, 1958).
15. C. Meinhof, *Die Sprachen der Hamiten* (Hamburg, 1912), 2; J. D. Fage, *An Introduction to the History of West Africa* (Cambridge, 1959); R. A. Oliver and J. D. Fage, *A Short History of Africa* (Baltimore, 1962), 46.
16. Fage, *West Africa*, 14, 18; Oliver and Fage, *Short History*, 62, 64.
17. Kroeber, *Anthropology*, 561.

ticipants, suggested several criteria which should be met before giving credence to migration as an explanation of a cultural change.[18] Most of these criteria should certainly be applied rigorously in Africa.

Rouse's first demand is for a demonstration that there actually has been an intrusion into an area by new cultural groups or communities ("components, foci, or phases in archaeological terminology") and not simply one or more individual cultural elements. Secondly, it is necessary to establish that the intruding community or culture shows an actual relation to some other region and, ideally, to show that there are some traces of it along the presumed migration route. Thirdly, it is obviously necessary to prove a reasonable chronological relationship between the culture of the "donor" and the "recipient." Rouse's fifth point is that "it is incumbent upon the person who wishes to demonstrate migration to consider and eliminate the possibility that some other hypothesis may better fit the facts at his disposal . . . I submit that in any study of migrations the differences as well as the similarities in culture between areas need to be considered, for if these differences are great enough they would favor trait-unit diffusion over site-unit [i.e., total culture or community] diffusion." [19] Of course, where there is clear-cut evidence of a genetic relationship between the languages found in two separate areas, we are bound to accept this as evidence of migration. Then our problem is not whether migration occurred, but how.

Linguistic and cultural evidence leave no doubt of the migration of Malayo-Polynesian-speaking peoples to Madagascar. Linguistic, archaeological, and cultural evidence confirms the reality of the great Bantu dispersonal throughout a third of the continent. No one would deny the occurrence of these great migrations. But a migration is just one form of historical event and process to be discovered by techniques of historical reconstruction. It is not an all-purpose explanatory device, although it has often been used as such.

18. I. Rouse, "The Inference of Migrations from Anthropological Evidence," in R. Thompson (ed.), *Migrations in New World Culture History* (University of Arizona Social Science Bulletin No. 27, 1958), 63–68.
19. *Ibid.*, 66.

Race, Language, and Culture in African Historiography

A major premise of American ethnology, growing partly from work with American Indian history and culture area analysis, is that race, language, and culture may and frequently do vary independently of one another. Historical reconstructions which lean heavily on an assumption (implicit or explicit) of an inherent connection between them is immediately suspect. Unfortunately, a great deal of African historiography has assumed the identity of these phenomena. Baumann and Westermann, for example, state:

> Les Chamites orientaux ont porté leur sang éthiopien partout où nous rencontrons des manifestations de leur civilisations particulière; l'apparition de leurs traits physique est même un critère de la possibilité de la présence de leur civilisation et l'inverse se trouvant être également vrai, la thèse de l'identité de la civilisation et du sung paraît pleinement justifiée.[20]

It is on the basis of this circular reasoning that Baumann and Westermann, as others before them, discern the former presence of "Hamites" among the Hottentot, Herero, Southeastern Bantu, in the Rhodesias, throughout the Lake District of East Africa, and among the Kenya Bantu, the Nilotes, the so-called "Nilo-Hamites," and others. This tendency to use race, language, and culture interchangeably has seriously hampered both the classification of peoples and historical reconstruction in Africa. (I will discuss the misuse of the term "Hamite" later in the paper.) Seligman, for example, expresses regrets about basing his racial classification of Africa largely upon linguistic data.[21] Ironically, he more often allows his judgment regarding linguistic affiliations to be guided by his ideas on racial and cultural grouping than vice-versa. In any case, he does not hesitate to equate pastoralism or divine monarchy with "Hamites." Although there certainly is some correlation between particular races, languages, and cul-

20. H. Baumann and D. Westermann, *Les Peuples et les Civilisations de l'Afrique* (Paris, 1947), 48.
21. C. G. Seligman, *The Races of Africa* (London, 1930), 9-10.

tures, we know that there is no inherent connection and that the correlation is not high enough to allow historical conclusions on this basis alone. There is no reason to consider pastoralism, divine monarchy, Capsian blade tools, blood-drinking, or building in stone as characteristics of "Hamites," Arabs, Nilotes, or any other racial or linguistic group.

The experience of Americanists with culture areas and culture history offers a lesson for African history. Culture area delineation, although not meant as an aid in historical reconstruction, points to the fact that culture traits tend to spread in all directions from their center of origin and that culture areas frequently include peoples of different physical and linguistic characteristics. Whereas the emphasis of many writers dealing with Africa vacillates from physical to linguistic to cultural elements (rarely explicity separating them), culture areas are based solely upon cultural criteria.[22] In North America, we speak of the Plains culture area (which includes groups speaking Algonkian, Siouan, and Uto-Aztecan languages) or the Northwest Coast culture area (including speakers of Algonkian, Penutian, and Nadene languages). We do not hear of "Kwakiutlized Haida" or "Penutianized Tanoan." To use such terms in referring to groups whose only connection is a cultural one is to prejudice the historical analysis. The direction of influence in any given situation is a matter to be discovered by further analysis. Hastily applied ethnic labels tend to obscure our perception of the historical processes involved.

In the case of the relations between the so-called "Nilo-Hamites," the "Hamitized Bantu," and the Eastern Cushites of southern Ethiopia and northern Kenya, it seems to this writer that it would be wiser to consider this as one culture area, possibly of some antiquity (with the Bantu joining it more recently), than as an example of the "Cushitization" or "Hamitization" of other peoples. This is especially true in view of the fact that the Central and Western Cushites have very little share in this culture area.

22. For African culture areas, see M. J. Herskovits, *The Human Factor in Changing Africa* (New York, 1962), 57.

Political Anthropology and African Kingdoms

One of the most striking aspects of African social and political organization is the extent to which African polities are organized monarchically and, furthermore, the fact that a great many of these monarchies, regardless of geographical region, share distinctive culture traits referring to kingship. For many years, it has been common for writers to speak of these kingdoms as "conquest states," thought to have been formed by the conquest of one ethnic group by another. Oliver and Fage claim that the type of state they call "Sudanic" (which includes the majority of African kingdoms) "was a superstructure erected over village communities of peasant cultivators rather than a society which had grown naturally out of them. In many cases such states are known to have had their origins in conquest; in almost all other cases conquest must be suspected." They cite Baumann to the effect that these states were areas that "had been overrun by later-comers of a higher culture that the original societies of cultivators." [23]

This well-established concept, partly supported by outmoded ideas of state formation, fails to pass the test of ethnographic fact. In Buganda, Swaziland, Nupe, Benin, Kafa, Ashanti, Zululand, and among the Shilluk and Bemba, there is no question that the ruling house belongs to the ethinic group it rules. In many African states the relationships between ruler and ruled are so direct that the idioms of kinship are the idioms of kingship as well. Fortes and others have pointed out that in Africa descent groups frequently hold corporate rights to political offices, and the ruling hierarchy often represents local kinship groups.[24] As Fallers has noted, the cultural gap between nobles and subjects in Africa is nowhere as great as in Asia or Europe.[25] There are remarkably few solid data on the continent to support a general theory of state formation through conquest.

23. Oliver and Fage, *Short History,* 46.
24. M. Fortes, "The Structure of Unilineal Descent Groups," in S. and P. Ottenberg (eds.), *Cultures and Societies of Africa* (New York, 1960), 163–187.
25. L. A. Fallers, "Are African Cultivators to be Called 'Peasants'?" *Current Anthropology,* II:110 (1961).

There is in existence an extensive and increasingly sophisticated literature on African political systems including, of course, many "Sudanic" states. This material, collected largely by British social anthropologists, gives us detailed accounts of how these countries are ruled, the relations between rulers and subjects, and, in some cases, how the kingdoms were formed. Unfortunately, the processual implications of these data have often been ignored in the search for particular formal cultural traits associated with kingship.

Given the presence of one kingdom in an area, there are many ways of extending the monarchical form of political organization.[26] Established kingdoms constantly expand their borders to control their neighbors (generally regardless of the ethnic affiliation of those neighbors.) Alternately, tributary states, provinces, princes, and successful generals frequently rebel, breaking off to create new polities when they succeed. Evidently, non-monarchically organized peoples, in the process of fighting against neighboring kingdoms, sometimes develop leaders with administrative staffs that can establish new political hierarchies, with or without conquest of others. And some groups do conquer established monarchies or non-monarchical neighbors. The expansion and multiplication of states seems to be a constant process in history, but it is clear that this process need not regularly involve conquest by ethnically and culturally foreign peoples. And there is absolutely no evidence to suggest that any people from one ethnic or geographical background ("Hamitic," Egyptian, Berber, or otherwise) made a series of conquests that carried monarchical organization from place to place.

The fortunes of kingdoms may rise and fall rapidly over time. In cases without historical documentation we cannot be sure that kingdoms which we observe were not once part of great empires or are not now amalgamations of smaller states. The roots of any state we observed may go back far in time, and the ruling dynasties may have changed a number of times without bringing major

26. For a fuller discussion of this subject, see H. S. Lewis, "The Origins of African Kingdoms," unpublished paper presented at the 1964 annual meeting of the African Studies Association, Chicago.

changes of culture or political structure. We do not normally consider the Chinese political system a conquest state although we know historically that it was conquered by Mongols and Manchus. The concept of the conquest state with reference to African states seems to be unrealistic and not very useful. In the Lake Region of East Africa, it appears certain that several conquests of Bantu-speaking kingdoms by pastoral peoples occurred, but in every case the preexistence of the state seems clearly established. Furthermore, in cases where pastoralists actually have conquered other kingdoms, we are faced with exactly the opposite situation from that envisioned by Baumann, Oliver, and Fage: it was the culturally less-developed people who conquered the more developed ones. This was true of the Mongols in China and the Galla in Ethiopia.

For purposes of historical reconstruction it seems useful, even necessary, to distinguish between two aspects of monarchy. On the one hand, monarchies consist partly of cultural and structural elements which grew from the exigencies of rule in non-industrial societies and which, in one form or another, are universal or extremely widespread. Examples of such phenomena are royal courts, systems of taxation, territorial and palace officials, and the right of eminent domain. On the other hand, there are formal traits which are not inherently connected with the process of rule. Examples of these traits include greeting the king by throwing dust upon one's head, the use of the double-bladed spear as a sign of the king's authority, and queen-mother and queen-sister courts. Although all kings have regalia, inaugurations, and court protocol, some historical relationship, no matter how indirect, may be postulated between two kingdoms that share ritual or material forms which bear no necessary relation to the purpose they serve.

Differences between states with regard to centralization and decentralization, allocation of rewards to officials, or organization of military force *may* owe more to a premonarchical heritage, ecological factors, and other internal developments than to diffusion. The trappings of kingship, court life, and ritual may owe more to diffusion, fashion, the spread of Islam, or other external factors. A kingdom which has borrowed a great many traits of divine kingship from one culture need not necessarily owe its origin as a state to the same source. Once a kingdom is in existence it is free to borrow secondary embellishments and ideas from any available source. It is clear, for example, that Moslem influences on the states of the Sudan were historically later than and secondary to the processes of state formation.[27] The same could be true (hypothetically) of Egyptian influences on the Nubian states.[28]

Ecology, Pastoralism, and African History

Pastoralists have occupied a vital place in African historiography. Cattle nomads have been accorded a role far in excess of their numbers, geographical dispersal, or observable political importance. Pastoral nomads have been credited with founding, through conquest, many of the states of Africa. They have been considered the carriers of the traditions of divine kingship, of iron to the Negro, and of "Hamitic blood."[29] A look at the ethnographic record, with respect to both the nature of pastoralism and its distribution in Africa, suggests that we reconsider the role of the pastoralists.

Pastoralism, as Kroeber has noted, "can theoretically be construed as a special derivative form of other cultures, and is not necessarily a basic form of culture in its own right."[30] For one thing, pastoralists very often form a "part-culture," "a well-marked profession within cultures, something like smithing or doctoring, say, except for being raised to include a higher fraction of the total population and being more nearly self-sufficient." Pastoralists have impressed outside observers with their devotion to their animals and their disdain for cultivators, but most of them also depend upon their neighbors, wives, or their own labor to supply vegetable foods now and then. Such peoples as the Fulani of the Western Sudan and the Hima herders of East Africa are

27. J. H. Greenberg, "The Negro Kingdoms of the Sudan," *Transactions of the New York Academy of Sciences*, XX:Ser. II, 126–135 (1949).
28. H. Frankfort, *Kingship and the Gods* (Chicago, 1948).
29. Irstam, *The King of Ganda*, 193; Seligman, *Races*, 158; Baumann and Westermann, *Les Peuples*, 48.
30. Kroeber, "Historical Reconstructions," 397.

generally only minority group specialists among sedentary peoples. I. M. Lewis' account of the Somali, supposedly devoted pastoralists, shows clearly that a Somali herder is part of an intricate web of occupational and kinship relations and that any family or lineage may contain town dwellers (shopkeepers, bureaucrats, or elder-politicians), traveling merchants, sailors, and settled farmers.[31]

Secondly, pastoralism seems to have been independently "invented" on many occasions and in many areas as mixed agriculturalists split up their camps through transhumance, specialization, or movement into agriculturally unsuitable land. (Murdock speculates on several possible independent developments of pastoralism in East Africa.[32]) Thus the necessary precondition for pastoral nomadism is not the presence of "Hamites" but of mixed agriculture with the knowledge and custom of milking animals. Increasing dessication or movement to arid lands may militate toward increasing nomadism and dependence upon livestock; movement to hilly, well-watered areas may militate toward an increasing emphasis upon agricultural activity. The Galla of Ethiopia and Kenya, who are frequently considered to be prime examples of "Hamitic" pastoralists, are found practicing many degrees of pastoralism and mixed agriculture depending upon their geographical location.

The ethnographic data fail to support the idea that pastoralists have been great conquerors in Africa. Although a proportionately small number of African states (the Fulani emirates and a few of the interlacustrine kingdoms) were ruled by pastoral elites who seem to have taken over kingdoms already well-established, the majority of African states were not. Most African pastoral societies are small and their political systems relatively simple. The independent and nomadic pastoralists (e.g., Masai, Hottentot, Turkana, Somali) are all stateless groups, republican or segmented in constitution, under no commanders other than charismatic war or religious leaders. It is remarkable that such independent and egalitarian peoples should be credited with carrying

31. I. M. Lewis, *A Pastoral Democracy* (London, 1961).
32. Murdock, *Africa*, 314–341.

traditions of divine monarchy throughout Africa. The supposed identification of pastoral nomads with customs relating to divine kingship, court life, and monarchical administration is farfetched as well as empirically unsupportable.

It is true, of course, that pastoralists tend to be inveterate fighters, constantly feuding with their neighbors. But in Africa, by and large, their wars consist of small-scale raids involving a few men in search of pasturage, cattle, revenge, and glory. In the cases where pastoralists have gained control of kingdoms it would seem that they were probably stimulated to military and political success by both the opposition and the example of organized states.

On the map, pastoralists appear to cover a great deal of ground. But their territory is frequently scrub and dry grassland undesired by farming populations.[33] The herders need lots of room to wander, and their kind of land is ignored by others. While the Masai and Somali occupy large areas of East Africa, agriculturists often manage to hold the intervening areas which are favorable for farming.

When considering the relation between pastoralism and African history it seems clear that more weight must be given to ecology than to hypotheses that envision a relationship between race, language, and means of subsistence.

The Status of the "Hamites" in African History

It would not be very wide of the mark to say that the history of Africa south of the Sahara is no more than the story of the permeation through the ages, in different degrees and at various times, of the Negro and Bushman aborigines by Hamitic blood and culture.[34]

Seligman was neither the first nor the last to express sentiments of this sort. The attribution of "Hamitic" influence to virtually every cultural, linguistic, or physical phenomenon in Africa deemed worthy of respect has dominated African historiography. So avidly have evidences of "Hamitic" influence been pursued, so readily have they been repeated and accepted, that it would not

33. *Ibid.*, 416.
34. Seligman, *Races*, 19.

be amiss to suggest that virtually every allegation regarding the so-called "Hamites" should be critically reexamined. J. H. Greenberg began this reevaluation and placed it on a firm footing by producing a genetic re-classification of the Hamito-Semitic (Afro-Asiatic) languages and by separating out such non-Hamitic languages as those of the "Nilo-Hamites," Fulani, Hottentots, and Bantu.[35] In these works and in other articles, he laid the groundwork for a reexamination of "Hamitic" culture as well. Considering the pervasiveness of the Hamitic problem throughout African history, linguistics, ethnology, physical anthropology, and archaeology, it may not be out of place to briefly discuss who the "Hamites" are and what legitimate claims we may, at this point, make for them.

In origin, the term *Hamitic* has only a linguistic significance, and although it has been given many other meanings in the past one hundred years there is still no justification for any definition but a linguistic one. Greenberg's genetic classification gives us a definition which is "at once non-arbitrary, exhaustive, and unique."[36] According to Greenberg, "The language family traditionally named Hamito-Semitic has five coordinate branches: (1) Semitic, (2) Berber, (3) Ancient Egyptian, (4) Cushitic, (5) Chad."[37] In order to qualify as Hamitic, the language of a group must show genetic, not typological or borrowed areal, relationship to one of the above branches of the Hamito-Semitic family. Such a qualification immediately excludes from membership such peoples as the Masai, Nandi, Hima, Fulani, Hottentot, Zulu, Yoruba, Akan, and includes the speakers of the many Chad languages previously denied membership for cultural or physical reasons. In order for any groups not showing this linguistic relationship to be considered "Hamitic" in genetic origin, there would have to be extremely compelling evidence, probably requiring written documentation of a change in language. On this basis, we are not justified in seeing much, if any, specifically

---

35. J. H. Greenberg, *Studies in African Linguistic Classification* (New Haven, 1955); Greenberg, *Languages of Africa*.
36. J. H. Greenberg, *Essays in Linguistics* (Chicago, 1957), 66.
37. Greenberg, *Studies*, 51.

"Hamitic" influence south of central Tanzania, in the Lake District, on the Guinea Coast, or in the Congo.

One conclusion suggested by the present distribution of the subgroups and languages of the Hamito-Semitic family is that when they began differentiating from proto-Hamito-Semitic they were located in Northeastern Africa, probably in the Eastern Sudan. Such an inference derives from methods of analysis of linguistic distribution suggested by Sapir, Voegelin, Dyen, and others.[38] This hypothesis is of great importance for African historical reconstruction, for it maintains that there were no waves of Hamitic invaders from Asia, at least not within the past ten or twelve thousand years. On the contrary, it would appear that the Semites migrated *to* Asia. Such conclusions have been suggested before, usually on other evidence by some Orientalists.[39] Of course, the Ethiopian Semites (but not the Cushites) and the post-Islamic Arabs are exceptions.

Lest this conclusion be taken to imply that the "Hamitic" peoples alone were responsible for the early culture of the Sudan and the Sahara, we should bear in mind that application of similar linguistic principles suggests that this was also the general area of origin of the Nilo-Saharan language family.[40] This group of languages and subgroups includes Nubian, Nilotic (including "Nilo-Hamitic"), Central Sudanic, Songhai, Kanuri, Teda, Maban, and Furian. If this hypothetical reconstruction of the origins of these two families has any validity, then some cultural and physical similarities between these groups might well be the result of their common share in an Eastern Sudanic culture area several thousand years ago. We certainly cannot assume a one-way transmission of culture elements from one group to the other.

The implications of this definition and classification of "Hamite" for African history are many. In the realm of ethnology, a reconsideration of the supposed cultural correlates of "Hamitic blood"

38. Sapir, *Time Perspective;* Dyen, "Language Distribution"; C. Voegelin, "The Dispersal Factor in Migrations and Immigrations of American Indians," in R. Thompson, *Migrations in New World Culture History* (University of Arizona Social Science Bulletin No. 27, 1958), 47–62.
39. G. A. Barton, *Hamitic and Semitic Origins* (Philadelphia, 1934).
40. Greenberg, *Languages,* 130.

indicates very different conclusions from the accepted ones. For one thing, the correlation between "Hamite" and pastoralist becomes negligible, restricted to a very few examples in the Horn of Africa and northern Kenya. For another, when the test of linguistic relation plus the criteria for establishing migrations are applied, the connection between "Hamites" and dynasties of conquerors of non-Hamitic peoples virtually disappears. There is no justification for attempts to establish "Hamitic" influence in Monomatopa, the interlacustrine area, Yorubaland, or ancient Ghana. Unquestionably, further investigations will show that many other supposedly typical "Hamitic" culture traits have no more relation to the "Hamites" than these do.

Such conclusions are causes for optimism about the possible uses of ethnography for culture-historical reconstruction. On the basis of what we know from work in the New World, we would immediately suspect reconstructions crediting the "Hamites" with all sorts of one-way contributions. It now seems much more likely that African history has been affected by the same processes as other world areas and that we may understand it by applying what we have learned: the relations between race, language, and culture; migrations; ecology; and political process from living and historic cultures.

III

African Languages and African Prehistory

Roger W. Wescott

Lecturer in Sociology and Anthropology
Wilson College

In Africa, as elsewhere, linguistic relationships may be expected to yield at least inferential information about non-linguistic relationships between peoples during periods for which no documentary evidence exists. But in Africa, as elsewhere, such inferences are beset with scientific hazards. One of these is the obvious —though often oddly underestimated—factual hazard created by paucity of data. There are still only a few African languages for which we have sufficient synchronic (or descriptive) information, much less sufficient diachronic (or historical) information. Another hazard is the procedural one created by explicit or (more often) implicit identification of language with race or culture. Still another problem is the sub-classificatory hazard created by failure to distinguish adequately between types of linguistic relationships. In this area, the crudest confusion, of course, is between typology and genealogy. Yet subtler confusions between sublevels within the domain of either typology or genealogy also confront us and impede our progress toward clarity and consistency in the elucidation of linguistic prehistory.

Broadly speaking, linguistic typology may be defined as the study of resemblances between languages; but, since linguistic resemblances are of several different kinds, typology itself must necessarily be divided into sub-disciplines. When two languages resemble each other, their resemblances may mean any of at least three quite different things: (1) that the two languages had a common ancestor and must, in fact, at one time have constituted a single language; (2) that in the course of historical culture contact the two languages became partially assimilated to each other; or (3) that as a result of unrelated internal dynamism the two languages have, quite coincidentally, developed similar vocabulary items or syntactic structures.

Unfortunately, terminology usage in linguistics has so fluctuated that, when linguists have tried to narrow the reference of the term *typology,* they have divided over the issue of whether to include or exclude the study of the results of process (2) above. However, on the grounds that the narrowest usages are usually the most precise and consequently the least likely to lead to confusion, we shall, during the remainder of this paper, refer only to the results of process (3) above as *typological.* The results of process (2) we shall call *areal* criteria, and the results of process (1) we shall henceforth call *genetic.*

Of these three criteria of relationship—the typological, the areal, and the genetic—most linguists have been most interested, during the past century and a half, in the genetic and least interested in the typological. What this fact probably represents is not so much the intrinsically greater significance of genealogy over other factors (after all, our friends may be more important to us than our kinsmen) as the intellectual prestige of biology generally and of Lamarckian and Darwinian evolutionism particularly. In view of this consideration, the frequent popular (and even scientific) confusion of language with race is, if not justifiable, at least comprehensible.

Even if, however, we agree pro tem to consider only genetic relations between languages as "true" relations, there remains the considerable question of which method of assessing genetic relations is best. The glottochronologists or lexicostatisticians usually consider that only whole "words" (free forms or lexemes) or, at the very least, word-bases are legitimate items for genetic comparison. Greenberg, on the other hand, gives at least equal weight to affixes—usually segmental prefixes and suffixes but also tonal superfixes in cases where these have been competently analyzed and consistently superscribed.[1]

Examples of word-correspondence are the following three Kwa-group lexemes, all of which mean *I*:

1. J. H. Greenberg, *Studies in African Linguistic Classification* (New Haven, 1955), 2.

Yoruba   èmī
Bini   ìmè, mè
Ibo   mé

Examples of affix-correspondence are the following three Adamawa-group morphemes, all of which are noun-class formatives representing body parts:

Vere   -k
Sari   -ko
Voko   -go

Within the camp of the lexicostatisticians, all of whom agree on preferring lexeme comparisons to morpheme comparisons, there are also divergences of method and viewpoint.[2] Of these, the most striking is that between Morris Swadesh, who calls his procedure glottochronology, and H. A. Gleason, who has devised two alternative lexicostatistic procedures which he calls "the method of counterindications" and "characteristic vocabulary index."[3] The principal theoretical difference between the Swadesh approach and the Gleason approach is that the former ostensibly yields absolute time depths, while the latter avowedly yields only relative time depths. That is, Swadesh's lists are designed to give the linguistic investigator approximate dates for language splits occurring at least as far back as five millennia ago, whereas Gleason's methods make no pretense of telling him anything more than, among a group of language splits, which preceded which. Crudely speaking, Gleason's two methods are reciprocals of one another, in that the first states negatively that "C is not as close to A as B is," while the second states positively that "B is closer to A than C is." Details of technique, however, are sufficiently different in the two procedures to allow the second to give a more complete family tree of languages than the former can.

Applying all three methods to the problem of sub groupings within the Mande branch of the Niger-Congo family of languages,

2. See D. Hymes, "Lexicostatistics So Far," *Current Anthropology*, I:3–44 (1960).
3. M. Swadesh, "Lexicostatistic Dating of Prehistoric Ethnic Contact," *Proceedings of the American Philosophical Society*, XCVI:452–463 (1952); H. A. Gleason, "Counting and Calculating for Historical Reconstruction," *Anthropological Linguistics*, I:22–32 (1959).

we find that Gleason's counterindicative method divides the branch into three subbranches, one consisting of Mano and Busa, another of Maninka and Vai, and a third of Kpelle and Mende. Gleason's vocabulary index, however, takes us back a little further into prehistory by revealing that the Mano-Busa subbranch separated from the other two subbranches before the other two subbranches separated from each other. And Swadesh's glottochronology gives us still more detail by revealing, first, that Mende and Kpelle separated from each other more recently than did Maninka from Vai and, secondly, that all the above separations can be roughly dated: the separation between Mano-Busa and the rest of Mande occurred about four millennia ago, that between Maninka-Vai and Mende-Kpelle about three millennia ago, that between Mano and Busa about two millennia ago, and that between Mende and Kpelle about one millennium ago.

More recently I produced two abridged versions of Swadesh's longer glottochronological test lists. In a sense, they do not offer the same degree of absoluteness and precision that the Swadesh lists do, yet they follow the Swadesh approach more closely than the Gleason approach in retaining the uniformity of a fixed word list the results of which can be compared from one language group to another. (Although Gleason naturally prefers to work with large bodies of lexical material, his methods are so constructed as to permit utilization either of very small or of very haphazard vocabularies.)

Since the writer's two lists are only one-tenth as long as Swadesh's shorter test list, space permits both to be included, as follows:

A Ten-Word Glottochronological Quick Test of Linguistic Cognation by R. W. Wescott, January, 1960

1. a pronoun (name-substitute)   *I*
2. a numeral (count-word)   *one*
3. a modifier (descriptive word)   *big*
4. a kinship term   *mother*
5. a body part   *head*
6. a sub-human organism   *dog*
7. a tool (technological item)   *fire*

8. a celestial body — *sun*
9. an anagogic activity — *eat*
10. a katagogic activity — *die*

An Alternative Ten-Word Glottochronological Quick Test ("the Swadesh-Wescott list")[4] by R. W. Wescott, July, 1961

1. numeral — *two*
2. descriptive — *old*
3. kinship — *brother*
4. body part — *hand*
5. animal — *worm*
6. plant — *leaf*
7. nature — *wind*
8. time — *year*
9. movement — *come*
10. miscellany — *name*

The difference between the first ("the Wescott") and the second ("the Swadesh-Wescott") ten-word list is that the first is based on the writer's assessment of the most basic semantic categories, while the second is based on Swadesh's assessment, although the list itself was produced by the writer and not by Swadesh.

The obvious disadvantage of ten-word lists is that their brevity precludes dating linguistic events in terms of time periods shorter than a millennium or estimating time depths greater than five millennia. Yet, in view of the devastating critiques of orthodox glottochronology recently published by Douglas Chrétien and Knut Bergsland and Hans Vogt,[5] it may be that this very imprecision is a virtue rather than a defect: results obtained from them seem less likely than those from longer lists to lead non-linguists to believe that glottochronology can, in the absence of corroborative non-lexical data, yield tight and detailed prehistoric chronologies. In addition, of course, the ten-word lists have an obvious prac-

4. Based on the maximally persistent items listed in Table 1 of Morris Swadesh's article, "Towards Greater Understanding in Lexicostatistic Dating," *International Journal of American Linguistics*, XXI:121–137 (1955).

5. D. Chrétien, "The Mathematical Models of Glottochronology," *Language*, XXXVIII:11–37 (1962); K. Bergsland and H. Vogt, "On the Validity of Glottochronology," *Current Anthropology*, III:115–153 (1962).

tical advantage as they can be gathered more quickly and easily for larger numbers of languages than the longer lists. In a field such as African linguistics, which is beset by acute shortages of both funds and investigators, such an advantage cannot be lightly dismissed, however much we may wish eventually to make more detailed comparisons.

Another modification of Swadesh's glottochronology has been suggested by R. G. Armstrong, who recommends that when the Swadesh hundred-word list is employed it be supplemented by a second hundred-word list, drawn up by a trained and locally-experienced ethnographer for the particular culture area in which glottochronological field work is being carried out.[6] He also advises that the supplementary list include names for local plants, animals, dishes, tools, and institutions. Thus, along the Guinea Coast of West Africa, for example, the list would include words for yams, leopards, *fufu,* digging sticks, and litigation.

Even Swadesh himself, of course, has had second thoughts about the adequacy of his original hundred-word list. The very existence of his two hundred-word list attests to this fact. He and his associates planned eventually to produce a more comprehensive thousand-word list, but the recent decline in the prestige of glottochronology among linguists and anthropologists will probably result in the abandonment of the project.

Areal—that is, assimilative or acculturative—contact between languages is harder to date than genetic relationships, not only in absolute but in relative terms as well. Nonetheless, the fact of its occurrence (or non-occurrence) can usually be established.

Linguistic acculturation can take place on either of at least two levels: the phonotypic or the lexical. In the first of these realms, two conspicuous examples of assimilative contact are the acquisition of lexical tone by Hausa (a member of the atonal Afro-Asian family) and the loss of lexical tone by Swahili (a member of the tonal Niger-Congo family). In each case, the influence of contiguous but genetically unrelated languages apparently brought about a change in the prosodic character of the language.

6. R. G. Armstrong, "The Idoma Dialect Cluster," Typescript, Oturkpo, Nigeria, 1953.

On the basis of assimilative developments of this sort—which are roughly analogous to what biologists call "convergent evolution"—one can discern and describe linguistic areas which often crosscut genetic families. In Nigeria, for example, Hans Wolff hypothesizes two highly distinct language zones which he calls "Plateau" and "Delta."[7] Of these, the second contains languages of several different Niger-Congo branches and subbranches (*viz.,* Ijaw, Edo, and Central), while the second contains languages of two distinct families (Afro-Asian and Niger-Congo).

Of the two forms of linguistic acculturation, the better known, and in some ways still the more useful, is lexical borrowing. For loan-words are good indicators not only of language contact but also of cultural inventories and cultural lacunae in both the borrowing and the lending languages. L. F. Maingard, for example, found that the Xhosa borrowed from the Hottentots large numbers of words for localities, cattle herding, and magic, but none in the domains of social structure, metallurgy, or tillage.[8] From this he concluded that the Xhosa and related tribes brought agriculture with them into South Africa but learned pastoralism from the peoples they conquered.

Although careful analysis usually enables the clearheaded investigator to keep genetic relationships distinct from areal relationships, it is not always so easy to keep areal phenomena distinct from typological phenomena (in the restricted sense of that adjective). When, for example, languages A and B, which we know to be genetically distant from one another, display almost identical phonemic inventories, we may safely infer areal assimilation between them. But when language D, which is both genetically distinct from A and B and geographically isolated from them, shows the same inventory, this may be explained in either of two quite different ways: as evidence of prehistoric language contact, or as evidence only of coincidental typological convergence. A decision can then be made, if it is made at all, only on the basis of non-phonological evidence.

Yet the further we move from phonology, the less rigorous our

7. H. Wolff, "Subsystem Typologies and Area Linguistics," *Anthropological Linguistics,* I:1–88 (1959).
8. L. F. Maingard, "The Linguistic Approach to South African Prehistory," *South African Journal of Science,* XXXI:117–143 (1934).

methods tend to become and the less convincing our inferences consequently appear. A fascinating parallelism between languages from three different branches of Niger-Congo is the following:

Vai	Kalabari	Efik	
kun-	-bi-	-et	hair
kuŋ	-bi	-ot	head
kɔŋ	be-	utu-	ear
		eto	tree

What we seem to see here is a remarkable correspondence of semantic patterning among three languages whose genetic relationships are distant and whose areal contacts are unlikely to have been extensive in the last millennium. Whether we should infer a genetically inherited semantic pattern, an ancient acculturative contact, or an astonishing triple coincidence, few linguists would currently venture to say.

Beyond genetic kinship and areal contact, there is a third linguistic phenomenon which may be of interest to prehistorians—technical vocabulary, especially as it is reconstructed for parent languages. Such vocabularies are usually reconstructed on the basis of lexical correspondence between languages already known to be genetically related. If all of them share one lexical item, it is assumed to have existed in the parent language from which they sprang, although only if the expected phonological correspondences obtain between them. According to Father Fortune, for example, we may safely assume, on the basis of modern Bantu vocabularies, that the speakers of Proto-Bantu were familiar with elephants and giraffes, raised beans and melons, and domesticated dogs and chickens; they made beer and porridge, hunted with spears and arrows, carved drums, smelted iron, prized cowrie shells, had chiefs and medicine men, and venerated their ancestors.[9]

In conclusion, it appears that while linguistics, even with the aid of glottochronology, is no "open sesame" to the overall study of African prehistory, it can, when judiciously combined with the findings of history, archaeology, and paleontology, materially assist us in our collective enterprise of reconstructing Africa's past.

---

9. G. Fortune, "The Contribution of Linguistics to Ethnohistory," in E. T. Stokes (ed.), *Historians in Tropical Africa* (Salisbury, 1962), 28.

IV

The Use of Oral Tradition

in

African Culture History

Jan Vansina

Professor of History
University of Wisconsin

Oral traditions are orally transmitted testimonies concerning the past. Excluded are eyewitness accounts of more recent events and rumors; the former have not yet been transmitted and the latter are not concerned with the past but with the diffusion of sensational news. Oral tradition includes most of the oral literature, insofar as it is transmitted and is believed to have come down unaltered from the ancestors.[1]

As any other source, oral traditions cannot be utilized until they have been scrutinized by the historical method and their relative value established. The student who collects and studies the traditions must know the language in which they are told and be well acquainted with the culture in which they flourish. Since oral traditions form part of that culture, he has to place them in their natural setting as genres of oral literature.

The traditions also fulfill certain functions for the society, in that their content is often influenced by the demands of literary conventions and style. These functions can be of a general nature, such as those proposing cultural values or justifying models for action. But very often specific traditions do have specific functions, usually of a political or social nature: to validate the right to rule for a certain family; to establish the rights of a village over

---

1. Jan Vansina, *De la tradition orale* (Tervuren, 1961), 22–23; H. Moniot, "Pour une histoire de l'Afrique noire," *Annales Economies Sociétés Civilisations*, I:50 (1962), would exclude all traditions which are not concerned with groups and handed down within groups ("le legs socialement organisé des générations passées").

tracts of territory; to be used as precedent in court, etc.[2] African traditions are so closely linked to the political structure that cultures without state structures or kingdoms seldom carry many traditions of any depth or scope.[3] The transmission of traditions is heavily influenced by their specific functional importance, and their contents may be drastically altered or at least influenced by their role.

It follows from the preceding points that the collection of traditions should be carried out in such a way as to provide all the linguistic, philological, cultural, and social data required as well as all relevant data on the nature and the techniques of transmission. All the variants of a tradition should be collected and comparison of variants should yield archetypes and provide a test of the faithfulness of the transmissions.

These requirements have not been met by many collectors and editors of oral tradition, with results which led G. P. Murdock to state that traditions are undependable.[4] Since in practice one has to rely often on published traditions without any indication of their value, it will be useful to indicate some of the most common difficulties which arise in interpretation.

Clichés (Wandersagen). Traditions, like other oral data, can be influenced by diffusion. It is therefore not surprising to find a similar story told in widely different areas. A good example is the Tower of Babel theme. A group of people build a tower to go to heaven, the tower falls, and the people either die or are scattered in different tribes. Such a cliché is met with in the whole of central Africa, where it is used to justify and explain the presence and location of other peoples around their country. Its historical value is therefore close to nil. But sometimes such clichés do cover historical facts. For example, the Imbangala of Angola

2. Jan Vansina, "De funktie der overlevering in de Maatschappii," *Bijdragen tot de Taal-land-en Volkenkunde,* 117, I:80–92 (1960).
3. J. Fage, "Some Notes on a Scheme for the Investigation of Oral Tradition in the Northern Territories of the Gold Coast," *Journal of the Historical Society of Nigeria,* I:15–19 (1956).
4. G. P. Murdock, *Africa: Its Peoples and their Culture History* (New York, 1959), 43.

tell that their first king invited a Pende chief, whose lands he wanted to conquer, to visit him in order to settle their dispute. He made a hole in his hut and covered it with a mat, so that the chief fell into the hole and was killed. The tradition seems to indicate that the Imbangala overcame the Pende, a fact which is known from other traditional sources and is confirmed by anthropological criteria. The same cliché is used among the Yaka-Suku of the Kwango to explain an episode in the transformation of the first Luba empire into the second; and the cliché appears again in a Kuba (Kasai) tradition. In each of these cases it is only a convenient literary figure to explain how A lost his land or rights to B.[5] It would be very useful to compile a list of these clichés as folklorists have done with themes in folktales.

Interpolation. This difficulty occurs not only in narrative traditions but also—and more often—in poetry. Usually when a word occurs in a praise-name which has itself a praise-name, the second one is then interpolated in the first name or substituted for the latter part of the first praise-name. In narratives, interpolation occurs when confusion is possible between traditions which are similar in plot or are concerned with the same hero.[6]

Part-for-a-whole substitution. Many traditions, especially traditions of origin, claim to be concerned with the whole people but are in reality traditions relating only to the ruling clan or lineage or to the clan or lineage of the narrator. Somehow, anthropologists have visualized tribal migrations as mass movements, which is not necessarily true. A good case in point are the Kuba.[7] According to official tradition, the Kuba came from "down river," and a list of place-names is given for the regions through which they passed. But when family traditions were collected, it appeared that the 400-odd clans had more or less migrated on their own and that the traditions above apply only to the chiefly clans and a few others who are associated with them. Expressed

5. On *Wandersagen* and this particular cliché, see Vansina, *De la tradition orale*, 66.
6. *Ibid.*, 103–104, for interpolation of a praise-name.
7. Many other examples will be quoted for the Kuba, among whom the author did fieldwork from 1953–1956. See Jan Vansina, *De Geschiedenis der Kuba* (Tervuren, 1962).

in percentages relating to the 1953–1956 population, the origins of the Kuba are as follows:

Lower Kwango	81.6 per cent
Lulua (Central Kasai)	9.5 per cent
Aboriginal	3.8 per cent
Mongo (north)	3.6 per cent
Southwest (and before that due south)	1.5 per cent

But all these immigrations, even those from a single direction, did not occur in one or two waves. For example, the immigration from Lulua, Mongo, and the southwest has been going on constantly for about two centuries through infiltration. Distribution maps show how clans originating from those quarters infiltrated not only the border areas of the kingdom but all parts of it. In fact, the family traditions show that the process of settlement in the area has been extremely complex and that the royal and chiefly traditions are to be applied only to their own clans. This sort of error seems to occur widely in Africa and can be explained by the fact that the political existence of a chiefdom or kingdom is equated with the kingship, and therefore the history of the chief—or kingship—is the history of the people. We are convinced that the lack of reliability in using traditions as evidence for migrations is generally due to this kind of error.[8] They are reliable as far as the chiefly family goes; they are not so with regard to the rest of the population.

Idealization of roles (interference of particular cultural values). The effect of current cultural values on traditions must always be considered. One of the most common distortions results from the specialization and idealization of the character of different rulers. In Lunda history, Kibinda Ilunga is the ideal of the successful hunter, Mwaant Yaav the ideal of the organizer. In Kuba history, one king is The Magician, another The Warrior, still another The Tryant, etc. Sometimes all wars will be attributed to The Warrior, and this kind of attribution can lead to extreme

8. It would seem that Murdock, *Africa,* used traditions only to establish the origins of migrations.

distortion. But conversely, if an ideal king, such as The Magician, is said to have done things which belong to the type of The Warrior, there is a very high probability that he did perform them indeed. In addition to this type of idealization, all traditions are influenced by particular concepts of historical truth, time, the role of the sacred, and so on. In Rwanda, time is conceived of as cyclical, and every fifth reign is seen as a duplication of the first one. Fate is important and explains the inexorability of history as well as the possibility of knowing it beforehand through divination. Truth for the Kuba or the Kongo is what has been told by the ancestors. If somebody repeats correctly a story told by his father, it is true because it is a correct repetition. Of course, the ultimate conception of history colors all traditions. Generally it is believed that first there was chaos—the opposite of the world as it exists now—which was terminated by a general culture hero. He instituted society and was in turn followed by a special culture hero who gave a people its own peculiar cultural characteristics. This period is followed by an epoch of more normal history which lasts until the beginning of colonial rule. This view of history is held by the Kuba and to some extent in Rwanda or Burundi as well; it ties in with the idealization of individual kings, a sentiment about fate, and the idea of the cyclical development of time.[9]

Etiological explanations. Many traditions explain existing circumstances in terms of a simplified historical development. Rwanda history relates how a culture hero, Gihanga, founded the kingdoms of Bugesera, Burundi, Ndorwa, Bushi, and Gisaka which surround Rwanda. This narrative must have been composed at a time when Gisaka, Bugesera, and Ndorwa were still independent kingdoms, not yet absorbed by Rwanda or Burundi, showing that even this type of tradition may have historical value.

Functional adaptation. Traditions of all sorts are influenced by the functions they fulfill. A classic example of this is found in segmentary lineage societies such as the Nuer or Tiv, among whom a set of genealogies validates the standards of relations between present-day groups of people. Ancestors who did not give rise to opposing segments are forgotten, and a general tel-

9. Vansina, *De la traditionorale,* 83–92.

escoping of the past condenses the whole of history into twelve generations or so.[10] Other examples are to be found in African states. In Ashanti history one king, Osei, successor to the first king, Osei Tutu, apparently has been omitted. It is suggested that this omission is not due to the resemblance in names but to the fact that the second Osei lost his life in the only major defeat the Ashanti suffered during the eighteenth century.[11] In Rwanda, the lists of kings do not include Rwaaka or Rutarindwa, although each of them ruled the country. Both are excluded because they were overthrown by their brothers and a king cannot be overthrown; therefore, they were not kings but usurpers!

On another level, village histories often claim land as the sites where former villages were built; these sites are close to valuable sources of raw materials (iron, clay) and the traditions constitute proof that the deposits belonged to the village. In such instances, it often happens that several present-day villages claim the same spot as an ancestral site. Obviously all but one of them are lying (at least in the Kuba context, from which this example is derived) and for clear reasons. But there is one which is not lying, although the tradition has all the earmarks of having been falsified! One of the villages must have had rights over the deposits. In all cases, therefore, suspicion of falsification is no proof, and proof must be adduced before such traditions can be rejected.

Rumor. A tradition can be of value only if it goes back ultimately to an eyewitness. Most of them do, although some may have been invented long after the facts they allegedly report. However, some go back, not to an eyewitness or to a faker, but to a rumor spread at the time of the events. Traditions in Burundi report that (around 1900) King Mweezi overcame the rebels Macoonco and Kilima, cut off their heads, and had them placed on a pole near his palace. Other traditions, as well as written sources, show clearly that Kilima died much later (around

10. E. E. Evans-Pritchard, *The Nuer* (Oxford, 1940); L. Bohannan, "A Genealogical Charter," *Africa*, XXII:301–315 (1952).
11. M. Priestley and I. Wilks, "The Ashanti Kings in the XVIIIth Century: a Revised Chronology," *Journal of African History*, I:83–96 (1960), (especially p. 90).

1920) and that Macoonco was killed in the German camp of Usumbura by a German officer whom he threatened with a spear. Geographical plotting shows that the tradition exists in areas far removed from the scene of action of this civil strife; and there is little doubt that it arose out of rumors. A check on this possibility can be made by noting how far the setting of the event lies from the locale where the tradition is noted.

New commentary. Many traditions, especially poetic ones, are told in archaic language or relate the facts only in an indirect fashion, through allusions. Generally the allusions or obsolete words are explained by the narrator of the tradition, but often his commentary proves to be in error. One must therefore distinguish clearly between the text of the tradition and the explicative commentary which goes with it and which is the product of a separate tradition. This is not splitting hairs, for such divergence is more typical of commentaries than of other sources which are prone to subsequent invention or elaboration. What often seems to happen is this: A tells the poem to B with commentary; B tells it to C, and C forgets to ask for some explanations and does not receive a part of the original commentary. C tells the poem to D, and by the time G hears it his curiosity is aroused by the very feature of the poem C had not noticed and for which he had not received the commentary from B. So G asks F for an explanation, and F gives one he thinks to be correct, but which is in fact his own invention. Clearly, all commentaries should be taken with a grain of salt.

The foregoing is not a complete inventory of the pitfalls of oral traditions, but it shows well enough how difficult the interpretation and use of oral traditions can be. We can now consider the uses of these traditions, which are so numerous as to make it well worthwhile to tackle the difficulties of collecting and interpreting data.

First of all, the use of traditions is limited by the fact that few of them in practice go back to dates beyond 1200–1500 A.D., which means that the range of time for which they can be employed is much smaller than the time depths with which archaeology, linguistics, ethnology, or physical anthropology deal; the time depth covered by oral traditions is close to that of written sources for most of the sub-Saharan continent. A more important limitation is the fact that traditions are based on relative chronologies which are not always the same for all the traditions within a given culture. The equation of relative chronologies one with another and with the absolute chronology is often approximate; this is especially so when they are based on lengths of generation or when the case rests on average length of rule. It is relatively rare to find a direct equation at several points in time between the relative chronology of a body of tradition and some date in absolute chronology. But once that limitation is granted there are practically no limits to the utilization of traditional data. Examples follow of their use in reconstructing population movements, material culture, economics, social and political structures, religion, arts, and the life cycle.

Population movements. By studying the traditions of all the sections of all the Kuba clans it has proved possible to show that successful chiefdoms attracted people and that immigration into these areas tended to be much higher than emigration. The estimate that 81.6 per cent of the Kuba originally came from the lower Kwango tallies with the linguistic data, for that area as well as the present Kuba zone belongs to Guthrie's language zone B.[12] Kuba sculpture is classified with Kwango sculpture, and Kuba culture is classified in the lower Kasai cluster.[13] All data converge, then, to support the traditions, and the fact that certain other cultural distributions also appear in the Kuba area confirms them. The political titles *ipaancl* and *cikl* are found not only in the Kuba area but also in a broad band stretching from Lake Moero to the Kwango and to Lake Leopold II. The title *yeli* is found near Lake Leopold II and among the Ngongo (a

12. M. Guthrie, *The Bantu Languages of Western Equatorial Africa* (Oxford, 1953).
13. F. Olbrechts, *Plastiek van Kongo* (Brussels, 1946); Murdock, *Africa*, 290–306.

Use of Oral Tradition in Culture History • 65

Table 1. Population movements of clan sections within the Kuba kingdom, 1600–1965.

Tribe[a]	Former affiliation[b]	Present affiliation	Difference
Bushong	177	757	+580
Ngyeen	219	271	+52
Pyaang	266	106	−160
Bieeng Bulaang	352	87	−265
Kel	91	87	−4
Shoowa	117[c]	106	−11
Ngongo	184	89	−95
Ngoombe	26	8	−18
Maluk	26	47	+21
Bokila	7	20	+13
Kayuweeng	31	31	0
Kaam	0[d]	4	+4
Kete	168[e]	322	+154
unknown	136		−136
others	135		−135
Totals	1,935	1,935	0

[a] The tribe is in this respect a set of chiefdoms. The Bushong are all organized in one chiefdom which is the biggest of all. The Kete reorganized on a village basis and most villages were directly dominated by the Bushong. This correlates with their huge gains. The Pyaang, Bieeng Bulaang, and Ngongo were split into a number of small chiefdoms, as were the Southern Ngyeen, while the Northern Ngyeen had bigger chiefdoms. The Ngyeen gained from Ngongo losses but lost themselves to the Bushong and the Kete, as did all the other chiefdoms mentioned.

[b] The number of present-day clan sections which claim to have belonged to a particular tribe at the time of their arrival in the territory, generally around 1600–1650.

[c] In this figure the village *Wuupu* is not included but is incorporated in the following figure. The real difference is therefore −31, since *Wuupu* includes 21 sections.

[d] The clan Kaam from which the name of the village is derived came from an outside territory at a late date.

[e] This figure includes all Kete, Lulua, Kete-Bieeng, and aborigines. Since many Kete are late immigrants, the figure is too high. The movement here represents in part an influx into Kuba territory from the outside, especially from troubled areas and after 1700. (Vansina, *De Geschiedenis der Kuba*, Chapter 3.)

Kuba people). The inverted mortar as a seat for the judge deliberating cases of bloodshed is found among both the Kuba and Nkucu (southern Mongo); the title *iyol* (*dyulu*) is also Kuba and southern and southeastern Mongo. All these terms suggest that there were influences from the south and north, influences which are borne out by small percentages of population influx. The fact that they are small when compared with the total culture provides a nice parallel to the relatively small amount of immigration from these quarters as compared with that from the lower Kwango. This argument, however, does not mean that cultural diffusion cannot take place without population movement, but simply that some diffusion is likely to go along with population movements.

Material culture. The Kuba tell us that the techniques of making embroidered cloth and pilecloth came to them from the Pende in the southwest, who also were responsible for the origin of a small type of pottery. The objects in question are found in Pende country. The Kuba say that they got the American crops in the seventeenth century, and before that they grew bananas and millet and were fishermen. The American crops came from the west-southwest (correct as far as other data go). Chili pepper was introduced first, then in the next reign appeared all other American crops except manioc, which came two reigns later. This tallies exceedingly well with the fact that written sources from the coast indicate that manioc was introduced half a century or more after the introduction of the other imported crops.

Another tradition relating to material culture gives the description of a throwing-knife (*mpeengl*) which the tribe is said to have had in earlier times.[14] In 1956, we found such a knife in a Kuba home. The owner did not know what it was! But it tallied with the traditions and confirmed them. It has thus been possible to describe the evolution of Kuba material culture since about 1550 to the present day, and the possibilities of error seem

14. As reported by E. Torday and T. A. Joyce, *Notes Ethnographiques sur les peuples communément appelés Bakuba, ainsi sur les peuplades apparentées—Les Bushongo* (Bruxelles, 1910), 37, 43, from data collected in 1907.

slight. Traditions about material culture are often told as matter-of-fact comment and seem to be inaccurate only rarely, as when an informant in Rwanda said that eleusine was introduced by Rwaabugiri (after 1860), which is manifestly false.[15]

Economic development. Insofar as economic development can be deduced from material culture, it is obvious that the traditions will yield considerable information about it. On the subjects of trade, trade routes, markets, and currency in particular, oral traditions can provide a good deal of evidence. The Kuba village of Ibaanc has a praise-name which extols its former market, where "heaps of cowries" were exchanged. The commentary has it that this was a big market in which cowries, *amandrilha* beads, and copper were used as currency; also given is a list of goods to be found in the market and from whence they came. These data are supplemented by some family traditions which tell about the trading activities of their immediate ancestors. The whole body of information refers to the late nineteenth century and agrees with the written sources we have for the period. In fact, the view it gives is much more complete and meaningful than the glimpses one can obtain from the written data. For earlier periods, markets are also mentioned and the introduction of cowries is attributed to the second culture hero, Shyaam (around 1650). Since this is the period during which American crops were also introduced, it is likely that the tradition is correct. In an indirect way, an eighteenth-century tradition refers to Portuguese beads, and the tradition which identifies particular drums of the royal treasury with particular kings is very useful for studying the introduction of copper. The earlier kings (eighteenth century) had drums with only one or two copper ornaments; the later ones had more and more copper and also some bead ornamentation; by the end of the nineteenth century almost the whole drum was covered with copper wire and beads.

Demography. Demographic trends can be reconstructed from

15. Traditions about material culture are short and hence, usually accurate; however, since their transmission depends on the asking of questions about origins of actual objects or usages, they are dying out more rapidly than other traditions under modern conditions.

genealogies and sometimes from village histories. But it must be realized that these histories usually begin at the middle of the nineteenth century. Earlier genealogical data have been found to be telescoped in such a way that only "relevant" ancestors are remembered.

Social Structure. First, family and village histories always provide case studies for the functioning of the social structure. Information of this kind is everywhere extremely rich from about 1850 onwards. For earlier periods, some essential changes are not reported at all, probably because the people at the time did not realize that the systems were changing. As far as we know, no oral traditions in Africa tell, for instance, of a specific change from matrilineality to patrilineality or vice versa, or from either of these lineage systems to dual descent or bilateral descent; and yet these things happened. Some written sources give evidence for such events (the Wolof case is one of the more spectacular ones), and anthropological data (survivals and distributions) are often very convincing. The same seems to be true with respect to other aspects of the social system. Age-grades survive in Kuba life as structural fossils. To the west, however, some Kuba tribes have age-grades which are still functionally important. The Lele, the people bordering on the west of those tribes, use their age-grades as a primary structure in their social organization. Yet no tradition attests to this decline in the importance of age-grades for the central Kuba.

Political structure. The traditions of populations in which political structure (mainly chiefs and kingdoms, also some age-grade societies) is distinct and separate from social structure have a wealth of material that often describes the evolution of the internal political structure in considerable detail. Such events as the creation of the state and the leading offices in the state and changes in law or in territorial organization are all related. The Kuba tell when their main political offices were instituted, but some of these are placed at the beginning of history (i.e., at the end of chaos), and such traditions do not mean much. But others are attributed to specific kings, and it is recorded that one king started to give offices to his sons and that another decided to change the fines for adultery in relation to his sons and daughters. The later king made the fines for commoners much higher and those for princes much less, thus underscoring the growing rift between classes in his time. In Rwanda, it is reported that X, favorite of King Z, invented around 1830 a system whereby political control of the district was given to two officials instead of one—"a chief of the land" and a "chief of the pastures." In an earlier period, according to tradition (around 1650), King Y instituted new rules for the college of medicine men who helped the king rule. As for quarrels about the succession and their structural significance for the whole political system, there is nowhere any tradition which omits these altogether. In most states, on the contrary, they are carefully recorded.

With regard to external political history, little needs to be said. The traditions give complete accounts of all wars or raids and territorial conquests, although they are, of course, often twisted for the sake of national honor or similar motives.

Religion. Although religion is similar to social structure in that people are often unaware of changes in their beliefs or rituals, there are traditions relating to changes in religion. Some of these are preserved by accident. The Kuba used to believe in two God-creators, Mboom and Ngaan, one for the good and "heavenly" things, the other for the bad and "waterly" things. There is still a traditional classification of animals into two sets—those created by Mboom and those created by Ngaan—as well as other indications of the earlier beliefs. Ngaan has now become a mere nature spirit, and Mboom is the sole creator. In this case, we can trace the change in belief but not identify the period during which it happened. A similar case has to do with the praise-name of the sun. In it are listed a number of spirits which are supposed to reside in the sun. Nowadays nobody believes in spirits of the sun; but some of these spirits also are said to have been "national" spirits, one or two for the Bushongo, one for the Ngyeen, one for the Pyaang, and so on. History tells that a given king in the eighteenth century performed an appropriate ceremony by which these national spirits were killed.

Taking all the data together, one is able to reconstruct some of the changes in the religious practices and beliefs. That the Kuba case is not unique is borne out, among others, by the Rwanda, among whom the introduction of the Ryaangombe cult can be roughly dated and its evolution followed. Wherever there are special colleges or guilds of religious specialists to watch over the kingship and transmit the ideology of kingship, their ritual formulae and traditions embody a great deal of data on the evolution of these beliefs.

Arts. Traditions are seldom concerned with art, but there are a few cases in which they yield some data on the subject. The Kuba say that one of their greatest artists, Miele, lived in the seventeenth century. He was a master of ironworking and made iron figurines of houses and canoes as well as of people; his figures were kept for a long time at court but are now lost. A few of these iron sculptures from the Kuba were found around 1900. Informants also will tell one that certain figurines were first carved at the time of King So-and-so for this or that purpose. Nineteenth-century traditions are, however, much richer; they record who made a certain masterpiece, when he made it, and what he wanted to express.

Life cycle. Data on rituals connected with the life cycle and changes in those ceremonies are not very numerous. The Kuba do know that formerly there was more bride service and less bride-wealth, but they do not say anything about possible changes in marriage ceremonies. The same is true for ceremonies at birth or at death. It is only with regard to initiation ceremonies that some traditions are found. These ceremonies are said to have been instituted by the founder of Kuba culture; but another tradition admits that the ritual came from the Kete, which is evident because of the use of the Kete language in the ceremony. The Kete say that they acquired the ceremony from Kete groups outside the Kuba territory who practice a similar initiation ritual. The first tradition is necessary to validate the ceremonies themselves; the founder *must* be seen as instituting them so that the boys can go "back to the source" during the ritual.[16] The second

16. The author outlines in detail the myth of origin connected with the ceremony in "Initiation Rituals of the Bushong," *Africa*, XXV:138–155 (1955).

tradition, of course, is the correct historical statement. We suspect that in many other instances traditions dealing with this type of material will show a tendency to associate it with the origins of the culture. This occurs with respect to the burial ceremonies of the Kuba in Rwanda and Burundi. However, that such traditions need not necessarily be true or even the correct historical tradition, as opposed to the mythological dogma, is shown by the case cited.

It remains now to discuss the relationships between oral traditions and other sources of culture history, notably archaeology, linguistics, cultural anthropology, and written documents. Since the sort of evidence these sciences (with the exception of historiography) can provide culture historians is discussed elsewhere in the book, we can take them for granted and focus on the problems of comparing their data with those from oral tradition.

Archaeology. The comparison between archaeological data and oral tradition can be fruitful; but it can also be misleading. One of the most common problems occurs when archaeological objects are discovered which the non-specialist can attribute, at first glance, to human activity (pottery, bricks, iron objects, etc., but less often stone artifacts). The usual response of local inhabitants is to attribute them to populations which once lived there but are now extinct. The reasoning is simple: (a) these are things made by humans; (b) they do not belong to our culture; (c) they are found on our land. (d) Since they are not ours, they must belong to people who lived here before us; (e) these people are the X (identified from oral tradition). (f) Therefore, the objects belong to the culture of the X people. This conclusion is then presented to the archaeologist as a definite tradition: "These things were made by the X people."

This tendency explains how in Rwanda the same prehistoric culture is reported in one place to be the work of the Abareenge and fifteen miles away to be the work of the Abahoondogo. By the same sort of reasoning, all the different cultures dug up in one spot are said to be the work of one group. A second pitfall occurs when monuments are still visible, since people tend to ascribe a history to them even if they have forgotten the real history. Thus a site could conceivably be called the capital of King So-and-so (generally a founder or a culture hero) without any real basis. This universal human tendency has led many to see the footsteps of famous men carved in the rock: Flemish peasants, for example, have invented a story about Julius Caesar because a tree in the neighborhood is "Caesar's tree," and Swiss herders have concocted a biography of Pilatus to explain Mount Pilatus.

Because of these tendencies, an archaeologist must be exceedingly careful in the interpretation of oral data relating to his findings. On the other hand, tradition can often help him. The interlacustrine traditions explain where the capitals of kings were located, and, using them, an archaeologist can discover the sites. If the sites are no longer visible, a correlation between the tradition and the actual finds provides strong corroboration. M. Posnansky found two superimposed capitals in Ankole where the traditions said they were;[17] the earlier capital was some feet under the more recent one, both being reduced to little more than potsherds and postholes. Even when the tradition is obviously unreliable as history, an archaeological find can sometimes be made with its help. The Lunda told how they sprang from a cave, Dyaal dya Maandam; and the cave was shown to contain a large assemblage of Neolithic materials. The Kuba tell us that they separated at a place called Iyool, indicating the location of the three earliest village sites; and unusual pottery did turn up at the sites.

From what has been said above it is clear that if a corroboration is genuine, it produces convincing evidence. In the absence of a corraboration, the purely archaeological data seem to carry more weight. In Rwanda, migrations are traditionally seen as an immigration of Tutsi into a country occupied by Hutu and Twa. But the archaeological record shows that there was not only a culture with pottery A and pottery B (the latter coming close to modern pottery), but also a pottery C. The differences in pot-

17. M. Posnansky, "Progress and Prospect in Historical Archaeology in Uganda," *Uganda Museum Occasional Paper*, IV:32–36 (1959).

tery A are very marked and the whole picture suggests a complex pattern of settlement. Obviously, the tradition has to be corrected. When examined, it turns out that the arrival of Tutsi is equivalent to the arrival of the royal clan and that no tradition explains when and in what order Tutsi, Twa, or Hutu arrived. Just to indicate the difficulties involved, it may be pointed out that the archaeological data are based mostly on pottery; and in present-day Rwanda, pottery is made only by the Twa and not by any members of the Hutu or Tutsi; therefore, no prehistoric pottery can be traced to any group other than the Twa.

Linguistics. The data derived from historical linguistics are often irrelevant for oral traditions because they refer to a very remote period.[18] However, the use of the concept of common origin can yield results comparable with oral data. A case in point is the situation on the lower Kasai. From its mouth to Port Francqui and the Kuba area, the left bank is occupied by peoples who speak related languages forming a cluster in zone B. The Kuba and Lele form another cluster which is related to this one (the Yans-Ding cluster). The traditions of the Yans, Ding, Ngul, and Lwer of the Yans-Ding cluster indicate that they came from the mouth of the river and the opposite right bank of the Congo River, where in fact the bulk of the B group is located. Kuba traditions agree with this. A comparative chronology would show a chain of movements involving first Kuba, then Ding, and then Yans—all of them in the sixteenth century. The traditions do not contradict each other, and they agree with the linguistic distribution. This part of zone B is a long finger extending from the main part of the zone, and presumably the latter is linguistically more splintered than this finger. One set of traditions, however, does not agree. The Mbun, south of the Ding, speak a language of the Yans-Ding cluster but claim an origin from the south Kwango, not from the lower Kasai. A study of the clan traditions shows that many of their clans did in fact originate in

18. For instance, French, Spanish, and Italian are closely related, but their separation is more than 1500 years old. Separation between Flemish and German dates from about 1000–1200 A.D. The split is then 700 years old or more; yet the differences between the two languages are no greater now than those between different Bantu languages.

Peoples and Languages of the Lower Kasai Area

the Ding area; the general tradition may be therefore an overlay from the politically dominant clans, which have taken over the language of the mass of the population. Most of the population, however, comes from the lower Kasai. A similar hypothesis with some additional evidence from traditions is postulated for the Tsong, whose main traditions also refer to the south instead of the northwest.[19] In these cases, then, it can be shown that the traditions are not essentially incorrect but that the "part-for-the-whole" error must be avoided.

The evidence derived from loanwords is generally very strong. In this case, traditions should correspond to the linguistic findings. If they do not, the reason for the divergence must be found. A typical case involves the political titles *ipaancl* and *cikl* which

19. Data on traditions of origin, clan origins, and cultural resemblance for the Mbun are from J. De Decker, *Les clans Ambuun* (Bruxelles, 1950); for the Tsong, from E. de Beaucorps, *Les Basongo de la Luniungu et de la Gobari* (Bruxelles, 1941). Although a southern origin for the Tsong is posited by the latter author, he admits that some groups claim to be derived from the Yans ancestor and use Yans as another name for their group.

are two of the four most important territorial titles in the Kuba chiefdom. Tradition says that they were invented at the time the chiefdoms were set up. Comparative study, however, shows that they are found from Lake Moero to Lake Leopold II and the southern Kwango in a continuous, or almost continuous, stretch; this suggests an early and very widespread diffusion. The Kuba tradition is mainly etiological; the real origin of the titles has clearly been forgotten. In other cases, the tradition bears out the linguistic facts in a very indirect fashion. The Yaka from Kwango, the Cokwe, the Lunda, and even the Luapula peoples have a special signal drum called *mondo;* and there are political traditions relating to the spread of Lunda dynasties in all the areas where the *mondo* is found. The traditions thus offer indirect support for the linguistic facts.

Evidence from dialectology is weaker. But when it is confirmed by oral tradition it can become helpful, especially if anthropology confirms its conclusions. For example, the central Kuba chiefdom has a chief (the king) who cannot be deposed. Surrounding chiefdoms have a custom called *mayay* by which a chief may be deposed. The age-area hypothesis suggests that the central chiefdom changed, and tradition confirms that it did. Most Kuba dialects present common features which do not occur in the central dialect, and the suggestion is that the central dialect has changed. Here there is no direct ethnological or traditional evidence, but the center is the center of a kingdom (ethnological data) which grew out of the central chiefdoms (traditions), and the language of the court became the norm in the central area (traditions). According to tradition, the kings even tried to impose it on other populations. This fits in very well with a theory of development of the central dialect.

Finally, evidence derived from semantic significance in the protolanguage seems weak to us. If such evidence is contradicted by traditional data, preference should be given to the latter, for later language-borrowings could seriously distort the picture. The more we know about Africa, the more we are impressed by the very extensive borrowings which seem to have occurred since very early times.

Cultural anthropology. Information derived from the study of plant or animal genetics seems to constitute very good evidence. Evidence from oral traditions correlating with these results will be limited, however, primarily to the introduction and diffusion of American crop complexes and probably certain types of cattle. There are some exceptions. The Ganda claim that Kintu, their first king, brought bananas to them in about the fifteenth century. But as far as we know, the great variety of bananas in Uganda contradicts this view, which should be classified as purely etiological. But the Rwanda claim that they received bananas from Bunyoro during the Nyoro wars of the sixteenth century, and this is quite possible. So is the claim that they have known zebu cattle only since nineteenth century raids, for the number of zebu cattle is low (only a few well-known herds), and these cattle are found only north of Rwanda in the Nyoro-Nkore area. The example of Kuba crops has already been given. In our view, few traditions will be found to contradict the genetic data, and oral tradition is the ideal means to learn about the spread of the American food complex.

Data based on inferences from cultural survivals are always hypothetical, although reconstructions based on them should certainly carry greater weight when corroborated by tradition. Unfortunately, this is not often the case when change has been gradual and unconscious and has not registered on the memory of tradition except in an indirect way, which is of course the case with most of these survivals.[20] However, the very presence of a survival can lead to the confirmation of an independent tradition, as in the instance of the Kuba throwing-knife. There is, of course, a distinct danger that special traditions may arise to explain such survivals *ex post facto.* Thus the Kuba have ingenious explanations for the wearing of barkcloth in funeral ceremonies, in spite of the obvious inference that it is a remnant of Kuba costume

20. A good example of such a lack of tradition is illustrated by the fact that the introduction of the horse was not recorded in most of the Plains Indians' traditions. When the horse later became of paramount importance to them, etiological origins were accordingly invented to account for its introduction. See R. Lowie, "Oral Tradition and History," *Journal of American Folklore,* XXX:101–107 (1917).

before the introduction of weaving. When traditions are contrary to such evidence they usually may be discounted; data based on survivals often carry a high degree of probability. It should be added that in many cases, such as the Kuba age-grades, evidence of this sort can be tested and substantiated by a study of distributions.

Techniques which reconstruct former structures by logical inference have been used in African history.[21] These seem to us weaker than any other approach because in so many instances there are more than one or a few probabilities of development. Such reconstructions should, therefore, be substantiated by evidence from other sources, among them oral tradition. Such a possibility will, however, be very rare since structural evolution (as shown by hypothesis in this case) is largely unconscious and therefore not reflected in tradition.

Anthropological data have been used extensively to reconstruct history on the basis of distributional evidence, using age-area or other working hypotheses. This seems legitimate provided the distribution is corroborated by evidence of semantic borrowing and that data are available for every part of the area under consideration, which is, in Africa at least, very seldom the case. Here, corroboration by oral tradition can be very valuable. An example of the use of a distribution pattern strengthened by semantic borrowing (*mayay*) was given for a feature of Kuba political organization. Oral traditions not only suggest a trend of change similar to the one which can be reconstructed from the anthropological evidence, but also help date this reconstruction, in this instance at about 1600 A.D.

Skillful use of a combination of distribution patterns, linguistics, and oral tradition seems to be the most likely way to elucidate in detail culture change in a set of related societies and cultures over a maximum depth of five to ten centuries. This as yet has not been attempted.

The history of specific diffusions can generally be investigated by tradition. The spread of Lunda political practices to the

21. See G. P. Murdock, *Social Structure* (New York, 1949) or Murdock, *Africa*.

Cokwe or Lwena, for instance, is attested by ethnological similarities, by the titles (*mwaant a ngaand*), and by the traditions.[22] A more specific case is the spread of the *mungongo-mukanda* boys' initiation, which exists among the Yaka, the Cokwe, Western Lunda, Pende, Kete, and Kuba. Kuba tradition and linguistic evidence connect it with the Kete, who are neighbors of the Pende. The Pende got it from the Cokwe and Lunda, as did the Yaka.[23] All elements—anthropological distribution, linguistic data (such as the name for the institution), and traditions—agree. A similar case is the spread for the girls' initiation from the Bemba to the Lunda (*cisungu* initiation), except that no traditions concerning it have been recorded so far.[24] This may be because nobody ever collected them and also indicates the possibility that the diffusion took place too long ago. This seems to be the case with the diffusion of the belief in *kalunga,* which is found throughout Angola and among the Kongo, Yaka, Lunda, and "Lundaized" peoples, including even the Holoholo on the shores of Lake Tanganyika. *Kalunga* is the expanse without boundaries of the underworld (the sea or the place where the dead live) and has a religious connotation. In some groups a mask with two faces is associated with it (Kuba, Kete, possibly Pende and Cokwe). The diffusion of the name and the concept over such a large area must be complex and in part very old.

22. M. McCulloch, *The Southern Lunda and Related Peoples* (London, 1951); data for the central Lunda will soon be published by M. F. Crine in a monograph of the Académie royal des sciences d'outre Mer, Brussels.
23. In the southern-southwestern half of its disturbution it is known as *Mungongi.* See L. de Sousberghe, *Les Danses rituelles Mugonge et Kela des Papende* (Bruxelles, 1956). For the Yaka, see M. Plancquaert, *Les Sociétés secrètes chez les Bavaka* (Louvain, 1930). For the Kuba, see Vansina, *De Geschiedenis der Kuba,* where further bibliography is given for the area. Also, see I. Cunnison, *The Luapula People of Northern Rhodesia* (Manchester, 1959), 66, on the Luapula, where *mukanda* is the initiation hut rather than the initiation, and I. Struyf, "Kahemba, envahiseurs badjok et conquerants Lunda," *Zaïre,* I:386–389 (1947), on the Lunda, where *mukanda* is the initiation for girls.
24. See A. Richards, *Chisungu* (London, 1956), Appendix A. The distribution ranges from the Ambo and Nsenga in Northern Rhodesia and Mozambique to the Cokwe in Angola. Among the Cokwe and Lunda of southern Kwango, the girls' initiation seems similar but is called *mukanda.*

The Kuba received the notion with the initiation *mukanda*. But this is just one part of the spread. How could the southern Angolan peoples, the Kongo, and the Holoholo have received it? Tradition can be of no use here, not only because tradition tends to be weaker with reference to religious matters than to political affairs, but primarily because the antiquity of the bulk of diffusion is too great.[25]

Written sources. In principle, oral traditions and written sources bearing on the same set of data should coincide. This does not happen very often, although some instances are known. Traditions collected in 1850 from the Imbangala relate the facts of the period 1600–1625; these traditions do give the names of Manuel (governor of Angola) and Miguel (first captain of Ambaca), but cases of this sort are very infrequent. One often gets the impression that oral traditions and written data relating to periods before 1800 are seldom interested in the same facts as later traditions; so, although they exist side by side they do not overlap.

A typical case from the old kingdom of Kongo may be cited. The tradition tells that King Alvare Pango, a Lukeni, had a nephew, Nzinga; Nzinga killed one of the king's wives and fled to Soyo where there was a king named Nkumbi. In time, Nzinga went back to Alvare and promised that he would conquer Soyo for Kongo. The king gave him the insignia of a "count" and agreed. But the family of the deceased wife asked for justice, and Alvare was obliged to order the death of Nzinga. The executioners

25. For the Kongo, see H. van Roy, "De godservaring bij de Bakongo," *Aequatoria*, XXII:134–136 (1959), who also gives evidence for its existence among peoples in the Kwango area, the Luba of Katango, and the Holoholo of Albertville. Evidence for the Kuba comes from the author's own field notes. For Angola, where the name is known everywhere, see L. Marquardsen, *Angola* (Berlin, 1920), 126; McCulloch, *The Southern Lunda*, 72, and the bibliography quoted there; C. Estermann, *Ethnografia do Sudoeste de Angola* (Lisbon, 1954), I, 212, for the Ambo and p. 232 for the Nyaneka Humbe groups as well as the Herero. See also Struyf, "Kahemba," 381–382; R. Burton, *Luba Religion and Magic in Customs and Belief* (Tervuren, 1961), 401; P. Colle, *Les Baluba* (Brussels, 1913), II, 428; and A. van Malderen, "Crimes et superstitions indigènes: La Secte du 'Bukazanzi,'" *Bulletin des Jurisdictions indibènes et du droit coutmier congolais*, III:38 (1935); A. van Malderen, "Crimes et Superstitions Indigènes: 'Bwanga Bwa Mawesa,'" *ibid.*, IX:116 (1941), for the Lomotwa.

tricked him, however, and Nzinga fled to Soyo. When he found out, Alvare was so outraged that the executioners themselves fled and founded lineages and villages in the Soyo area and north of the mouth of the Congo. Nzinga instituted matrilineality because his sons lacked proper respect for him. He "bought" the crown of Soyo at the death of Nkumbi. After that, he unified Soyo and fought the king of Kongo at San Salvador.

There were several Alvares in the seventeenth century, and one of them, Alvare Affonso (1636–1641), had to face a successful rebellion of the Count of Soyo. An earlier Alvare made war on Count Miguel of Soyo in 1614. The episode seems to refer to one of these two periods. An analysis of the tradition shows that the statement that Nzinga fought the king of Kongo does not make sense in terms of the story. Therefore, it might be one of the most authentic elements. It is one which is inherently plausible, and it is even possible that the use of the title "count" is correct since Soyo was a country in the seventeenth century and the titulary in Kongo seems to have come into use at the end of the sixteenth century. This is all the help we can obtain from written documents. An analysis of the tradition shows that it attempts to explain why the succession to the Soyo throne is matrilineal while some Asolongo are patrilineal and why one finds Kongo lineages in Soyo mixed with Asolongo ones. As its stands, the story of the murder of the king's wife, with its consequences, is more unlikely. A more plausible explanation would be that Alvare's nephew became involved in a political plot and fled with other nobles who were also implicated. Soyo was the obvious place to go since it was in dispute with Kongo. If this interpretation is correct, the "true" elements of the story are: the name of the king, the strife between Soyo and Kongo, and the Kongo origin of a number of lineages in Solongo country. "Untrue" elements would be the theme of the killing of a king's wife and the institution of matrilineality by Nzinga. But, of course, the death of the king's wife is a possibility. The story about matrilineality is less so, since it is a widespread cliché in the whole of the matrilineal belt.

The case shows how written and oral accounts can exist side by side and not necessarily cover the same facts. It also demonstrates the mixture of "true" and "false" elements possibly present in a tradition.[26]

Traditions of the nineteenth century generally belong to different types than earlier ones. They often cover the same ground as written documents and are frequently much more complete and meaningful. The Kuba revolt of 1904, for instance, is described by the written sources as a sudden outburst, motivated by faith in a special war-magic. The rebellion primarily involved the missions, and in fact its motives were much more complex: the principal reason was that the local Protestant mission had unwittingly helped one of its converts, a king's son, to power. He was the leader of an anti-successor faction and wanted to take the throne although he had no right to it, the succession being matrilineal. Not only are the motives better understood from the oral record but so are some of the subsequent events. As far as we know, no military record is left of the operation to suppress the revolt. But the Kuba traditions tell the road the troops took, through which villages they passed, details of skirmishes, when and why the king capitulated, and the mood of the would-be usurper when he decided to abandon the fight. There is little doubt that for the history of the latter half of the nineteenth century, oral traditions are the most valuable, diverse, and complete sources of all those available.

Our conclusion can be brief. Oral traditions are useful for the culture-historian, if he realizes they must be submitted to the acid test of the historical method and that they are based on relative chronologies. Their main use lies in the fields of population movements, material culture, economics, and religion. They are especially good for political history, weak on the history of ceremonials linked with the life cycle or the history of the arts, and especially weak for the history of social structures. But even in these latter fields, oral traditions are extremely rich from about

26. P. G. Marchal, "Sur l'origine des Basolongo," *Aequatoria*, XI:121–124 (1948); J. Cuvelier, in "Alvare," *Biographie Coloniale Belge*, II:6–11 (1951). "True" and "false" are relative notions in that a "false" element in a tradition is often as significant for the historian as a "true" element.

1850 onwards. Finally, it is evident that the wealth of information to be derived from traditions has barely been tapped. What is most needed is intensive and prolonged field work by many scholars before this source of history vanishes from the minds of men.

V

The Use of Music as a
Technique of Reconstructing
Culture History in Africa

Alan P. Merriam
Professor of Anthropology
Indiana University

Recent developments in the study of African history indicate that historians must begin to use a wider variety of analytic tools than has commonly been employed in studying history, even in those areas for which written records exist.[1] To this end, a number of aids to reconstruction have been suggested at various times by various authors: among them are archaeology used in conjunction with whatever historic records are available, oral literature, ethnographic distributional analysis, linguistic relationships, and botanical studies. The question of whether music can contribute to such studies has not, to the best of my knowledge, been seriously discussed, and there are some problems which must be carefully considered.

The first of these problems is to define what is meant by the phrase "reconstructing culture history" and to determine how we may use music to do so. The use of any special tool in such an investigation involves at least three separate possibilities. In the first place, part of the culture history of any group consists of a description of a way of life at a given point in time; that is, at any particular time the culture inventory of a people contains certain items, and these items, in turn, tell us something about the people and their way of life. Such descriptions, whether broad or narrow in terms of the number of items described, can be reached either through the use of historic accounts, which in the case of Africa seem to be of limited time depth, or through archaeology,

---

1. See Alan P. Merriam, *The Anthropology of Music* (Evanston, 1964), ch. XIV.

in which the time depth is theoretically unlimited. From such an approach we learn certain things about a way of life, subject, in the case of music, to the limitations to be noted below.

But inevitably, in considering the reconstruction of culture history, a dynamic is implied which involves the wider framework of development through time. In this case we look at culture change, and thus history, as a *process* of time, and we are interested in any theory which implies process and which enables us to reconstruct what has happened in the past. Music can be used this way too, though again only within certain limitations.

Finally, in using specific tools—in this case music—we must raise the question of whether there is anything unique or special about the tool which makes it particularly relevant to the problem of reconstructing history.

I should like to consider each of these approaches in turn; but it must first be clear that the potential importance of music to this kind of problem varies widely because of its special characteristics. So far as is known, no African culture ever independently developed a notational system for its organization of culturally-defined musical sound; this means there is relatively little hope of reconstructing the aural shape of African music with any accuracy. As will be noted below, some attempts have been made along this line, either through special archaeological techniques or through the application of a priori anthropological theory, but such attempts do not seem particularly effective or reliable. The tracing of the actual sound of music to any substantial time depth does not appear, therefore, to be a very fruitful avenue toward reconstructing culture history as a whole.

Of course, music is represented not only by sound but by musical instruments as well, and some of these instruments have survived over considerable spans of time. Thus, in dealing with music as a tool for historic reconstruction, we must consider the music and the instruments and be prepared to use either or both as the possibilities present themselves.

Finally, musical sound as an entity has three major characteristics which seem to make it potentially valuable to the reconstruction of culture contact; these characteristics, which culminate in the reliability of the reduction of sound to statistical terms, may in the future give us a particularly sharp tool for analysis. This aspect of music study will be discussed as the final section of this paper.

I have noted above that one approach to the culture history of a people consists in describing that culture at a given point in time. The question is whether this can be done with music, and if so what kind of information it can yield.

Though examples are few, there is some evidence indicating the use made of song texts in Africa to bring historical information to mind. Waterman and Bascom, for example, in commenting on the topical song in Africa, write:

> Topical songs have been known to persist for generations when they commemorate some historic event or when they treat with some incident of lasting interest. Thus, songs referring to battles of the 18th century are still current in Nigeria, just as calypsos were composed in Trinidad deriding certain slave overseers or commemorating the first visits of *The Graf Zeppelin* or *The Duke and Duchess of Kent*.[2]

Similarly, Herskovits notes the historic usages of song in Dahomey:

> Songs were and are the prime carriers of history among this non-literate folk. In recounting the ritual associated with the giving of offerings to the souls of those who were transported into slavery, this function of song came out with great clarity. The informant at one point could not recall the sequence of important names in the series as he was giving. Under his breath, to the accompaniment of clicking finger-nails, he began to sing, continuing his song for some moments. When he stopped he had the names clearly in mind once more, and in explanation of his song stated that this was the Dahomean method of remembering historic facts. The role of the singer as

---

2. R. A. Waterman and W. R. Bascom, "African and New World Negro Folklore," in M. Leach (ed.), *Dictionary of Folklore, Mythology, and Legend* (New York, 1949), 21.

the "keeper of records" has been remarked by those who visited the kingdom in the days of its autonomy.[3]

Further examples could be cited, although the study of song texts with the particular problems of African history in mind has not been frequently or exhaustively undertaken. The difficulty of this approach lies in the problem of the authenticity of the texts in terms of the accuracy of the message or description conveyed. This is a similar difficulty to that involved in the acceptance or rejection of the evidence of African oral literature. But we do have at least one example of a song text which has remained unchanged over the past sixty-three years. This is "Nkosi Sikelel' iAfrica" first sung publicly in 1899 at the ordination of Reverend M. Boweni, a Shangaan Methodist minister; more recently it was adopted unofficially as a nationalist anthem in parts of Central and South Africa, as reported by W. Rhodes.[4] It appears, then, that song texts are capable of existing unchanged in the folk idiom over substantial periods of time, although we do not know for how long. A study and analysis of this problem might well lead the investigator into some relatively important areas of historic information, though I personally doubt that the time span would be long, despite the Waterman and Bascom claim for what appears to be a period of approximately two hundred years. At the same time, historic reconstruction of relatively recent periods is in its way as valuable as that of great epochs of earlier history; given the limitations of the song text, it appears that music may be most useful in this way.

The use of music and musical instruments as described in historic accounts is a second kind of reconstruction of culture history in this same general category. Kirby, for example, reports information concerning the xylophone in East Africa dating back to 1586;[5] and considerable numbers of references since that time

3. M. J. Herskovits, *Dahomey: An Ancient West African Kingdom* (New York, 1938), II, 321.
4. W. Rhodes, "Music as an Agent of Political Expression," *African Studies Bulletin*, V:16–17 (1962).
5. P. R. Kirby, *The Musical Instruments of the Native Races of South Africa* (Johannesburg, 1953), 47.

give us rather remarkable information concerning African instruments over the past four centuries.

In respect to musical sound, the time depth is much shorter, although fragments of notated songs appear from time to time in the accounts of early travelers, explorers, missionaries, and others. The validity of these transcriptions, however, is in considerable doubt, and it was not until more recent times that large and reliable samples of African music, transcribed from phonograph records, began to appear. Thus in 1917, Erich M. von Hornbostel transcribed and analyzed songs collected in 1907–1909 by the Deutschen Zentral-Afrika-Expedition headed by the Duke of Mecklenburg. Various other bodies of song from a similar time period are now available to us.[6]

The question is whether such materials help us markedly in reconstructing culture history and, if so, how. It seems clear that we do not profit greatly from knowing that the Rwandese had music in 1907, or even knowing precisely what form that music took when reduced to notation by a European expert, although this knowledge is of considerable significance when cast in the framework of a theory of culture change. Yet, if we were to find an instance in which such early materials differed drastically from those we can record today, we would be faced with a problem of great importance; for given the generally conservative nature of music, we should be forced to conclude that historic events of considerable impact had taken place in the meantime. To the best of my knowledge, no such sharp differences exist between past and present music sound systems in Africa; but again to the best of my knowledge, no really detailed comparative studies of such materials have been undertaken.

Much the same sort of information is available from the study of historic records of musical instruments. We should expect to find, and so far as I know do find, cultural continuity in musical instrument forms; but again, the studies have not been exhaustive.

This kind of reconstruction from historic accounts tells us cer-

6. E. M. von Hornbostel, "Gesänge aus Ruanda," in J. Czekanowski, *Ethnographic-Anthropologie* I, *Wissenschaftliche Ergebnisse der Deutschen Zentral-Afrika-Expedition 1907–1908,* Band VI, Erster Teil (Leipzig, 1917).

tain things about the history of the people involved. The information gleaned is obviously primarily directed toward the history of music and musical instruments as things in themselves; that is, music is a part of culture, culture moves through time, and thus through music we can approach certain kinds of history. Further, as pointed out above, we expect the processes of change to proceed in a more or less orderly fashion; when the available record shows discontinuities, in this case in the course of music, we should expect to find reasons for the discontinuities.

A third approach to the reconstruction of culture history in terms of the description of a culture at any given point in time and through the use of music depends upon the findings of archaeology. Two kinds of problems have been approached in using this method in African studies. The first is virtually restricted to the field of Egyptian studies and has been carried on primarily by European scholars who combine interests and talents in antiquarianism and musical instrument studies. It has been pointed out by Curt Sachs that research in Egyptian instruments is particularly rich because of two major factors:

> The extreme aridity of the desert soil and the Egyptian belief in the magic power of painting and sculpture. Aridity has preserved hundreds of instruments from decomposition, and many musical scenes are depicted on tomb walls . . . Egyptian art works are explained by short, naive texts written between the human figures wherever an empty spot is left. "He is playing the harp," they read, or, "He is playing the flute." Thus, we know the authentic names of practically all Egyptian instruments.[7]

Because of these two factors, it has been possible to reconstruct not only the instrumentation of the early Egyptian orchestra but, according to the investigators, the kinds of scales and even possibly the orchestral sounds produced. Instruments themselves provide the student with measurable acoustic quantities which can give a high degree of precision; and where instruments are not themselves available, scholars such as Sachs and Hickmann, among others, have reconstructed both forms and probable musical

7. C. Sachs, *The History of Musical Instruments* (New York, 1940), 87.

sounds from finger positions of harpists, for example, as these are depicted in a substantial number of paintings and bas-reliefs.[8]

In African areas outside Egypt, the archaeological record is far less rich as most musical instruments are made of wood and the aridity of Egypt does not prevail. Even so, however, some instruments have been preserved and have come to form part of the archaeological record. The most notable examples are iron gongs and rock gongs, of which the latter can be discussed briefly here; the former will be discussed below.

A considerable number of publications has been devoted recently to what is sometimes called the "rock-gong complex."[9] These are ringing rocks characterized by so-called "chatter marks," which are small, cuplike depressions caused by repeated nonrandom striking of the rock with a hammerstone. Rock gongs have been located in Nigeria, the Northern Cameroons, Uganda, the Sudan, Portugal, Brittany, Wales, and England.

Interpretations of the rock gongs, rock slides, and rock paintings, which are sometimes assumed to be associated phenomena, vary widely. Fagg characterizes them as a megalithic, prehistoric complex, and calls attention to the common interpretation that stone instruments are among man's earliest musical modes of expression;[10] Conant, on the other hand, argues for a more limited interpretation:

8. C. Sachs, *Die Musikinstrumente des Alten Aegyptens* (Berlin, 1921); C. Sachs, *History of Musical Instruments; The Rise of Music in the Ancient World East and West* (New York, 1943); H. Hickmann, "Miscellanea Musicologica," *Annales du Service des Antiquités de l'Egypte*, LII:1–23 (1952); H. Hickmann, "La Flûte de Pan dans l'Egypte ancienne," *Chronique d'Egypte*, XXX:217–224 (1955); "Le problème de la notation musicale dans l'Egypte ancienne," *Bulletin de l'Institut d'Egypte*, XXXVI:489–531 (1955).

9. B. Fagg, "The Rock Gong Complex Today and in Prehistoric Times," *Journal of the Historical Society of Nigeria*, I:27–42 (1956); B. Fagg, "Rock Gongs and Rock Slides," *Man*, LVII:30–32 (1957); F. P. Conant, "Rocks that Ring: Their Ritual Setting in Northern Nigeria," *Transactions of the New York Academy of Sciences*, Ser. II, XXIII:155–162 (1960); J. H. Vaughan, Jr., "Rock Paintings and Rock Gongs among the Marghi of Nigeria," *Man*, LXII:49–52 (1962).

10. Fagg, "The Rock Gong Complex," 42.

May the use of rock gongs represent a substitution of abundantly available ringing rock for the double hand gong made of iron, a much more scarce material? The quality of notes produced by both instruments is so similar that it is sometimes difficult to tell them apart . . . In other words, it would be most suggestive if rock gongs and iron gongs eventually prove to have roughly the same distribution. The significance of rock gongs then might be largely in terms of the diffusion of iron metallurgy in Africa, associated by some prehistorians with the spread of Bantu-speaking peoples.[11]

Given the current state of uncertainty as to the antiquity of the rock gongs, it is clear that only further research will establish their usefulness in reconstructing Africa's culture history. At the moment, however, there appears to be a tendency to attempt to solve the puzzle of the uses of rock gongs in the past by describing current practice. Vaughan describes the current use of the rock-gong complex among the Marghi of Nigeria, and holds that the parts of the complex "should be viewed as distinct variables in a much larger behavioural context—rites of passage." He lists the following patterns which he feels may characterize the complex: social rebellion, symbolic death to childhood, birth into adulthood, fertility rites, and publicity. He concludes his discussion of the complex among the Marghi by noting:

Extrapolation from the Marghi materials to all other rock paintings in Nigeria would be unwise, but these data are suggestive of possible behavioural bases to rock paintings and gongs. More importantly they indicate that a shift in emphasis from antiquarian studies of material traits to studies of rites of passage may lead to new discoveries of paintings, gongs and associated phenomena, and could certainly lead to a broader understanding of just what these non-behavioural artifacts mean.[12]

All the approaches discussed so far are those which fall under the general rubric of description of culture at a given point in time. Song texts may preserve historic occasions and events; descriptions of music and music instruments in literate sources tell

11. Conant, "Rocks that Ring," 161.
12. Vaughan, "Rock Paintings," 52.

us much about change and development in forms as well as of continuities and discontinuities through time; and archaeological reconstruction, whether through the discovery of instruments or the discovery of paintings and carvings depicting instruments, can tell us the same kinds of things as historic records but presumably with a greater time depth.

Two major kinds of information emerge from materials of this sort. The first relates to the history of African music itself; here the emphasis is upon a single aspect of culture and its development through time. The second relates to music as an aspect of culture which is descriptive of one phase of culture and useful, primarily through extrapolation, for determining the relationship of that aspect to other aspects of culture. The last is a reconstructive process which depends not only upon evidence but also upon controlled comparative analysis and logical deduction.

The second major approach to the reconstruction of culture history involves the possibility of using music to establish theories of grand processes which operate throughout time. Anthropology has seen the rise and fall of many such theories in the past, and some of them will be discussed here. These are discussed, first because theories of evolution or *kulturkreis* form a part of the history of ethnomusicology; second, because such theories have all left their imprint, although we may be unwilling and unable to accept them as originally phrased; and third, because, though the broader patterns of such theories are now rejected, they contain some truths and some speculations which are clearly not without merit.

Least acceptable today are evolutionary theories of the development of music, particularly those which, through the use of what is now regarded as an invalid comparative method, array facts from cultures around the world into systems which "prove" a deductively formulated theory. We need not consider such formulations—which have devised systems of cultural stages through which mankind is said inevitably to move.

Of almost equal difficulty are theories of the particular and ultimate origin of individual music styles or instruments. Balfour, for example, held that the African friction drum originated from the stick-and-membrane bellows and found the two to have a roughly coterminous distribution on the continent.[13] While he may conceivably be correct, it is as logical to suppose that the stick-and-membrane bellows developed from the friction drum as vice versa, and there seems little that is useful in this kind of search for origin.

A more controlled, but still largely speculative kind of evolutionary analysis is found in the work of Kirby, who postulates a developmental sequence for the musical bow but restricts himself primarily to applying his analysis to the Bushmen. He speculates that the hunting bow is probably at the origin of a number of stringed instruments. The first stage is the twang emitted by the bowstring when the arrow is fired; the second appears when it occurs to the hunter "to tap his bow-string with an arrow, thus applying a new method of sound-production to the string."[14] The third stage comes when a number of bows are placed together on the ground and are tapped by a single person. Further evidences of evolution are postulated as the performer learns to use his own body as a resonating chamber, adds outside resonators, and so forth. It should also be pointed out that, according to Kirby, a Bushman rock painting exists in which the third stage is illustrated.[15]

Similar formulations have been made for musical sounds; for example, Phillips postulates a series of stages in the development of music in general and attempts to apply them to Yoruba music in particular.[16] One of the most determined formulations, though used in a cautious manner, is that of Bruno Nettl about Shawnee Indian music of North America. In this case, Nettl has put together historic data and music structural materials to reach conclusions about the history of the Shawnee. Basic to his work, however, and basic to all evolutionary schemes, is the assumption that culture develops chronologically from the simple to the com-

13. H. Balfour, "The Friction-Drum," *Journal of the Royal Anthropological Institute*, XXXVII:67– 92 (1907).
14. Kirby, "Musical Instruments," 193.
15. *Ibid.*, 194–195.
16. E. Phillips, *Yoruba Music* (Johannesburg, 1953).

plex; thus Nettl postulates that the simplest songs are the oldest—simplest being those with "small range, simple form, and two or three tone scales."[17] Later in style are more complex songs, still later are those whose style appears to make it possible to postulate that they were borrowed from southern Plains tribes; newest of all are the Peyote songs whose origin in time is known.

Although the equation of old and simple is not, in my view, a fixed one, Nettl's study does indicate a possibility which will be discussed later in this paper. That is, he works from the basic fact that Shawnee style is internally diverse, with some songs showing certain constellations of traits and others showing other constellations. Given the diversity of the present repertoire, it is logical to assume that differing influences have come to bear upon it. In the case of the Shawnee, the various diversities of the style give clues to the influences which have shaped it; these in turn can be coupled with the historic record of the migrations of the Shawnee in order to help fix their history. In short, the diversity of style in the present Shawnee repertoire gives clues about contacts they have had with other peoples and enables us to buttress incomplete records. The scheme is not in itself evolutionary, except in the use of the "simple-old" syndrome.

The possibilities of using evolutionary schemes in reconstructing culture history are not particularly bright. In order to do so, we must make assumptions which do not seem tenable; for example, if one finds the stick-and-membrane bellows in one location, and the friction drum in another, it must follow, according to Balfour, that the culture of the first people is older than that of the second. Similarly, the culture of people who use the simple hunting bow as a musical bow must be older than that of people who use instruments of several strings. Or people who use two- or three-note melodies have older cultures than those who use six- or seven-note melodies. We can follow the logic of such propositions without difficulty; the problem is that logic and deductive theory are not substitutes for empiricism.

The same kind of criticism can be applied to *kulturkreis* theories

17. B. Nettl, "The Shawnee Musical Style: Historical Perspective in Primitive Music," *Southwestern Journal of Anthropology,* IX:284 (1953).

of the origin and history of various elements of African culture; but because music played such a large part in formulations of this kind, some discussion of these theories is necessary.

It will be recalled that Friedrich Ratzel established the first step in a series of speculations by drawing attention to the similarities between West African and Melanesian bows, in the cross section of the bow shaft, in the material and fastening of the bowstring, and in the feathering of the arrow. Leo Frobenius, however, took the idea a step further, calling attention to other culture elements which he considered similar in the two areas. Without going into detail concerning the arguments advanced by Frobenius, I should like to call attention to the fact that musical instruments (but apparently not music styles) formed the basis for a considerable amount of this speculation. In at least one instance Frobenius uses the drum as a primary piece of evidence:

> Our investigation of culture-anatomy may begin with African drum forms. By far the larger part of African drums consist of a log scooped out, one or both ends covered with hide. We need not enter into details here, and I do no more than state the fact that the Indonesian method of bracing drums reappears on the West African coast. Besides these commonest drum forms, others occur made entirely of a log, hewn round or with angles; in the latter case usually wedge-shaped, the broad surface resting on the ground. The logs are hollowed out within through a cleft, made always on the broad side. Often the cleft is enlarged at its ends, the enlargement forming a round aperture in the drums of the Congo, an angle in those of the Cameroons. The famous signaling or telegraph drums of the Cameroons belong to this class. The drums covered with hide are found throughout the whole of Africa, with the exception of its southernmost part, but the wooden drums occur only in the Congo Basin and in Upper and Lower Guinea. The hide-covered drums are a development of the famous millet mortar, which points to East India. The civilization of the Mediterranean shores has similar drums made of clay, and related to those found in Persia and in prehistoric tombs of Germany. Now, the wooden drums belong to the Malayo-Negrito elements of African culture. They recur in Melanesia and frequently in Poly-

nesia. Their home obviously must be the same as that of the lofty bamboo cane, for these drums are developed from the bamboo.[18]

Using musical instruments as one of his criteria for resemblance, Frobenius develops four culture circles in Africa: the Negrito culture, Malayo-Negrito culture, Indo-Negrito culture, and Semito-Negrito culture. In like order, each of these includes the following music instruments: (1) staff as music instrument; (2) bamboo lute, tangola and drum, wooden kettledrum, and marimba; (3) violin, guitar, earthenware base drum, iron kettledrum, tambourine; (4) gubo, gora, hide as drum, mortar drum, and pot drum.[19] Similar uses of music instruments were made by others, among them, Ankermann.[20]

Once established, the idea of the Melanesian–West African relationship, as well as of that of culture circles, was elaborated by other theorists, and musical instruments inevitably functioned as part of the schemes. Thus George Montandon devised a system of ten culture circles, postulated an original development in and near the Himalayan region which led through Oceania to Africa and, as usual, cited musical instruments as a major part of the reconstruction.[21]

For Africa specifically, he arrived at a series of five circles, as follows: (1) African primitive (15,000–20,000 years or more before our era) [including boomerangs, bull-roarers, whistles, trumpets, and other idiophones as instruments]; (2) Negrito period (15,000 or more years before the present era) [Pan pipes, primitive xylophones, wooden drum, musical bow]; (3) proto-Hamitic period (10,000 years or more before our era) [musical instruments developing out of 1 and 2]; (4) Hamito-Semitic period (7000–8000 years before our era) [same instruments plus those of

---

18. L. Frobenius, "The Origin of African Civilizations," *Annual Report of the Board of Regents of the Smithsonian Institution*, I:640–641 (1898).
19. *Ibid.*, 650.
20. B. Ankermann, "Kulturkreis und Kulturschichten in Afrika," *Zeitschrift für Ethnologie*, XXXVII:54–90 (1905).
21. G. Montandon, "La généalogie des instruments de musique et les cycles de civilisation," *Archives suisses d'Anthropologie général*, III:1–120 (1919).

India]; (5) Neo-Semitic (from about 700 A.D.) [instruments of Western Asian origin including the rebab, various lutes, etc.].[22]

These theories led to the postulation of further schemes involving similar principles but devoted exclusively to musical instruments. In his *Geist und Werden der Musikinstrumente* published in 1929, Curt Sachs, using the *kulturkreis* approach, laid out a worldwide theory of the history of all musical instruments which involved the creation of twenty-three strata; this was later to be "corroborated" by André Schaeffner among the Dogon and formed the basis for an extended study of African music instruments by Hornbostel.[23]

Hornbostel gave considerable attention to the comparison of his groups with Sachs strata, and found, in general, that they agreed, although there were differences on particular points. Using apparently the single criterion of extent of distribution of instruments, and assuming that the instruments with the widest distribution were also necessarily the oldest, Hornbostel arrived at a total of twelve groups, arranged as follows:

I. *Earliest Cultures.* 1. Universal: strung rattles, bull-roarer, bone-flute, scrape idiophones; 2. Universal—sporadic in Africa: end-blown conch trumpet; 3. Sporadic everywhere it occurs: percussion-rod. II. *"Ancient Sudan."* Extensive but not universal: gourd rattle? Cylindrical drum, mouth bow. III. *"West African."* W. and Central Africa, S. and E. Asia, South America: slit-drum, globular-flute, log-xylophone, nose-flute. IV. *"Mid-Erythraean."* E. Africa, S. and E. Asia—S. America: Pan-pipes, stamping-tube, central-hole flute, (gourd drum), single-skin hourglass-drum. V. *"Pan Erythraean, Early."* Indonesia—Africa: gourd-xylophone, iron bell, cup-shaped drum. VI. *"Pan-Erythraean, Late."* India-Africa: bow with gourd resonator, harp-zither with notched bridge. VIa. *"Hova."* Indonesia—Madagascar: flat-bar zither, tube-zither. VII. *Ancient Southwest Asia—Ancient Egypt:* 1. Proto-Hamitic? Animal

---

22. *Ibid.*, 93.
23. A. Schaeffner, "Ethnologie musicale ou musicologie comparée," in P. Collaer (ed.), *Les Colloques de Wégimont* (Brussels, 1956), 29–30; E. M. von Hornbostel, "The Ethnology of African Sound-Instruments," *Africa,* VI:277–311 (1933).

horn. 2. Pre-Islamic. Bow-harp. 3. Post-Islamic. Double clarinet, tanged lute. VIII. *Buddhism.* Buddhist Asia, sporadically in NW. Africa: double-skin hourglass-shaped drum. IX. *Pre-Christian, West Asiatic.* Arabia, E. Asia, Sudan: bowl-lyre. X. *Post-Christian, Pre-Islamic.* W. Asia—Indonesia, W. Africa: hooked drumstick. XI. *Islam.* NE. Africa, W. Asia—Indonesia; tanged fiddle with lateral pegs, kettledrum.[24]

Finally, Sachs later gave a concise explanation of his method and reduced his twenty-three strata and Hornbostel's twelve groups to three major ones. In respect to the method used both by himself and by Hornbostel, he noted as the chief axioms: "(1) An object or idea found in scattered regions of a certain district is older than an object found everywhere in the same area. (2) Objects preserved only in remote valleys and islands are older than those used in open plains. (3) The more widely an object is spread over the world, the more primitive it is."[25] In his three-part scheme derived from these principles, he reached the following conclusions:

The early stratum comprises those instruments which, prehistorically, occur in paleolithic excavations and, geographically, are scattered all over the world. These are:

Idiophones	Aerophones	Membranophones	Chordophones
rattles	bull-roarer		
rubbed shell?	ribbon reed		
scraper	flute without		
stamped pit	holes		

No drums and no stringed instruments appear in this early stratum.

The middle stratum comprises those instruments which, prehistorically, occur in neolithic excavations, and, geographically, in several continents, though they are not universal. These are:

slit-drum	flute with	drum	ground-harp
stamping tube	holes		ground-zither
	trumpet		musical bow
	shell trumpet		

---

24. *Ibid.*, 299–301.
25. Sachs, *History of Musical Instruments,* 62–64.

The late stratum comprises those instruments which, prehistorically, occur in more recent neolithic excavations, and, geographically, are confined to certain limited areas. These are:

Idiophones	Aerophones	Membranophones	Chordophones
rubbed wood			friction drum
basketry	nose flute		drum stick
rattle	cross flute		
xylophone	transverse		
jews' harp	trumpet		

This rough chronology, though established on the objective data of distribution and prehistory, gives satisfaction also to the mind concerned with workmanship and cultural level.[26]

How useful are theoretical formulations such as these? There seems, first of all, little reason for accepting the propositions forwarded by Frobenius and Montandon. This is partly because factual information is now available which did not exist some sixty years ago and which makes certain of their assumptions untenable, but mostly because both appear to have been dealing with a priori schemes for which they were intent upon supplying facts. The severest criticism must be directed toward assumptions of "layers of time." At the same time, the relationships between Africa and other parts of the world, in terms of migrations of peoples or of cultures, have never been clearly proven false or acceptable; and the criteria of form and quantity proposed by the Kulturhistorische Schule remain criteria better adapted to studying diffusion problems of more restricted scope.

The same strictures may be applied to the work of Hornbostel and Sachs, and yet it is clear that their formulations are based upon more reliable information more cautiously applied than those of Frobenius and Montandon. In both cases, one is struck by the extraordinary range of knowledge of music instruments brought to the theories; and it seems clear that the results may well be reasonably accurate in the broadest perspective. Logic is on their side, and in this case, logic is carefully buttressed by fact; the major difficulty, again, is in accepting the three premises regarding the diffusionary process; and if we cannot accept them

26. *Ibid.*, 63–64.

on the scale proposed by Sachs, then the theory must fall. The approaches taken by Hornbostel and Sachs appear more reasonable than those advanced by Frobenius and Montandon because they represent a step in the direction of far greater control of materials within the framework of diffusion studies.

There is no need here to summarize the increasing restrictions placed upon the study of diffusion and the reconstruction of culture history by a more rigorous methodology. But the result has been a controlled use of distribution and diffusion based upon certain principles which have been succinctly and simply expressed by Herskovits:

> It would seem, all things considered, that the effort is worth the return provided 1) *that the area selected for analysis should be one whose historic unity can be assumed,* and *the probability, not the absolute fact of historic developments, be recognized as the aim.*[27]

Under these conditions, we can examine one or two of the more recent diffusion studies of music instruments in Africa and assess their value in the reconstruction of culture history.

The concept of culture clusters as a taxonomic device for ordering cultures was suggested in 1952 by P. H. Gulliver, and further discussed by the present writer in relation to the cultures of the then-Belgian Congo.[28] In the latter article, I contrasted the cluster with the concept of culture area, and noted that:

> The cluster concept, however, adds a dimension lacking in the area concept in that it *suggests* generic relationship on the basis of historic fact and in what we have called commonality. In a culture area, diffusion from one or more centers is assumed and can often be traced, but in a cluster, by definition, we find not only diffusion but also the factor of commonality. Thus, for example, the fact that the Mongo say they are all re-

27. M. J. Herskovits, *Man and His Works* (New York, 1948), 521 (his italics).
28. P. H. Gulliver, "The Karamajong Cluster," *Africa*, XXII:1–22 (1952); A. P. Merriam, "The Concept of Culture Clusters Applied to the Belgian Congo," *Southwestern Journal of Anthropology*, XV:373–395 (1959).

lated and have myths and other means to 'prove' it, makes them quite different from the Flathead and Sanpoil Indians who are grouped together in the same Plateau area of North America but who deny any relationship to each other. The cluster involves an acknowledged historic unity, while an area shows unity, but of a descriptive nature only.

If the existence of the culture cluster can be accepted, and if it is further realized that music instruments inevitably are among the material traits characterizing a cluster, then it follows that instrument and cluster distributional boundaries should be very similar. This, in fact, turns out to be the case in the Congo where J. S. Laurenty in 1960 attempted to map the distribution of some musical instruments.[29] In reviewing Laurenty's work, the present writer attempted to draw attention to the correlations between clusters and instruments.

> In the first place, he [Laurenty] finds that in instrument distribution the peoples to the north of the Congo River and to the east of the Lualaba River are quite sharply differentiated from those in the Congo basin whose area is south of the Congo and west of the Lualaba: the differences are found in the form of affixing the drum head; the fact that the xylophone, zither and harp are found together in the north and somewhat to the east and not in the basin; and that the pluriarc is found in the basin and not to the north and east. Thus the boundary formed by the rivers makes a sharp distinction between harps and zithers on the one hand, and pluriarcs on the other. On the basis of ethnic divisions, this distinction is not particularly surprising; the pluriarcs are found among the Mongo peoples of the basin who form an enormous cluster of interrelated groups . . . while the harp, zither and xylophone belong to such well-defined clusters as the Mangbetu-Azande and the related Mamvu-Lese.
>
> It is generally felt that the Mamvu-Lese were pushed into their present location from the northwest probably before the 17th and 18th centuries, while the Mangbetu established themselves about 1750–1800 and the Azande about 1830, both com-

---

29. J. S. Laurenty, *Les Cordophones du Congo Belge et du Ruanda-Urundi* (Annales du Musée Royal du Congo Belge, Sciences de l'Homme, Vol. 2, Tervuren).

ing from the northwest and north. On the other hand, it appears that the Mongo have been in their present location for "several hundred years," having come from the northeast. The Mongo, then, must have moved through the present Mangbetu-Azande and Mamvu-Lese areas before the two latter clusters had arrived there, and thus the instrument distribution accords with what we know of the history of some, at least, of the peoples involved.

M. Laurenty's second conclusion is that there are some sharp distinctions between the Equator region north of the Congo River in the great bend of the Uele River, and those of Lake Leopold II: again evidence from the study of culture clusters accords with this conclusion. Further, Laurenty sees Ruanda-Urundi, the Lower Congo, and the Katanga as generally separated from each other and as distinct from all other populations as well in terms of musical instruments; again this is not surprising in view of what we know of populations and population movements. Ruanda-Urundi seems clearly to be East African in origin and affiliation, and thus separate from the Congo itself; the Kongo people in the Lower Congo are one of the earlier groups in the Congo region, having reached the Kasai about 500 AD, and thence moved into their present location by about 1150 AD; the Luba of the Katanga came into the area from the northeast while the Lunda peoples came from roughly the same area but before the Luba.

I am not trying to argue a necessary racial or even tribal correlation with musical instruments, of course, but it does seem logical that migrating groups would carry with them their musical instruments, which may or may not be like those of their earlier neighbors, and that thus we should expect some correlation to exist. But such correlation, it seems to me, can best be expected where culture clusters are involved, and not so much where we deal only with culture areas or even ecological areas. Thus the distribution of instruments noted by Boone and Laurenty and brought together by Laurenty, seem clearly to accord with what we already know about clusters in the Congo.[30]

I have quoted here at some length in order to make two points: first, that the culture cluster seems to be a valid concept which is

30. A. P. Merriam, Review of Laurenty, *Les Cordophones, Ethnomusicology*, VI:48–49 (1962).

much more precise than the older area concept in handling distribution of culture traits and the movements of peoples; and second, it appears that the presence and distribution of music instruments is predictable within a cluster. Reversing the latter point, it would then seem feasible to predict that the distribution of music instruments within limited African areas can be used both to establish clusters and to trace, either alone or preferably in conjunction with other evidence, the movements and history of the particular people involved. And the proposition as presented here seems to accord rather precisely with the restrictions on distribution and diffusion studies noted by Herskovits.

A second example of the use of music instruments in distribution and diffusion studies, as it applies to the reconstruction of culture history, concerns iron gongs. This subject is probably better known to prehistorians interested in African studies than it is to ethnomusicologists.

The first series of articles concerning the iron gongs was published by James Walton, and in it he established three gong classes: "double gongs joined by an arched link, single gong suspended from both ends, single gong with handle." [31] He found these gongs archaeologically distributed at Zimbabwe, Imnukwana, and Dhlo Dhlo in Southern Rhodesia, and from their distribution and development postulated that:

> Stratigraphical evidence at Zimbabwe shows that the arrival of these double gongs in Southern Rhodesia took place after the foundation of the Monomotapa Empire by Hima invaders at the end of the fourteenth century. The distribution pattern indicates that they spread from the Congo along the Kasai to Kazembe and thence southwards to Zimbabwe, and the Kazembe peoples, according to their own traditions, migrated from Mwato Yamwo on the Kasai to Kazembe.[32]

Barrie Reynolds raised some questions in a later article concerning Walton's descriptive typology and dating, as well as the

---

31. J. Walton, "Iron Gongs from the Congo and Southern Rhodesia," *Man*, LV:30 (1955).
32. *Ibid.*, 30.

diffusion route.[33] On the basis of this and other evidence, Walton changed his formulation both about the date and the means of introduction of the gongs into the Rhodesias:

> Studies subsequent to the publication of my original paper confirm that the iron gongs were introduced into Northern Rhodesia and further south by peoples who migrated from the Congo basin. This introduction took place sometime after A.D. 1500 when the first peoples began to migrate from the Congo into Northern Rhodesia and iron gongs may well have reached Southern Rhodesia by the middle of the sixteenth century . . . The people concerned could not have been the Lunda unless the gongs did not reach Southern Rhodesia until after A.D. 1740.[34]

Further studies on the problem were carried out by Brian Fagan, particularly in Northern Rhodesia, and he reached roughly the same conclusions.

> The Lusitu gongs open the question of the ultimate origin of these instruments, and the date of their arrival in Northern Rhodesia. It seems that they were introduced from the Congo by some reasonably early settlers, such as the Chewa/Maravi groups, who arrived in Northern Rhodesia from the Southern Congo about A.D. 1500 or earlier . . . It seems probable that gongs were introduced into Southern Rhodesia from the Congo by elements which entered the country around A.D. 1500–1600.[35]

And finally, using the gongs as well as other iron implements, Fagan was able to establish three phases of ironworking in Northern Rhodesia. "(1) The Earliest Period (*c.* A.D. 0 to ? A.D. 1000). (2) The Middle Period (*c.* ? A.D. 1000 to A.D. 1740) . . . and a few ceremonial objects including gongs are rarely found; at

33. B. Reynolds, "Iron Gongs from Northern Rhodesia," *Man*, LVIII:255 (1958).
34. Walton, "Iron Gongs," 30.
35. B. Fagan, "A Collection of Nineteenth Century Soli Ironwork from the Lusaka Area of Northern Rhodesia," *Journal of the Royal Anthropological Institute*, XCI:228–243 (1961); B. Fagan, "Pre-European Ironworking in Central Africa with Special Reference to Northern Rhodesia," *Journal of African History*, II:199–210 (1961).

Lusitu and in Southern Rhodesia, they are more common. The Chewa/Maravi migration brought in new ideas and tool forms around A.D. 1500. (3) The Late Period (A.D. 1740–1900)." [The source here is the Luba who came in repeated migrations.] [36]

In the case of iron gongs in Central Africa, then, a musical instrument recovered from archaeological sites and analyzed in stratigraphic and distributional terms has assisted materially in establishing dates and phases or periods of ironworking. Again the criteria proposed by Herskovits—for working in limited areas where historic unity can be assumed and for taking the probability rather than the absolute fact of history—have been clearly met.

It is clear that music instruments can be of considerable use in reconstructing culture history, both in connection with larger cultural units as in the study of culture clusters, and in archaeological investigations where musical instruments are part, or perhaps even all, of the materials recovered.

Up to this point three major uses of music in reconstructing the culture history of Africa have been discussed; the first of these is the reconstruction of the history of music and musical instruments through the utilization of various historic and archaeological techniques. It is assumed that such reconstruction for a particular aspect of culture is of value to the general historic picture since the analysis of a single complex such as music reveals patterns of change indicative of the culture as a whole. The second is the use of music and musical instruments as an adjunct to other kinds of investigations; and third is the role of music and musical instruments which, as in archaeology, point the way toward hypotheses which can be corroborated by additional information. All of these techniques are essentially additive, that is, they contribute to our knowledge of African history through analysis by methods which are basically non-musical—i.e., historic documentation or archaeological techniques.

A further question is whether music or musical instruments in themselves can present us with any unique method for reconstructing African culture history. The answer to this question is

36. *Ibid.*, 209.

positive, though many details remain to be worked out. If the method discussed below is rather highly technical, it is because of the nature of the materials to be presented. It would appear that music offers one extraordinarily precise way of reconstructing contacts between peoples as well as the migrations of cultures through time. If this is so, the diffusionists were wise indeed in their choice of music instruments to help to illustrate their theoretical culture circles; what was lacking was a precision of method which now seems potentially within our grasp.

It was noted previously that music has three special attributes which make it particularly valuable in the reconstruction of history. The first of these is that music is carried below the level of consciousness and therefore is particularly resistant to change. To the best of my knowledge, this aspect of music was first suggested by Herskovits who phrased it as follows: "The peculiar value of studying music . . . is that, even more than other aspects of culture, its patterns tend to lodge on the unconscious level." [37] What is meant by this is that patterns of music do not seem to be objectified by most members of most cultures, including our own, even though they are thoroughly learned. It seems to make no difference that most of us cannot make sharp definitions of consonance and dissonance, or speak with real knowledge of the perfect cadence; we recognize what is consonant and what is dissonant in our music, and we have learned the patterns of our music well enough to know when the closing measures of a musical composition are brought to a satisfying or to an "unfinished" end. Thus, we learn what kinds of sounds satisfactorily fit into our music without necessarily knowing anything at all technical about music; so music structure is carried subliminally, and it is resistant to change.

Two further points must be noted. First, this does not mean that music does not change; it does change, but except for cultural accident, it changes within what seems to be a culturally determined framework. In other words, barring unusual exceptions, we can expect music over a period of time to retain its general

37. M. J. Herskovits, "Patterns of Negro Music," *Transactions, Illinois State Academy of Sciences,* XXXIV:19 (1941).

characteristics. This is borne out in studies of New World Negro cultures whose music differs from the original African but retains the characterizing traits of African music.[38] The second point is that I am not convinced that music is unique in this respect; it may well be that other arts share the characteristic. In any case, it is clear that music operates in this manner.

The second attribute of music which makes it especially useful in studying culture contact is the fact that it is a creative aspect of culture which, through recording, can be frozen as it happens. Thus it can be repeated over and over and studied in detail.

Finally, and perhaps most importantly, music is one of the relatively rare aspects of culture whose structure can be transcribed to paper and expressed precisely through arithmetic and statistical means. While some questions remain to be answered in this connection, a number of such studies have been carried out with the result that there is a strong possibility of obtaining extremely fine and precise measurements of music pitches, as well as reducing song structure to a series of arithmetic measures which are subject to statistical analysis.

One of the earliest such studies was carried out by Hornbostel, who made comparisons between the absolute pitches of music instruments in Burma and Africa and in the Solomon Islands and Brazil.[39] In approaching the problem, Hornbostel set up three criteria necessary for significant comparison: these he refers to as exact determination, absence of purpose, and variability. Since the rate of vibration of various tones can be set out with what appears to be absolute precision, the first criterion, exact determination, is fulfilled simply in music. The criterion of absence of purpose is met by the fact that what is important in music is not the absolute pitch of any given note, but rather the intervallic relationships

---

38. A. P. Merriam, *Songs of the Afro-Bahian Cults: An Ethnomusicological Analysis* (Unpubl. diss., Northwestern University, 1951); A. P. Merriam, S. Whinery and B. G. Fred, "Songs of a Rada Community in Trinidad," *Anthropos*, LI:157–174 (1956); R. A. Waterman, *African Patterns in Trinidad Negro Music* (Unpubl. diss., Northwestern University, 1943).

39. E. M. von Hornbostel, "Über ein Akustisches Kriterium für Kulturzusammenhange," *Zeitschrift für Ethnologie*, XLIII:601–615 (1911).

among the various steps of the scale. That is, it does not matter (since it appears that some 70 tones can be distinguished within the octave) whether the first tone of a scale is at 236 or 250 vibrations per second; the human ear distinguishes both, and comparison on a world basis indicates that almost every possible absolute pitch is used by one or another culture. Therefore, absolute pitch seems to fulfill the requirement of absence of purpose. Finally, since pitch is infinitely variable theoretically, the criterion of variability is met. In sum, any single absolute pitch is an extraordinarily complex matter since pitch in general is theoretically infinitely variable and since it is intervallic relationship rather than any single pitch which is of vital concern in constructing a musical system. Thus, if absolute pitches are found in different musical systems, the possibility of coincidence, convergence, or parallel invention is very slight.

Hornbostel used the tones of four Burmese xylophones and two African xylophones, one from the Bavenda and one from the Mandingo. It is not necessary here to indicate the various computations made, but the result is a series of three figures, expressed in terms of vibrations per second, which represent the Burmese, the theoretical, and the Bavenda figures. These are as follows: 672, 669, 675; 738.5, 739, 735; 408, 408, 408; 450, 450, 453. These figures are almost incredibly close, and given the complexity of the event, as well as the coincidence of absolute pitch, type of instrument, and character of scale, the relationship is difficult, indeed, to contravene. Similar coincidences, it may be noted, were reached for Melanesian and Brazilian pan pipes.

More recently, A. M. Jones has made a similar study in which a somewhat broader range of musical characteristics has been used.[40] Jones, too, notes the almost exact similarity of beginning absolute pitch in comparing xylophone pitches of the Chopi, Malinke and Bakuba in Africa, with xylophones of Cambodia and Java. At one point he charts the pitches of the scale of six xylophones from these various regions and finds that in all cases the octave is divided into equitonal steps which are almost pre-

40. A. M. Jones, "Indonesia and Africa: the Xylophone as a Culture Indicator," *African Music*, II:36–47 (1960).

cisely the same size, and that the variations in no case exceed the smallest fraction of a semitone. Again, he notes the two Javanese scales, the *pelog* which is the seven-toned equidistant-stepped, and the *slendro,* an artificial pentatonic scale whose steps are either equitonal or nearly so, and finds examples of similar tunings in Africa. Finally, Jones adds information and comparisons of other kinds, i.e., the distribution of the techniques of singing in thirds as opposed to singing in fourths, fifths, and octaves, correspondence of physical form of music instruments found only in Java and West Africa, linguistic evidence, decorative patterns, game forms, and others. Jones closes his argument by saying:

> The thesis we have propounded alters our perspective of Africa; it calls for a map with the Indian Ocean in the centre—a basin whose rim is Indonesia on the east, Madagascar in the south, and Africa on the west, all, to a greater or less extent, sharers in a common sphere of influence. The theory calls for the collaboration of scholars working all round this rim. Perhaps African studies have tended to be too much confined to Africa . . . Let us all come into the open with evidence for or against. We would welcome discussion and criticism, but, as a musician, with one *caveat,* that those who would demolish the non-musical evidence must at the same time account for the musical phenomena if their argument is to stand . . . Perhaps all this is mere coincidence: but if so, will someone tell us what has to be its coefficient of frequency before chance coincidence changes overnight to become positive evidence? [41]

The single response to Jones' plea has come from M. D. W. Jeffreys who, however, does not argue the merits or demerits of Jones' evidence but rather confines himself to discussion of the point of view that Indonesia has not influenced Africa but Africa has influenced Indonesia through the Arab slave trade: "The similarities in music between Indonesia and Africa are due to the impress that African Negroes, imported into Melanesia by the Arab slave trade, exerted on the culture traits of Indonesia." [42]

41. *Ibid.,* 46.
42. M. D. W. Jeffreys, "Negro Influences on Indonesia," *African Music,* II:16 (1961).

Jones' final remark leads me to a last consideration of the potential use of music in the reconstruction of culture history. I have previously indicated that precision of technique and result can characterize the study either of music pitch or music structure as a whole; Hornbostel and Jones have used the former, but the latter is of equal potential importance.

The analysis of a music style depends upon breaking down a structure into its component parts and understanding how these parts fit together to form a coherent whole. Thirty or forty different parts can be isolated, measured, and expressed in arithmetic terms; for example, tonal range, melodic movement, melodic level, ascending versus descending intervals, proportions of wide, medium and narrow intervals, proportions of kinds of intervals used, and so forth. Given the fact that such measurements are significant, a problem to which I will return in a moment, it is clear that precise comparisons can be made between music styles. For example, the following figures were reached in a study in which Gêge (Dahomean-derived music of Brazil), Rada (Dahomean-derived music of Trinidad), and Ketu (Yoruba-derived music of Bahia, Brazil) were compared, and in which the three groups were contrasted to Cheyenne Indian music which was used as a control group. The figures below refer to the proportionate use of the intervals named, expressed as a percentage of the total number of intervals.[43]

Total	*Gêge*	*Rada*	*Ketu*	*Cheyenne*
Minor second	——	——	1.3 per cent	——
Major second	31.5 per cent	25.3 per cent	39	33 per cent
Minor third	35.5	39.6	22	28
Major third	12.3	14.3	13.5	10
Perfect fourth	13.5	14.3	21	15
Perfect fifth	4.4	3.9	2.3	5

It does not take a practiced eye to see that for this small number of measurements taken alone, the differences between the samples

43. Merriam, Whinery and Fred, "Songs of a Rada Community," 170.

are almost precisely what one would expect. That is, Cheyenne music stands apart in almost every respect, falling either above or below the Africa-derived figures. Further, the Gêge and Rada groups, both of which are Dahomean-derived, place themselves together in almost all respects, and are opposed to the Ketu (Yoruba-derived) music. I say that this is what we would expect because experience has shown that music does differ and also that a music system has continuity and integrity through time.

If we can accept figures of this sort, then it is clear that we have an extremely fine set of measurements which expresses a music style with great precision. If we can express a music style with this precision, and if the style does have individual integrity, we should be able to use the technique for the reconstruction of culture history. That is, given an unknown body of song in the New World, for example, we should be able to tell whether it is American Indian or African in derivation—common sense would tell us this, but through the application of this kind of analysis we can be more certain. But more important, it is apparently possible, once we know that the song body is African-derived, to know that it is Dahomean or Yoruba or Bakongo specifically. Similarly, if the method is correct, we should be able to take a Mongo group in the Congo, for example, and given the requisite quantity of comparative material, trace its antecedent forms in other parts of Africa, providing they still exist. And still further, given all the suppositions of the reliability of method and assuming refinement of technique, we should be able to disentangle the component parts which have contributed to the establishment of any given music style.

Since I have cited no examples from the literature concerning Africa, it is evident that none exists; and yet the technique has been used in New World Negro studies enough to indicate its high potential. It should be re-emphasized also that the examples noted above in connection with Gêge, Rada, Ketu, and Cheyenne music represent but a fraction of the items used for comparison, and that virtually all those used in the complete study give the same kinds of results.

There is, however, one set of problems which is still of concern, and this involves the questions of sampling and of which elements of music style are significant. The question of sample is universal in handling problems of this nature, and no further discussion of it need be undertaken here. The question of significance, however, is more pressing and more difficult.

Given thirty or forty items of music structure which can be isolated and expressed quantitatively, which of them are significant? Further, if we accept a particular trait as characterizing, do we have any right to assume that it is also unique? The answers to these problems lie in two directions, the accumulation of much more material than is presently available, and the submission of the results to tests of statistical reliability. The problem of the accumulation of further materials is a question of time, but there has been one case, at least, in which the arithmetic figures have been tested for reliability through the application of statistical means.

This test was undertaken by the present author and Linton C. Freeman, and the materials used were the interval counts for the Ketu and Rada materials noted above.[44] Without recapitulating in detail, the study is an attempt to discern the possible error in identifying the two song styles on the basis of the proportionate use of major seconds and minor thirds. The result, obtained through the application of Fisher's discriminant function, is that the probability of error in discriminating between the two styles is .09. That is, but 9 per cent of the cases in a distribution will be misclassified, and the authors note that "It is reasonable to believe that further reduction in error may be accomplished merely by adding more variables. In the final analysis it should be possible to reduce error in classification to less than one in one hundred." [45]

It would thus appear that the proportionate use of specific music intervals, calculated in relation to the total body of intervals in any given style, is both a characterizing and significant trait, and

44. L. C. Freeman and A. P. Merriam, "Statistical Classification in Anthropology: An Application to Ethnomusicology," *American Anthropologist*, LVIII:464–472 (1956).
45. *Ibid.*, 470.

given the large numbers of traits in a style which can be handled in the same way, it is clear that the precision of the tool is remarkably high. While its specific application to music styles within Africa has not as yet been carried out, its potential is enormous.

Music study, then, contributes in a number of ways to the reconstruction of African culture history. In certain uses it is corroborative; that is, its own history contributes to the knowledge of history in general, and both music sound and music instruments can be and are handled through techniques of historic documentation and archaeological investigation. It has reflected anthropological theory and history in that it has been widely used in evolutionary and diffusionist theories and, as with all other traits and complexes of culture, it can be used in diffusion and distribution studies. Its greatest potential contribution, however, lies in the fact that both music sound and music instruments, are subject to analysis of an extremely precise nature through the use of statistics.

VI

African Art and Culture History

Roy Sieber

Associate Professor of Fine Arts
Indiana University

Two comments must precede any discussion of the role of art in reconstructing the culture history of sub-Saharan Africa. Both are based on the relatively small number of archaeological art objects available from this area; this dearth is in contrast to the comparative wealth of material from Egypt, Greece, Rome, China, and the Americas.

Aside from rock engravings and paintings dating at most from 5000 B.C. and some terra cottas and bronzes from about 500 B.C., there are discouragingly few objects to discuss. This paucity is the result of the small amount of systematic archaeology carried out for cultures that produced nonperishable arts in any quantity. It is no exaggeration to say that nearly all archaeological art has been stumbled upon, not excavated. Most of the Nok terra cottas, all but a few of the finds at Ife and Benin, and the Igbo horde, were found under circumstances calculated to make strong archaeologists (and art historians, for that matter) weep. Bernard Fagg working at Nok and Frank Willett at Ife have done much in the past few years to recover information and to institute controlled excavations.[1] However, the nature of the sites themselves compli-

1. B. Fagg, "Primitive Art of Problematic Age," *London Illustrated News,* April 26, 1947, 442; B. Fagg, "An Outline of the Stone Age of the Plateau Minesfield," *Proceedings of the Third International West African Conference, Ibadan, 1949* (London, 1956), 203–222; B. Fagg, "A Life-size Terracotta Head from Nok," *Man,* LVI:95 (1956); F. Willett, "Bronze Figures from Ita Yemoo, Ife, Nigeria," *Man,* LIX:308 (1959); B. Fagg and F. Willett, "Ancient Ife: An Ethnographic Summary," in G. Mortelmans and J. Nenquin (eds.), *Actes du IV⁰ Congrès Panafricain de Préhistoire et de l'Etude du Quaternaire* (Tervuren, 1962), 357–374.

cates the issue. Thus far, most of the "controlled" Nok finds are well rolled in a river bed and isolated from occupation sites. At Ife, stratigraphy is all but impossible to ascertain except in instances where there are successive shard and/or pebble pavements (to my knowledge no more than two occur at any one site). Further, the Yoruba practice of reusing old building materials, such as mud from collapsed houses, has produced a hopelessly mixed debris at occupation sites. (I have seen maize-impressed pottery fragments in the bricks of recently built houses.) It should also be noted that the terra cottas excavated at Ita Yemoo, Ife, by Willett in 1957 are extremely soft. Fired at low temperatures, their texture is nearly indistinguishable from the surrounding soil.[2]

Thus, the first point is that the scarcity of art objects and clear stratigraphy echoes a scarcity of systematic excavation. The second is that it would perhaps be unrealistic to anticipate the existence of great quantities of archaeological arts. More finds are to be expected, of course, but if it is possible to judge from the recent African emphasis on arts of perishable media, over-optimism would seem distinctly out of order. At the same time, the assumption that even perishable arts existed in large quantity may be unwarranted. Gordon Eckholm expressed a widely-held view when he stated:

> It would appear to be generally the case that as soon as any culture has risen above the level of the primitive, objects of art of more durable materials begin to appear. An improved technology or an unusually favorable environment, or whatever it might be that allows larger groupings of people, usually results in the appearance of more specialized arts and crafts. Stone and fired clay, or perhaps metal comes into use in the realm of art, and objects of such materials can, of course, be preserved for the archaeologist to find.
>
> Perhaps an illuminating example of this observation is to be seen in Negro Africa. The art of the area as we know it is

[2]. In conversation, Willett has stated that they take on the character of a dry digestive biscuit in the dry season and a wet digestive biscuit in the rainy season.

basically wood-carving, a perishable medium, so we cannot see back into the past of this sculptural art. For most parts of Negro Africa there appear to be no archaeological remains whatsoever that would give us any indication of its history except a few minor and unimportant stone carvings and some occurrences of modelled pottery. By themselves they would probably have no aesthetic interest to us whatsoever. As we well know, however, fired clay and metal objects of extraordinary quality do occur under archaeological conditions at Ife in Nigeria. They appear here, it would seem to me, because this portion of Negro Africa is and has been for a considerable period an area of high population density and the most highly developed in its socio-political organization of any part of Negro Africa. It is here that we have something on the order of kingship and real cities, and as a consequence, I would say, a notable archaeological art.[3]

In addition to Eckholm's failure to mention the Nok complex and other ceramic and/or metal sculpture-producing groups, it is possible that he generally underestimates the case in expressing a view based on his observations in another geographical area of specialization. Sub-Saharan Africa could upset the assumed relationship between "kingship and real cities" (the latter usually implying "real," i.e., permanent, architecture), particularly where the materials for monumental architecture and a "notable archaeological art" are absent.

Further, it may be proven that the appearance of iron resulted in a florescence of woodworking (see below). The great quantities of wood sculpture reported in relatively recent times might lead then to a false estimate of the quantity of art objects produced before the introduction of iron. Indeed, Africa could even contradict the assumption that art forms necessarily move from less permanent to more permanent media.

With this prologue, we can turn to the problem at hand with the warning that much of the discussion will be—for the reasons

---

3. G. Eckholm, "Art in Archaeology," in *Aspects of Primitive Art* (Lecture Series Number One, Museum of Primitive Art, New York, 1959), 75–76.

given above—hypothetical and methodological rather than descriptive. Also, it will necessarily draw on non-African examples to make its point.

Tatiana Proskouriakoff, in a special symposium of the American Anthropological Association on "Middle American Anthropology," stated:

> I think many of my colleagues will agree that critical study of art is not for the archaeologist. Aesthetic values have little bearing on immediate archaeological problems, and their elucidation in works of art has always been and should remain the function of art critics and art historians. Few of us can bring to bear on these subjects the heightened perceptions and the intuitive interpretations that they require.
>
> Occasionally there are persons who do encompass both points of view successfully. Such studies as Spinden's on Maya art or Covarrubias's on the Olmec style, are both critical and anthropological. The synthesis, however, rests on conclusions reached independently by the two disciplines and does not of itself offer a practical method of research. In the field of art criticism, our responsibility ends with supplying for the critic the necessary information on chronology and cultural affiliation of works of art and in publishing them with the least possible loss of aesthetic values.
>
> As a student of culture, the archaeologist is concerned primarily, not with the creative and expressive aspects of art, but with the incidental anthropological information it contains and with the stable artistic conventions, techniques and mannerisms by means of which he can trace continuities in tradition.[4]

Granting that this "objective" attitude exists among many scientific archaeologists, this is perhaps not the occasion to demur.[5] Yet both H. J. Spinden and George Kubler protest this attitude

  4. T. Proskouriakoff, "Studies on Middle American Art," in *Middle American Anthropology* (Social Science Monographs, No. 5, Pan-American Union, Washington, D.C., 1958), 29.
  5. Eckholm, "Art and Archaeology," 78 and *passim,* uses the term "scientific archaeologist" to distinguish the "anthropological archaeologist" from the classical archaeologist and others whose work, though not unscientific, is generally more closely allied to that of the art historian.

According to the line of reasoning I have been following, this lack of interest among archaeologists in the arts of Middle America stems primarily from their background in scientific disciplines. In other words—if we look at the history of the development of archaeology that is done in the area, we see the reasons why its orientation has become channeled in the direction it has. There are, of course, other factors that are involved. Although interest and activity in the area has been increasing greatly in recent years, there have been relatively few institutions and persons engaged in the study of its ancient cultures, and much of the work that has been done has been directed toward developing basic chronologies and distributions, as necessary here, because of the lack of written records, as it is in the areas of more primitive cultures. Some of the more fundamental problems are indeed more readily solved through the detailed study of objects that occur in large numbers and whose occurrences in stratified deposits permit more objective analysis.

It is significant that earlier in this paper, discussing the training of an archaeologist, he noted: "most likely he will get no formal training in the fine arts."

Under the circumstances it is perhaps necessary to note—indeed, to insist—that art-historical studies are by no means as subjective and unscientific as Proskouriakoff and Eckholm indicate. In fact, Eckholm singles out two studies by Proskouriakoff as "completely acceptable to most Middle American archaeologists, I believe, and are considered to be significant contributions to the archaeology of the area."[7] In no way minimizing Proskouriakoff's excellent studies, it should be added that they are, as art history, not particularly exceptional for their disciplined approach. Her fine sense of discrimination of form, style, and subject implications find counterparts in studies ranging over the whole history of world art. Hers are exceptional in two respects: first, their subject (Middle American archaeological arts) and, second, her adaptation of the well-known art-historical technique of relating style to chronology.

7. *Ibid.*, 83. The works he refers to are *A Study of Classic Maya Sculpture* (Carnegie Institute of Washington, Publ. 593, 1950) and *Varieties of Classic Central Veracruz Sculpture* (Carnegie Institute of Washington, Publ. 606, 1954).

in their discussions of Proskouriakoff's paper, Kubler as an art historian and Spinden in a general protest against disciplinary separatism. Eckholm touched upon this point when he stated:[6]

> The archaeologist must take cognizance of what we call works of art, but they must be analyzed, of course, in a scientific manner. Why were they made, what role do they play in the community that produced them, and how can they be used to show that one culture was related to another? Subjective evaluations of them are not permissible or at least are not recognized as valid evidence leading to a particular conclusion. By the same token, the scientific archaeologist is never interested in an object as of importance in itself. To him it only provides an illustration of ideas that he may have about culture or culture history. This is an ideal, of course, and all archaeologists do not come up to it. It is characteristic, however, that an archaeologist of this kind has no desire to collect objects of art and to have them about him in his daily life, for in themselves they have no meaning to him. Taking this a step further we can also see why exhibitions devoted exclusively to objects of primitive art are something of an incongruity according to his lights.

He does, however, add:

> It does happen, though, that anthropologically-trained archaeologists with this dominantly scientific orientation do operate in some regions of more advanced cultures where objects of considerable aesthetic merit are found. As we might expect, such archaeologists are usually not able nor are they interested in fully exploring these more complex phenomena. They are unaccustomed to dealing with things of this kind and are untrained in the methods and insights that have been developed by the art historians.
>
> This is true of Middle and South America where most of the archaeological investigation is being done by Latin American scholars trained in methods developed in the United States or by scholars from this country. . . . Knowing these better would be of exceptional importance to our understanding of the cultures of Ancient Mexico, but they have not been subjected to the kinds of studies they deserve.

6. The passages quoted are from "Art and Archaeology," 79–83 *passim*.

It is thus evident that the archaeologist distrusts, as he should, art criticism and connoisseurship rooted in esthetic values and judgments that are western and contemporary in origin (even though they are probably *less* subjective than the archaeologist suggests). Such an ethnocentric approach, although unimpeachable with regard to contemporary western esthetics, is not to be considered a useful tool in the analysis of the arts of non-western societies or in the reconstruction of culture history.

On the other hand, the archaeologist should realize, perhaps more than he does, the potential worth of objective analyses of subject, symbol, type, and style as developed by art historians. It is to these aspects of the study of the arts and to their value in the recovery of culture history that the remainder of this paper is devoted.

Despite her exclusive concern with Middle American art, Proskouriakoff has offered some suggestions on methodology well worth the attention of Africanists concerned with culture history.

Middle American art furnishes us with three distinct kinds of data. The first comprises ethnographic details presented in a realistic manner. Thus Tozzer, on the basis of sculptures at Chichen Itza, distinguished the Maya and the Toltec peoples. Thompson, in a more recent paper on Bonampak, discussed the ethnographic implications of the detail drawn on the murals. Although such grand pictorial scenes are rare in Middle America, its minor arts are full of scattered ethnographic data, constantly used to amplify interpretations of ancient customs and to trace their continuity in time.

Even richer than the descriptive content, though much more difficult to interpret, is the symbolism of Middle American art, and this constitutes another field of interest, closely akin to an interest in epigraphy. Caso and Bernal's presentation of the funerary urns of Oaxaca leans heavily on this approach. Rand's study of the water symbol is an attempt at a more analytical method, which follows a single symbol in its variations. Occasional fantastic excursions into this field do not detract from the more serious work on which archaeologists habitually rely.

It is the third kind of data, however, that I would like to

stress in this discussion: data inherent in the formal properties of design, considered without reference to aesthetic values or to symbolic meaning. In Middle America we have scarcely begun to explore the potentialities of this field, although it is directly applicable to archaeological problems.[8]

Each of these—subject matter, symbolism and style—merit close scrutiny; yet some terminological adjustment seems necessary. For the purposes of this paper, symbolism will be considered as an aspect of subject matter and a new third category, type, will be considered. Of these, the easiest to discuss and of most immediately apparent value to historical reconstructions is the realistic (or at least identifiable) depiction of a subject matter which illustrates one or more aspects of the culture.

Proskouriakoff's reference to "ethnographic details" is perhaps too limiting a view. In a broader sense, "subject matter" is a better term, for it implies not only the ethnographic details depicted (hairdo or clothing, fishing-spear or bow-type) but the thing or event depicted as well (man, deity, animal, hunting scene, or ritual act).

J. Desmond Clark has used the subject matter of South African rock paintings extensively (but by no means exclusively) in his reconstruction of the daily life of the Later Stone Age.[9] He spells out his sources thus:

> It is possible to reconstruct with a certain degree of accuracy the life of Later Stone Age times, since more of the perishable equipment has survived and *in the rock art there is preserved an invaluable record of the people's hunting methods, the different kinds of weapons and domestic equipment they used, their customs and their ceremonies.* Also, in the Bushmen and Bergdama, we have still surviving hunting people who were once making and using stone tools, and the numerous records of them and of the Hottentots in the writings of the early travellers and missionaries help to bridge the gap between history and pre-history and so to clothe the bare bones of Later Stone Age culture

8. Proskouriakoff, "Studies on Middle American Art," 29–30.
9. The following extracts are from J. D. Clark, *The Prehistory of Southern Africa* (Hammondsworth, 1959), Chapters 9–10, pp. 217, 219, 220, 231, 220–223, 229, 228–229. Italics are the author's.

with flesh and blood and to give us an insight into the daily life of the people of those times.

It should be noted that he uses both scenes (subject matter broadly taken) and details. For example, the following three references may be cited to indicate his use of subject matter (scene):

Like the Bushmen to-day, groups from different bands were probably brought together for certain special purposes. Paintings occur of possible marriage scenes, rain ceremonies, and burials of important persons, and such occasions may have implicated more than one band. Paintings also show that, at friendly meetings between bands, arms and sandals were put down at some distance away from the meeting place, as in Bushman custom. Many are the paintings of fights and these no doubt followed trespass on hunting preserves, the abduction of women, adultery, homicide, theft, or other such disputes.

Trade or barter was another cause of the bringing together of families and bands. As we have seen, the Wilton family that lived in the Amadzimba Cave in the Matopos may have been particularly skilled in making bone tools and so have supplied its own group; a painting on the wall shows what appears to be the exchange of bone points between two persons.

There is a strict division of labour between the sexes and this can be seen again and again depicted in the rock paintings. Only the men do the hunting while it is the women who are responsible for collecting vegetable foods, for the cooking, and for rearing the children.

Several rock shelters with paintings of fishes and fishing scenes are known from the eastern Free State. Some of these fish certainly appear to be dolphins and other sea fish and the two fishing scenes found in the Drakensberg Mountains also show what are apparently sea fish being speared by men each standing on a float or boat with a platform at one or both ends, no doubt to facilitate balancing.

The following quotation will serve to illustrate his use of details found depicted in the paintings:

The hunting weapons were, first and foremost, the bow and arrow. From rock paintings it can be seen that the bows may vary considerably in size between different regions but they are always made from a single piece of carefully chosen and worked wood. The unusually small size of the bow used by the Cape and other Southern Bushman peoples and the typical bone-pointed, unfletched arrows are seen repeatedly in the painted shelters of the south-eastern region . . . The type of bow depicted in the Rhodesias and further north in Tanganyika, however, is a long bow, sometimes almost as long as the man himself . . . The bow strings of the present-day Bushmen are usually made from sinew, but among the northern groups a twisted bark string is found and in the Congo the Pygmies and BaTwa use a rattan string.

The arrows were probably of complex structure and must have varied not a little in detail just as the modern Bushman arrows vary to-day. There are several different forms of arrow depicted in the rock paintings and it can be seen how arrows were sometimes feathered in the northern, more wooded, regions.

His description of arrows is based on more evidence than the paintings alone, such as nineteenth-century descriptions and artifacts themselves (points, fore- and link-shafts, etc.). For the most part, Clark uses the paintings as correlative or corroborative evidence. This, where possible, is undoubtedly a wise procedure for several reasons, chiefly the ease with which depictions from another culture can be misread or misinterpreted. At the same time, inferences can be in order when supporting (or contradicting) evidence is absent. For example:

> At least one rock painting exists of men spearing fish from the bank . . . but no bone harpoon-heads have as yet been found in South Africa, though it is possible that they will be discovered when an inland waterside site favourable for the preservation of bone is investigated.

Further, Clark uses a rock painting as negative evidence in the following observation:

> Nowadays dogs are commonly used by Bushmen for hunting, but it is uncertain whether these people possessed dogs in prehistoric times as, so far as I am aware, no early painting exists

showing Bushmen with dogs, though dogs are depicted in several late paintings in the Union. It is probable, however, that they were used in the north earlier than they were further south and may have been introduced by the earliest pastoral people.

It is evident that the subject matter of pictorial art can be useful in the reconstruction of culture history. In addition to the instances given, the following observations might be made.

1. *Depictions can indicate the basic economy of the culture,* as in the South African paintings. These show hunters, fishermen and women with digging sticks or other implements, indicating a hunting-gathering economy.

2. *Representations of ritual and deity at least intimate the beliefs and values of the culture.*

3. *Subject matter often reflects cultural change or foreign influences,* as in the appearance in South African rock paintings of fat-tailed sheep, cattle, horses, differing racial types (Bushman, Bantu, Hottentot, European) and what may be a sailing ship.[10]

4. *The relation of subject and date is a complex one.* In many —if not most—cases the art historian looks to the archaeologist for help in dating prehistoric art. Subject, as such, is seldom an aid in dating a culture, although at times it can be useful. For example, certain Saharan rock paintings and engravings depict extinct animals or ones no longer found in the area. These can be taken as clues to the climate of the area and serve as an aid to dating the pictures and the culture that produced them. In general, however, style is a far better criterion of date than subject matter. We will return to this problem later in the paper.

Thus far, examples of subject have been taken solely from rock paintings. Valuable as they are, their geographic distribution is limited, and for much of sub-Saharan Africa this tool is totally absent. (Painting elsewhere is restricted for the most part to perishable surfaces such as textiles and house walls.)

The usefulness of other archaeological arts needs to be explored. Despite the paucity of such artifacts it is possible to discover some

10. *Ibid.,* Figures 58 and 59.

potentially useful hints. Aside from painting, sculpture is probably the only art that is essentially depictive (subject oriented) in a manner useful in reconstructing culture history. The quantity of prehistoric sculpture is extremely limited, but what exists comes predominantly from areas where there are few if any paintings. Furthermore, instances of compositions, such as reliefs showing multiple figures or objects or groupings of three-dimensional figures or objects, occur rarely. Benin reliefs, Ashanti and Dahomean bronze figure groups, and similar art forms cannot be dated before the seventeenth century at the earliest. Associated but independent sculptures, as found on Benin altars or in Yoruba shrines, have been documented; but in no instance has such a complex been excavated *in situ*. In any case, interpretation based on subject matter could be extremely difficult if, as in Yoruba and Benin, the thread connecting the physically associated objects cannot be adduced from the objects themselves. (For example, the writer recalls a Shango shrine containing *ibeji* [twin-cult figures] and an Eshu shrine with Shango staffs and *ibeji*.)

The subject matter of sculpture in Africa rarely exists on the scenic level that is found in the rock paintings. On the other hand, sculpture displays a rich variety of detail that can be taken as depictive. Much of the archaeological sculpture illustrates costume, hair arrangements, scarification, and similar details.

It must be noted that for an art to prove useful to culture historians, it must be assumed that the details are essentially accurate. This probably can be assumed on the basis, for example, of the near identity of details of regalia depicted in Ife and Benin bronzes with the ceremonial costumes still worn by the *oni* and *oba*.[11] Moreover, it becomes increasingly apparent to the writer that more recent African sculpture displays a consistent and remarkable accuracy of detail. Himmelheber juxtaposes photographs of the head of a Senufo sculpture and a woman's head to indicate the precision with which details of hairdo, for example,

11. See, for example, the figure of an *oni* discovered in 1957 which depicts the "ceremonial regalia as worn, so the present *oni* tells me, at the coronation." Willett, "Bronze Figures," 308.

are copied.[12] I have observed that "old" scarification marks and costume continue to be accurately indicated in figure carvings among the Idoma and Goemai despite their nearly total disappearance from the contemprary scene. Thus, despite its allegedly "abstract" (or even "cubist") character discerned by some western critics, African sculpture is in fact more realistic than not.

Assuming then that details are accurate, it would seem that with regard to the Nok terra cottas certain observations by Bernard Fagg point to profitable inquiries. He states:

> There is much internal evidence of the material culture in the terra-cotta figurines themselves, many of which show a wealth of carefully executed details of dress and accoutrements comparable to some of the work of Ife and Benin.[13]

In his discussion of a particular head he notes:

> The five "buns" of hair resemble the present-day hair style of the Kachichiri and Numana, tribes living about 30 miles east of Nok. Four of these buns have holes which may have been used for the insertion of feathers—an inference from contemporary practice. Three strings of beads or plaited fibre across the forehead end at the temples, where something has been broken away at each side . . . The keeled ornaments on the buns of hair are probably plaited hair, though no modern parallels are known to me.

Further,

> Fragments of female figures show bangles around the neck and elaborate ornaments and strings of beads around the loins, with a bell hanging at the side—this has a modern parallel in a tribe living forty to fifty miles from Nok. Part of a human figure shows a hand clasping a hafted stone ax, stylistic corroboration for the presence of polished stone axes found associated in the same geological horizon.

12. H. Himmelheber, *Negerkunst und Negerkünstler* (Stuttgart, 1960), Figure 53.
13. Fagg, "Primitive Art," 442.

And, finally,

> This head suggests that the makers of the Nok figurines were physically as well as culturally closely parallel to the many pagan tribes living in Northern Nigeria today. There may in fact have been an extensive cultural unity, owing its existence perhaps to the introduction of metallurgy, from which many of the very diversified present-day pagan cultures of the Niger-Benue region have derived.[14]

Some corroborative evidence exists. For example:

> During the *Nep* rites (performed by married couples for fertility purposes) Ganawuri women wear an iron bell with a long iron clapper at their side, very similar to what appears to be a bell and its clapper represented on the side of one of the female figurines found at Nok. Moreover five interlocking iron rings have been found in old-tin-bearing deposits at Nok (the exact horizon is uncertain) similar to the iron chains worn as a decorative skirt by Ganawuri women before they have successfully completed the *Nep* rites.[15]

Parallels two thousand years apart should certainly be viewed with some suspicion, yet they are provocative and the search for links is to be encouraged.

Particularly in the depiction of perishable elements (for sculpture—hair arrangements, scarification, costume, etc.; for painting—similar details plus scenes and acts) which do not survive archaeologically, works of art contain data of potential use to the reconstruction of history. As yet, neither the paintings nor the sculpture have yielded extensive sequence of such details. A relatively uninterrupted sequence would, of course, reveal specific changes or modifications that would constitute an element (or aspect) of culture history such as exist for Greek or Mayan art. Careful analyses of paintings (of style, of materials, and of palimpsests) have begun to reveal such sequences. Whether sculpture will also yield such sequences depends greatly on future discoveries. So far, materials available for study are from geographically scattered and temporarily discontinuous sources.

14. Fagg, "A Life-size Terra-cotta," 95.
15. Fagg, "An Outline of the Stone Age," 217.

Next in the discussion of the aspects of subject matter, the problem of symbolism raises its provocative head. Without direct—written or equally reliable—evidence, the relation between the symbol and the idea symbolized is extremely difficult to ascertain. The symbolic content of a work of art is neither as apparent as its subject (a lamb may be distinguishable as a lamb but undistinguishable as a symbol of Christ without its literary reference, "Lamb of God"); nor is it as discernible or time-bound as its style (the lamb has been produced in many styles and sub-styles over the last fourteen centuries). Various suggestions that there exists a universality of symbolism which permits cross-cultural identification have produced no workable code or iconographic dictionary. Indeed, up to this point the associational inventiveness of humans in constructing symbols does not seem susceptible to analysis. "Every culture has developed configurations of associated ideas and symbols which appear illogical to an outsider. Our own associations of lambs, doves and crosses with a death cult, revealed in every cemetery, would look like the purest schizophrenia to an Eskimo." [16]

At best, in the absence of written sources, a combination of archaeology, the direct historical approach, and inference may at times permit an educated guess. But even such can be dangerous, as seen in the attempts to deal with symbols in Middle America (where a great deal more evidence exists than for Africa) or in the apparent over-symbolization of Griaule and his students in their analyses of the Dogon. These negative comments are not meant to throw symbolism out of court with regard to African culture history, but to indicate the need for more data, more thought on the subject, and better methods of verification before it can be used as a systematic tool.

Unlike symbolism, which requires external evidence, style is an intrinsic aspect of the material art object and open to careful analysis. Used as a basis for classification, it becomes an aspect of material culture studies, whether ethnographic or archaeologi-

16. Ralph Linton, in W. Fagg and E. Elisofen, *The Sculpture of Africa* (New York, 1958), 10. He could have added skulls, flowers, and cherubs.

cal. Artifact assemblages can be analyzed and classified on the principle that "every style is peculiar to a period of culture and that, in a given culture or epoch of culture, there is only one style or a limited range of styles. Works in the style of one time could not have been produced in another." [17]

This observation reflects a general agreement among art historians and, although less often expressly stated, archaeologists. The latter, for example, are to a great extent style-oriented in their analyses of ceramics. Sequences based on stratigraphy are cross-referenced in part to changes in shape, color, and decoration which are, of course, elements of style. In general, style may be said to be the sum of such elements.

In ceramics, the number of stylistic elements is limited, essentially to shape, color, and decoration, but their variation is great. Certainly other factors—size, function, and material for example—are open to analysis and have proved particularly useful in conjunction with stratification and style analyses. The basic concern of this paper, however, is with style and not primarily with the problems of cross-referencing style with other types of analysis.

Where stylistic elements are limited within an art such as ceramics, analysis of variation and its cultural correlatives is relatively simple. Particularly where a large quantity of material is available, as is often the case with ceramics, stylistic norms emerge that permit the identification and rejection of idiosyncratic variations (such as less or more than average skill or inventiveness on the part of the potter).

However, where the number of stylistic variables is greater, the problems of analysis are compounded. Analyses of sculpture, such as those of Proskouriakoff for the Mayan area and Olbrechts for the Congo, indicate the greater number of variables that must be treated.[18] With reference to Olbrechts' work: "Style

17. M. Shapiro, "Style," in A. L. Kroeber (ed.), *Anthropology Today* (Chicago, 1953), 288. Robert L. Rands quotes just this passage in his comment on Proskouriakoff's "Studies on Middle American Art," wherein he emphasizes the importance of style as an archaeological tool.

18. Proskouriakoff, "Studies on Middle American Art"; F. Olbrechts, *Les Arts Plastiques du Congo Belge* (Brussels, 1959).

to him was mainly the sum of factors like posture, bodily proportion and anatomical detail in a given figure or set of figures. This method applied with great consistency and single-mindedness, gave results which have stood the test of time remarkably well."[19] In addition to the stylistic elements analyzed by Olbrechts, Proskouriakoff includes details of costume and other associated attributes. She deals with stone sculpture and correlates style with time and place; Olbrechts, dealing with wooden objects of approximately the same age, relates style only to place (tribal, subtribal and, rarely, village provenance). It is possible, of course, that Olbrechts' data and his conclusions will prove to have valuable chronological implications precisely because the objects were all of approximately the same age.

It is significant that neither Olbrechts nor Proskouriakoff deals with individual artists' styles except peripherally. In fact, this introduces a major caution regarding the dangers of oversystematization in style analysis. The greater the precision attempted, the greater is the potential for error because of three factors: (1) *Quantity.* Rarely do sculptures (or paintings) exist archaeologically in the quantity of, say, ceramics; (2) *Variables.* The greater the number of variables treated the greater the difficulty of establishing fixed concordances; (3) *Idiosyncratic factors.* Whether sculpture and painting are more open to individual stylistic variations than other arts is a moot question. Nevertheless, in combination with fewer specimens and a greater number of variables, individual artistic differences in style (and technique, for that matter) loom larger and thereby seem to limit the scope of precise analysis.[20]

The combination of these three factors can produce, and in the writer's experience have produced, a situation in which it is difficult or impossible to determine whether certain stylistic details

19. Guy Atkins, review of Olbrechts' *Les Arts Plastiques, Man,* LXI:191 (1961).
20. Indeed, it may be that the extreme variations within a style unit can be greater than the variation between that unit and another. For example, the stylistic difference between two Senufo objects may be greater than the difference between a "typical" (or mean) Senufo piece and, say, a Bambara piece.

in a limited group of objects are historically or geographically significant or evidence of an individual artist's style. An examination of the Nok terra-cotta fragments reveals several styles or sub-styles. For each, some documented examples exist. The smaller stylistic variations between the examples of each style or sub-style may be significant historically or geographically or they may be idiosyncratic differences. If the distinctions are cultural, undocumented fragments may be assigned with some confidence to the same time or place on the basis of style. If, however, they are idiosyncratic, such assignment may prove impossible. Obviously, more data, more examples, and more systematic analyses are necessary before it is possible to decide this question.

Another caution is in order. It does happen that two or more styles exist at the same time and place. An imported style can thrive alongside a local style, or variant local styles can develop. An aristocratic style may develop alongside a folk style. Variations may be related to materials, size, or function. Works in clay and metal (wax or resin if cast by the "lost wax" process) *may* be closer stylistically to each other than either is to wood or stone because of the modes of manufacture: both processes build up forms rather than cutting them out of a block. A large wooden figure may be more pole-like, a small figure squatter because the form of the latter is less constrained by the cylindrical shape of the tree. Masks may differ in style from figures because of the manner in which they are used or because of differing rates of destruction and replacement. Finally, the association of form and function may serve to inhibit stylistic change where the type reflects a more conservative aspect of the culture; at the same time, another type is unaffected and experiences stylistic changes.

Despite these cautions with regard to oversystematization and oversimplification, style, because it is culture-bound and indeed because it may be carried subliminally, has proved an enormously useful tool in archaeology.

1. *The geographic distribution of a style* may corroborate or help determine the geographic distribution of a culture. Clark notes that the distribution of rock engravings in southern Africa coincides reasonably closely with that of the Smithfield culture and

rock paintings with the Wilton and Smithfield-C cultures.[21] The Nok culture is, to date, almost totally defined by the terra cottas which seem to interrelate stylistically. Further, it is perhaps significant that the linguistic areas of Africa as defined by Greenberg reflect the larger art style complexes more accurately than earlier linguistic analyses.

2. *The depth distribution of a style* may corroborate or help determine the temporal distribution of a culture. For example, the archaeology of the north coast of Peru exhibits a series of sequences, each with an identifiable art style which, in turn, can be related to a phase of the culture history of the area. This phenomenon has been observed many times over in the history of world art.

3. *The interactions, overlappings, and influences that occur in art styles* reflect exactly such interactions, overlappings, and influences in culture. These may occur geographically or temporally. The spread of a style often implies the diffusion of other aspects of culture. Its distribution can reflect, for example, the spread of language and quite probably other cultural traits; more significantly, the movement of a style seems often to reflect the movement of a people.[22] It may even be possible to determine from style—in conjunction with other factors—the size of a migration. If large, there is a tendency toward almost total style replacement; if small, the tendency is toward minor style enclaves, plebeian or aristocratic.

It is difficult to find a term that will apply to still another aspect of the art object. Art historians usually make themselves understood by using either "form" or, preferably, "type." Form often implies some contact or overlap with style, whereas type is taken to mean a class or subclass or objects (for example, easel paintings or bowl). Archaeologists have preempted certain spe-

21. J. D. Clark, *Prehistory*, 253.
22. Art historians may find this statement heretical, for in the history of Western art, styles seem to travel despite cultural differences. Yet in every such case known to the author, there has been either a lingua franca (e.g., Latin), shared religious beliefs, a shared aristocracy, or a combination of such factors.

cial meanings for "type" that makes its use here ambiguous. "Mode," because it includes both material and decorative (stylistic?) considerations is inapplicable. "Class," or "subclass" seem too broad to be useful, "motif" too narrow. Therefore, and with due deference, the term "type" will be used with reference to a group of objects sharing the same generalized shape or use. For example, door locks based on an imported (Arabic?) prototype are found widely in the Western Sudan; a series of subtypical variants are known, some of which include human forms, animal forms, or geometric decorations. Similarly, masks may be subdivided into face coverings, hoods or casques, horizontal headgear (with or without cap-like extensions), and crests, each with possible subdivisions.

Whereas style is closely culture and time-bound, type is not. For example, a mask subtype consisting of a combination of horns, human facial features, and a crocodile mouth exists in a number of tribal styles in West Africa. A distribution study of types (correlated with other data such as style, linguistics, and function) might well reveal data that would corroborate or amend other evidence.

Generally, it may even be proven that, whereas stylistic studies often reveal time and space extensions of people, typological studies will in some cases reveal the time and space extensions of concepts or beliefs.[23]

The study of materials, tools, and techniques of art is of minor concern to most art historians except as a style determinant. Yet accurate identification of materials and their sources may prove useful. Generally available materials, such as wood and ivory, are of relatively little value in contrast to those with limited but discoverable sources. Artifacts of clay, stone, and metal, however,

23. Again, this statement is not totally in accord with art-historical assumptions. Here it is meant to imply that groups once related culturally may continue to hold certain basic values and beliefs and, concurrently, continue to use the same basic forms (or types) even while other cultural traits such as style and language change. Furthermore, ideas and, concomitantly, types may be transmitted through peaceful contact or through conquest. It is also obvious that types may move between cultures with few or no value associations (as in the case of an object whose utility is apparent in itself).

if their origins were established, could indicate trade contacts. If objects were carried on a migration or the earlier site continued to serve as a source of supply, this could be determined or substantiated by such analyses.

Similarly, the study of tools and techniques of manufacture (often revealed by the object) could prove useful. A fuller knowledge of the methods of casting metals, for example, could help sort out the relationships among the various styles and cultures involved.

More broadly, it may be assumed that a correlation between material and quantity could be worked out. For example, considering both materials (availability and workability) and tools, one would expect to find in Africa less stone than brass (or bronze), and less brass than wood. Indeed, it is quite probable that the appearance of iron tools, as in the American Northwest, acted as an impetus to woodworking. Such a florescence may well have fostered a fairly rapid separation of styles and types, a factor as yet scarcely considered in the art history of Africa.

It should be noted again that although this paper attempts to indicate some of the uses of the visual arts in the reconstruction of culture history, and only peripherally makes reference to the enormous utility of archaeology and attendant sciences to art history, constant reference has been made to the interaction of archaeology, the direct historical approach, and the "reading" of art objects. Thus, identification of a particular tool depiction (as in the instances given above by Fagg for Nok terra cottas and Clark for Bushman painting) is confirmed by the artifacts themselves known to and excavated by archaeologists.

Finally, the collection of data for existing arts that have a direct contact with prehistoric or protohistoric periods can greatly enlarge our understanding of these periods. Such direct historical studies have been published by Bradbury and Vaughan and, as noted, Clark and Bernard Fagg have used such observations with reference to Southern Africa and to the Nok culture.[24]

24. R. E. Bradbury, "Ezomo's 'Ikegobo' and the Benin Cult of the Hand," *Man,* LXI:165 (1961); J. H. Vaughan, "Rock Paintings and Rock Gongs among the Marghi of Nigeria," *Man,* LXII:83 (1962).

VII

The Origin of the Sickle-Cell Gene

Frank B. Livingstone

Associate Professor of Anthropology
University of Michigan

When Allison produced the first evidence for the manner in which selection favored the sickle-cell gene, it triggered a spate of investigations to test his hypothesis that heterozygotes for this gene possessed a relative resistance to falciparum malaria.[1] Although some of the earlier investigations purported to disprove the relationship between sickling and malaria, critical studies, such as those by Raper and by the Lambotte-Legrands, have clearly demonstrated this relationship.[2] Investigations into the nature of the natural selection favoring the other hemoglobin genes have been almost nonexistent. But because there is some selection against homozygotes for these genes, those which attain notable frequencies are also considered to be balanced polymorphisms and by analogy with the sickle-cell gene to be balanced by malaria.

More recently Ingram's work on the chemistry of hemoglobin has shown that sickle-cell hemoglobin differs from normal adult hemoglobin by only a single amino acid out of the almost three hundred amino acids which comprise the two different polypeptide chains of the hemoglobin molecule.[3] With the exception of some unpublished reports, all samples of hemoglobin S which

[1]. A. C. Allison, "Protection Afforded by Sickle-cell Trait against Subtertian Malarial Infection," *British Medical Journal*, I:290–294 (1954).
[2]. A. B. Raper, "Sickling in Relation to Morbidity from Malaria and Other Diseases," *British Medical Journal*, I:965–966 (1956); J. and C. Lambotte-Legrand, "Notes complementaire sur la drepanocytose," *Annales de la Société Belge de Medécine Tropical*, XXXVIII:45–54 (1957).
[3]. V. M. Ingram, *Hemoglobin and its Abnormalities* (Springfield, 1961), 92.

have been analyzed have been found to be the same chemically.[4] Since the sickle-cell gene is only found in populations between which there is historical evidence of contact and between which gene flow is thus likely to have occurred, a single origin for all these genes appears possible, and, it is argued here, probable. Of course, mutation is a recurrent phenomenon, so that to explain the presence of any gene one must decide between the alternatives of gene flow or a separate mutation. But the fact that the sickle-cell gene is not found in many diverse populations in Asia and elsewhere, which for many generations have been subjected to severe natural selection by falciparum malaria, indicates that it is a rather rare mutant. In this regard the sickle-cell gene contrasts sharply with the genes controlling thalassemia, hemoglobin D, and the glucose-6-phosphate dehydrogenase deficiency which are much more widely and spottily distributed among the world's populations.

Although these conclusions are tentative, they imply that the sickle-cell gene had an origin and a history of expansion from that origin which has been determined to a great extent by the history of falciparum malaria. I will attempt to reconstruct the history of the sickle-cell gene. Specifically, the hypothesis will be advanced that the sickle-cell gene originated in East Africa at the time early Iron Age Bantu agriculturalists were decimating the forests and greatly changing the indigenous flora and fauna.

The argument for this hypothesis will center around two rather different kinds of evidence: first, the population dynamics and frequency distributions of not only the sickle cell but all human hemoglobin genes; and, second, a reconstruction of the history of human malaria parasites and their human host populations. I do not claim originality for the general hypothesis, since Singer in 1953 postulated that the sickle-cell gene arose in Uganda.[5] However, Singer did not take natural selection into consideration

4. The exceptions are noted in J. A. Hunt and V. M. Ingram, "The Genetic Control of Protein Structure: the Abnormal Human Haemoglobins," in G. E. W. Wolstenholme and C. M. O'Connor (eds.), *Biochemistry of Human Genetics* (CIBA Foundation Symposia, 1959), 133.

5. R. Singer, "The Sickle-cell Trait in Africa," *American Anthropologist*, LV:634–648 (1953).

in his reconstruction, and therefore the conclusions of this paper will be quite different from Singer's.

It will be assumed that appreciable frequencies of all the abnormal human hemoglobin genes are due to natural selection by malaria. However, not all of these genes are related solely to falciparum malaria, as the sickle-cell gene seems to be. In earlier studies I have attempted to show that the world distributions of these genes can be explained if one assumes that the genes of the thalassemia complex and the hemoglobin E gene confer some resistance to all species of human malaria, while the hemoglobin C gene seems also to confer some resistance to all malarias but perhaps more specifically to that due to *Plasmodium malariae*.[6] The relationships between the various abnormal hemoglobins which attain appreciable frequencies and the species of human malaria will be assumed in this paper. Appreciable frequencies of thalassemia or hemoglobin E can thus be maintained by the endemic presence of any human malaria whether it be due to *P. falciparum, P. vivax, P. malariae,* or *P. ovale*, the usual species of human malaria parasites. On the other hand, appreciable frequencies of the sickle-cell gene can be maintained only by *P. falciparum*, and in this regard the sickle-cell gene contrasts with other abnormal hemoglobin genes.

Population Dynamics of Abnormal Hemoglobin Genes

In the populations of West and Central Africa, the Mediterranean area, the Middle East, and India—which have appreciable frequencies of the sickle-cell gene—the genes for thalassemia and the other abnormal hemoglobins are also found. No population has the full complement, but in almost all those with high sickling frequencies at least one other abnormal hemoglobin gene is present. Thus, there is a strong tendency for the abnormal hemoglobin genes to be found together in populations which inhabit the tropical regions of the Old World. Surveys of these populations frequently uncover as many as six different abnormal adult

6. F. B. Livingstone, "Balancing the Human Hemoglobin Polymorphisms," *Human Biology*, XXXIII:205–219 (1961).

hemoglobins, while surveys comprising many more individuals from populations which inhabit the more temperate regions such as Northern Europe, Japan, or the Australian interior, very rarely encounter a single individual with an abnormal hemoglobin. These differences cannot be due to different mutation rates, but must in some way be associated with the environment and differences in natural selection. The possibility that these differences could be due to genetic drift will not be considered further although other scholars apparently consider it a distinct possibility.[7]

Although many different kinds of abnormal hemoglobin are found in most of the malarious areas of the Old World, there appears to be one striking exception—East Africa. Despite many surveys there, I know of no report of any abnormal hemoglobin other than hemoglobin S in the native populations, although hemoglobin D has been found in recent Indian immigrants to East Africa.[8] In addition, among other populations which have the thalassemia gene(s), paper electrophoresis surveys usually discover many individuals with an all-S hemoglobin electrophoretic pattern. These individuals are usually reported to be homozygous for the sickle-cell gene, but it seems more likely that the majority are simultaneously heterozygous for the sickle-cell and a thalassemia gene. The relative absence of such individuals in East Africa is further evidence of the absence of thalassemia there. However, it should be noted that individuals with an all-S pattern have been found in East Africa too. These individuals have been shown to be simultaneously heterozygous for the sickle-cell and a "high fetal" gene, which may be a thalassemia variant. But, although widespread in the indigenous populations of East Africa, this "high fetal" gene occurs at the very low frequency of .003.[9] More importantly, Lehmann and Raper's intensive study of the Bwamba tribe found no adults and only four children with an all-S

7. H. Foy and A. Kondi, "Anaemias in Africans," *Central African Journal of Medicine*, II:256 (1956).
8. G. F. Jacob, H. Lehmann and A. B. Raper, "Haemoglobin D in Indians of Gujerati Origin in Uganda," *East African Medical Journal*, XXXIII:135–138 (1956).
9. G. F. Jacob and A. B. Raper, "Hereditary Persistence of Foetal Haemoglobin Production, and its Interaction with the Sickle-cell Trait," *British Journal of Haematology*, IV:138–149.

pattern; all the children were shown to be homozygous for the sickle-cell gene.[10]

East Africa is also unique in that most of its populations are close to equilibrium for the sickle-cell gene. This is all the more remarkable when considered in conjunction with the fact that the intensity of malaria in East Africa is extremely variable. In contrast to West and Central Africa, where altitude and rainfall variability is much less and hence the endemicity of malaria comparatively constant, East Africa has extremes of altitude and rainfall, and these occur over very short distances. Even populations who are members of the same tribe are sometimes found in environments which differ greatly in the intensity of malaria. Thus, the equilibrium frequency of the sickle-cell gene also varies greatly from population to population in East Africa even within the same tribe. From the Masai pastoralists, who inhabit the dry, non-malarious plains of Tanzania and Kenya and have very low frequencies of the sickle-cell gene, to the Bwamba of the malarious Semliki River Valley and the Sukuma along the infested shores of Lake Victoria (who both have about 40 per cent heterozygotes for the sickle-cell gene), East Africa includes populations with the greatest extremes of sickle-cell gene frequencies to be found anywhere in the world. But, as Allison has demonstrated, the sickle-cell gene frequency of each population is correlated with the intensity of malaria and hence is close to the equilibrium value.[11]

Now the presence of hemoglobin S—and only this abnormal hemoglobin—in East Africa and the close approximation of the frequencies to equilibrium in these populations have clear implications for the history of the sickle-cell gene. It takes the sickle-cell gene about twenty-eight generations or seven hundred years to approach equilibrium, starting at a negligible frequency.[12] Thus,

10. H. Lehmann and A. B. Raper, "Maintenance of High Sickling Rate in an African Community," *British Medical Journal*, II:333–336 (1956).
11. A. C. Allison, "The Distribution of the Sickle-cell Trait in East Africa and Elsewhere, and its Apparent Relationship to the Incidence of Subtertian Malaria," *Transactions of the Royal Society of Tropical Medicine and Hygiene*, XLVIII:312–318 (1954).
12. F. B. Livingstone, "Aspects of the Population Dynamics of the Abnormal Hemoglobin and Glucose-6-phosphate Dehydrogenase Deficiency Genes," *American Journal of Human Genetics*, XVI:435–450 (1964).

this gene has been present in East Africa for at least this long and perhaps longer since all populations are close to equilibrium. In West Africa there are still many populations which are far from equilibrium, indicating that the sickle-cell gene has been present in East Africa longer than in West Africa.[13] In addition, the fact that the sickle-cell gene is the only abnormal hemoglobin gene in East Africa seems to imply that it was the first abnormal hemoglobin gene present and attained appreciable frequencies before others were introduced either by mutation or gene flow.

Heterozygosity for one abnormal hemoglobin gene confers a selective advantage on the individual in an endemic malaria area, but the effects of these genes are not independent or additive. Persons who are simultaneously heterozygous for two or more abnormal hemoglobin genes usually have a decreased fitness, although the amount of the disadvantage will vary with the individual abnormal hemoglobin genes involved. These genes thus tend to be in competition with one another and show a reciprocal relationship between their frequencies, as Allison has shown for the S and C genes in West Africa.[14] Given the most reasonable estimates of the fitness values for the various genotypes, the sickle-cell gene would also tend to replace all other abnormal hemoglobin genes and thalassemia.[15] It appears to have done this in East Africa but not elsewhere. East Africa is thus different from the other malarious areas of the Old World since in all others thalassemia seems to have been the first abnormal hemoglobin gene to attain high frequencies.

Of all the abnormal hemoglobins, the thalassemia complex is the most widespread, and at least one type of thalassemia is present in every endemic malaria area of the Old World except East Africa. There are also occasional reports of thalassemia in the

13. F. B. Livingstone, "Anthropological Implications of Sickle Cell Gene Distribution in West Africa," *American Anthropologist*, LX:533–562 (1958); J. V. Neel and Others, "The Frequency of Elevations in the A_2 and Fetal Hemoglobin Fractions in the Natives of Liberia and Adjacent Regions, with Data on Haptoglobin and Transferrin Types," *American Journal of Human Genetics*, XIII:263 (1961).
14. A. C. Allison, "Population Genetics of Abnormal Human Hemoglobins," *Acta Genetica et Statistica Medica*, VI:430–434 (1956).
15. Livingstone, "Aspects of the Population Dynamics," 435–450.

indigenous inhabitants of regions such as England, Germany, and Japan, which are not now malarious. This widespread nature of thalassemia is predictable in terms of genetic theory as thalassemia can be due to any one of several "genes." [16] Hence, one would expect to encounter more mutations to this trait. Thalassemia is similar to hemophilia or albinism in that the presence of any of these genes is determined by clinical or phenotypic characteristics. Most studies of gene frequencies or mutation rates for these genes are based on all cases of these conditions found in a large population; these cases are then all attributed to the same gene. More recently, however, biochemical studies have shown that these clinical conditions can be due to several different chemical alterations. Mutations to specific chemical changes, such as the sickle-cell gene, tend to be much less frequent than mutations to these other clinical conditions. For this reason, thalassemia is the most widespread of the abnormal hemoglobins, and sporadic mutants to this condition do occur. I know of no case in which the sickle-cell gene can be reasonably attributed to a sporadic mutant. When malaria first becomes endemic in a population the first favorable mutant it is likely to encounter, therefore, is a thalassemia gene.

Two areas where malaria has been spreading until fairly recently illustrate this concept of thalassemia. In West Africa, there has been a sharp decline in the frequency of the sickle-cell gene among the tribes of Liberia. In the north, the tribes have about 20 per cent heterozygotes for the sickle-cell gene, while in the southeast the frequency is almost zero. I attempted to show that this decline is due to the recent spread of the sickle-cell gene into this part of Africa and that the frequency increased in the area's populations only after endemic malaria was present.[17] Among the tribes which have few sickle-cell genes but now have endemic malaria, we have since found evidence of thalassemia being present.[18] Although the frequency of thalassemia seems to be higher

16. D. L. Rucknagel, "Current Concepts of the Genetics of Thalassemia," *Annals of the New York Academy of Sciences,* CXIX:436–449 (1964).
17. Livingstone, "Anthropological Implications," 556.
18. E. B. Oleson and Others, "Thalassemia in Liberia," *British Medical Journal,* I:1385–1387 (1959).

in central Liberia among tribes with appreciable frequencies of the sickle-cell gene, the data indicate that endemic malaria first encountered a thalassemia gene, which then began to increase its frequency, in the tribes of southeastern Liberia.[19] On the other side of the world, malaria also has been recently spreading through Australasia. Hemoglobin E, whose presence appears to be due to gene flow from the mainland of Asia, is found in the Indonesian archipelago as far as Sulawezi (Celebes). However, endemic malaria is found through New Guinea and out to the Solomon Islands. Recently, thalassemia has been found to be widespread in New Guinea where it is also correlated with the endemicity of malaria.[20] Thus, in the absence of the hemoglobin E gene, thalassemia has been selected for in New Guinea.

Another factor in addition to a higher mutation rate contributes to the widespread nature of thalassemia. This is the fact that heterozygosity for thalassemia seems to confer some resistance to all species of human malaria parasite, so that anywhere malaria took a toll of life thalassemia would be expected. On the other hand, the sickle-cell gene would be expected only where falciparum malaria was endemic. In the temperate regions of Europe, such as Holland and the Po River Valley of Northern Italy where *Plasmodium vivax* was the common parasite, thalassemia rather than the sickle-cell gene is present. Thalassemia is also found in Sardinia where both falciparum and vivax malaria occur, but the sickle-cell gene is absent. The presence of falciparum malaria and the absence of the sickle-cell gene here point up the differences between the population dynamics of thalassemia and those of the sickle-cell gene. While appreciable frequencies of thalassemia in many populations appear to result from the action of selection on a few mutant genes previously present in the population, high frequencies of the sickle-cell gene appear to be

19. Neel and Others, "The Frequency of Elevations," 263.
20. B. P. K. Ryan, "Thalassemia in Melanesia," *Nature,* CXCII:75–76 (1961); C. C. Curtain and Others, "Distribution Pattern, Population Genetics and Anthropological Significance of Thalassemia and Abnormal Hemoglobins in Melanesia," *American Journal of Physical Anthropology,* XX:475–483 (1962).

due to selection on genes which have been introduced by gene flow. It seems plausible that the absence of the sickle-cell gene in Sardinia can be ascribed to the absence of gene flow, since Sardinia is one of the more isolated areas of the Mediterranean.

Because the sickle-cell and thalassemia genes do not affect the resistance of the individual equally to all human malaria parasites, the distributions of these genes are dependent to a great extent on the distributions and history of the human malaria parasites. Of course, each of these parasites has a unique history; but the history of all is dependent on the cultural and ecological history of their mutual host, the human species. To reconstruct the history of the sickle-cell gene then, we will first attempt to infer the broad outlines of human parasitism in general and then attempt to reconstruct the history of the individual human malaria parasites.

The Hominidae as Malaria Parasite Hosts

During the long Paleolithic period man occupied an ecological niche similar to that of the large carnivores. Although the women of these human groups undoubtedly did a great deal of collecting, the crucial part of the food supply resulted from the hunting activities of the males or perhaps of the whole band. In the early proto-human stage, which is represented in the fossil record by the Australopithecines, man may have been for the most part a scavenger like the hyena and not a killer of game, but it is certain that later in the Paleolithic man relied on his own ability to kill game.[21] During this time the human population was undoubtedly sparse, and its density less than that of many other animals, even large ones. In terms of food chains, man would have been in more or less the same position at the very end as the large carnivores, which explains man's low population density. In addition to low population density, one further feature of early human society has implications for the extent of malaria parasitism at this time; that feature is the origin of bipedalism. Bipedalism is obviously an adaptation to open country, and this implies that the

21. G. Hewes, "Food Transport and the Origin of Hominid Bipedalism," *American Anthropologist,* LXIII:687–710 (1961).

early proto-hominids occupied either savanna, open woodland, or grassland. Only after successfully adapting to bipedalism in the open did man reinvade the forests.

The question arises as to whether or not this group of proto-hominids could have functioned as the host for a malaria parasite. I think the most reasonable answer is that it could not, not at least for *P. falciparum*. These human malaria parasites are quite host specific, and the human population must have a high density and a close association with the anopheline mosquitos which are acting as vectors in order for the parasites to be transmitted. As wide-ranging, sparsely distributed animals, the proto-hominids would have been very unsuitable malaria hosts, as are the large carnivores of the African savanna today. This situation among the early proto-hominids contrasts sharply with that of most primates, who because of their tree-dwelling habits and high population densities are, along with birds, the major carriers of malaria parasites. While early man is unlikely to have harbored any malaria parasites, his primate inheritance has made him very susceptible to the parasites of his cousins, even though in most cases man simply becomes infected with the parasite and does not transmit it.

If early man was not host to any malaria parasites, humans must have acquired them at a later date; the problem is then identifying where, when, and from whom they were acquired. Although this may seem to be an insoluble problem, many human malaria parasites resemble very closely those of other primates. Using these similarities as indications of evolutionary relationships, we can infer something about the history of human malaria parasites from an examination of their close relatives. It should be noted, however, that the evolutionary relationships of the protozoa in general and the *Plasmodia* in particular are not well worked out, and there is considerable disagreement among protozoologists. Not even the kinds of similarities between species which are indicative of common ancestry have been well-established for this phylum. The principal criteria are morphological and concern all phases of the life cycle; but, in addition, periodicity, number of segmenters or merozoites, number of exo-erythrocytic cycles, and host specificity are all used to determine phylogenetic relationships among the *Plasmodia*. In 1947, the discovery of the exoerythrocytic cycle by Shortt and his colleagues and the extensions of this work by Garnham and Bray introduced a whole new set of criteria for determining evolutionary relationships among the *Plasmodia*. Finally, renewed interest in the malaria parasites of man's close relatives during the last five years has emphasized the susceptibility of humans to simian parasites.[22]

The first human malaria parasite to be considered is *Plasmodium vivax*. This is perhaps the most widespread of the malaria parasites; because of its relapsing character, it is responsible for most of the malaria found in such temperate climates as those of Holland, the United States, and Korea. *P. vivax* is thus adapted to a host inhabiting a climate which only permits a seasonal transmission of malaria, although it is also found in the tropics. The chimpanzee and lowland gorilla are known to harbor a parasite similar to vivax; in fact it is considered to be the same species but of a different subspecies. Man may have acquired vivax malaria from either of these two animals; however, among the Old World monkeys, there is yet a better candidate for the pleasure of having given man *P. vivax*. Several species of macaque (genus *Macaca*) have a malaria parasite, *P. cynomolgi*, of which one subspecies, *P. cynomolgi bastianelli*, can infect man quite readily and can also be transmitted from man to man. This parasite is therefore also a human parasite, whose ability to simulate *P. vivax* almost exactly has only recently been recognized.[23]

At present macaques are found only around Gibraltar, in India, and further eastward; this distribution and the fossil record strongly suggest that the genus was previously much more widespread in the Middle East and has been driven back to these peripheral areas by man's competition and by his destruction of the monkey's habitat in the Middle East. In the past, macaques thus were common in those areas where *P. vivax* is the predomi-

22. G. R. Coatney, "Symposium on Recent Advances in Simian Malaria," *Journal of Parisitology*, XLIX:865 (1963).
23. D. E. Eyles, G. R. Coatney and M. E. Getz, "Vivax-type Malaria Parasite of Macaques Transmissable to Man," *Science*, CXXXI:1812–1813 (1960).

nant human malaria parasite today. This replacement of one species by another, with the subsequent transference of the former's parasites to the latter, is a common phenomenon in parasite evolution.[24] With the extinction of its normal host, a parasite must find another host in order to survive; it usually finds a closely related animal which is becoming predominant. It is obvious that those parasites which infect another host do in fact survive while those that do not find another host perish with the original host. As man has drastically altered the face of the earth, he became, first, the alternate host of many parasites; at this stage the parasite would be defined as a zoonosis. Later, when the other hosts became extinct or very diminished in numbers and confined to a few refuge areas, man became the sole host of the parasite.

Man's domesticated animals have also picked up many parasites from closely related wild animals which are rapidly diminishing in number. Domesticated animals have greatly increased the distributions of several parasites and also increased the different modes of transmission of these parasites. Hoare has shown that the African trypanosomes have been spread far beyond the range of their normal invertebrate host, the tsetse fly, by domesticated animals.[25]

Because of its more temperate character and its distribution in the Middle East, *P. vivax* is most likely to have been the malaria of antiquity. Another human malaria parasite, *P. ovale,* is very much like *P. vivax* but has a far more restricted distribution. *P. ovale* is found with appreciable frequency only in West Africa.[26] Its pre-erythrocytic schizont is very unlike those of other human malaria species. However, in West and Central Africa, but not in East Africa, many of the monkeys, drills, and baboons are infected with a parasite, *P. gonderi,* whose pre-erythrocytic schizont in particular is similar to *P. ovale.* These similarities

24. R. B. Heisch, "Zoonoses as a Study in Ecology," *British Medical Journal,* I:669–673 (1956).
25. C. A. Hoare, "The Spread of African Trypanosomes beyond their Natural Range," *Zeitschrift für Tropenmedizin und Parasitologie,* VIII:1–6 (1957).
26. P. C. C. Garnham, "Distribution of Blood Protozoa in Africa," *Proceedings of the Linnaean Society of London,* CLXV:61–66 (1954).

have led Garnham, Lainson, and Cooper to suggest that *P. gonderi* and *P. ovale* are related.[27] The distribution of *P. ovale* and the absence of similarities between it and any other simian malaria parasite suggest that it is an adaptation of *P. gonderi* to man. If *P. ovale* were the first malaria parasite to become highly endemic in man in West Africa, this may explain why hemoglobin C became very frequent in the rather primitive Gur-speaking peoples of the interior of West Africa.[28] Recently, however, Garnham has stated on other grounds that *P. gonderi* and *P. ovale* are not closely related, so the latter may have had a different origin.[29] In any case, there seems to be little chance of its having first infected man in East Africa.

The third human malaria parasite to be considered, *P. malariae*, causes quartan malaria. There are no similar parasites among the Old World monkeys, although in Asia some species do harbor a quartan parasite, *P. inui,* whose pre-erythrocytic schizont is quite different. In Africa, the monkeys have no quartan parasite, but the chimpanzee has quartan malaria from a parasite almost identical to *P. malariae* in man. There are some differences between the two parasites based on the ability of various anophelines to transmit them, but the morphology of the two is so close that they are considered the same species.[30] Hence *P. malariae* is a zoonosis with the chimpanzee as the other host. The fact that there are no close relatives of this parasite in the Old World monkeys seems to indicate that it has been an anthropoid parasite for a long time; it seems likely that man acquired this parasite from the chimpanzee. As a quartan parasite with a light, long-last-

27. P. C. C. Garnham, R. Lainson and W. Cooper, "The Complete Lifecycle of a New Strain of *Plasmodium gonderi* from the Drill (*Mandrillus leucophaeus*) Including its Sporogeny in the Rhesus Monkey," *Transactions of the Royal Society of Tropical Medicine and Hygiene*, LII:509–517 (1958).
28. Livingstone, "Balancing the Human Hemoglobin," 216.
29. P. C. C. Garnham, "Distribution of Simian Malaria Parasites in Various Hosts," *Journal of Parasitology*, XLIX:905–911 (1963).
30. R. S. Bray, "Studies on Malaria in Chimpanzees. VIII. The Experimental Transmission and Pre-erythrocytic Phase of *Plasmodium malariae*, with a note on the Host-range of the Parasite," *American Journal of Tropical Medicine and Hygiene*, IX:455–465 (1960).

ing infection, *P. malariae* represents an adaptation to a comparatively sparsely distributed host. For this reason it appears to have adapted itself originally to the lesser densities of a large animal such as the chimpanzee. At present the chimpanzee is infected with *P. malariae* only in West and Central Africa, but the chimpanzees of East Africa are isolated, relict populations.

The one common malaria parasite of the New World monkeys, *P. brasilianum,* is also very like *P. malariae.* In fact it may be the same parasite and is certainly a zoonosis since Contacos and Coatney have transmitted it by mosquito to man and then back to the monkey.[31] Man may have obtained *P. malariae* from the New World monkeys, but it seems much more likely that man gave the New World monkeys their one malaria parasite in the same manner in which he gave them yellow fever. The complete absence of malaria and malaria-like parasites in New World monkeys, with the exception of a few which look much like human parasites and can reasonably be attributed to recent transfers, indicates that the *Plasmodia* evolved in the Old World after the late Eocene Period when the primates of the two hemispheres were separated.

The final human malaria parasite, *P. falciparum,* is the one whose evolutionary history is of most concern here since the sickle-cell gene apparently confers a resistance to this parasite alone. *P. falciparum* is so different from the other malaria parasites that Bray has placed it in a different genus, *Laverania.*[32] The belief that *P. falciparum* is the most recent of the malaria parasites to evolve is one of the most accepted inferences concerning the history of human malaria.[33] This belief rests primarily on its greater pathogenicity in man, which is usually considered to be indicative of an unstable and recent host-parasite association.

31. P. G. Contacos and G. R. Coatney, "Experimental Adaptation of Simian Malarias to Abnormal Hosts," *Journal of Parasitology,* XLIX:912–918 (1963).

32. R. S. Bray, "Studies on Malaria in Chimpanzees. VI. *Laverania falciparum,*" *American Journal of Tropical Medicine and Hygiene,* VII:20–24 (1958).

33. M. F. Boyd, "Historical Review," in M. F. Boyd (ed.), *Malariology* (Philadelphia, 1949), I, 3–25.

P. falciparum has one very close relative among the simian parasites, *P. reichenowi* of the chimpanzee and lowland gorilla. Although these parasites have been regarded as different species, their differences are minor and Bray has placed them together in the new genus, *Laverania,* which indicates that the two are very different from other malaria parasites.[34] The chimpanzee is known to be infected with *P. reichenowi* in West and Central Africa, but east of Stanleyville it does not seem to be infected.[35] However, Garnham points out that some time ago Duke apparently found *P. reichenowi* in a chimpanzee in Uganda. Because of the great similarities between these two parasites and their great differences from the other malaria parasites, it does seem reasonable to infer that man got *P. falciparum* from the chimpanzee, and, according to the hypothesis of this paper, that this probably occurred in East Africa.

The history of the chimpanzee in East Africa is similar to the history of the macaque further north and provided the sequence of events which permits the transference of a parasite from one host to another. Today the chimpanzee is found in isolated forests in Uganda and Tanzania. These relict populations are small and scattered and hence are poor hosts for a non-relapsing form of malaria such as *P. reichenowi,* but there can be little doubt that in the past when the forests were much more widespread in East Africa the champanzee was more numerous. There is a recent report of a chimpanzee population in Malawi, which, if it represents a relict population and not simply some released individuals, would indicate a far wider range.[36] Since man is responsible for the decrease in the East African forest, the human populations would have been increasing simultaneously with the disappearance of the chimpanzee. It thus seems quite possible that *P. reichenowi* adapted to man in East Africa and became *P. falciparum.*

34. Bray, "Studies on Malaria in Chimpanzees. VI. *Laverania falciparum,*" 20–24.

35. R. S. Bray, "The Malaria Parasites of Anthropoid Apes," *Journal of Parasitology,* XLIX:888–891 (1963); Garnham, "Distribution of Blood Protozoa," 61–66.

36. B. L. Mitchell and C. S. Holliday, "A New Primate from Nyasaland," *South African Journal of Science,* LVI:215–220 (1960).

Although the origins of the various human malaria parasites have been pinpointed in this paper, it follows that such transfers would be expected any time the circumstances arose which cause parasites to adapt to different hosts. *P. falciparum* could have evolved elsewhere, and other malaria parasites could have adapted to man in East Africa. But *P. vivax* is more likely to have done this where the macaque was previously present, and *P. ovale* has no close relatives in East Africa. The origin of *P. malariae* in East Africa seems to be a strong possibility. However, none of these parasites attains its highest frequencies there, while *P. falciparum* is as endemic in East Africa as anywhere in the world. Even if *P. falciparum* did not evolve there, it could have become endemic there first.

The absence of thalassemia, hemoglobin C, or other abnormal hemoglobin genes which seem to confer some resistance to malarias other than falciparum is related to the great predominance of falciparum malaria in East Africa and the low densities of other malarias. Therefore, the hypothesis of this paper that the sickle-cell gene first mutated and attained high frequencies in East Africa gains some support from the phylogeny of the human malaria parasites. Of course, other phylogenies are possible, but the parasitological evidence, at least, does not seem to contradict the hypothesis. The last part of this paper will attempt to relate the culture history of East Africa to the proposed evolution of the human malaria parasites.

The Culture History of East Africa and its Relation to Malaria and the Sickle-Cell Gene

Some of the earliest evidence for the existence of the family of man, the *Hominidae,* comes from East Africa. Since the time of these Australopithecines, 1,750,000 years ago, there is archaeological evidence for the continuous occupation of East Africa by man or manlike creatures. During the long Paleolithic and succeeding Mesolithic periods, hunting and gathering peoples occupied most of East Africa; the Bushman and other Khoisan-speakers, who today are confined to the more arid and inhospitable areas of East and South Africa, are presumably the direct descendants of these earlier Mesolithic hunters. The spread to East Africa of the agricultural revolution, which seems to have occurred about 10,000 years ago somewhere in the Middle East or the Sahara, forced the hunters out of the cultivable areas and led to a great increase in the human population. However, the areas of East Africa man was able to utilize agriculturally depended to a great extent on the crop plants at his disposal and on his technological knowledge.

The original agricultural economy of the Middle East was based on grain crops, goats, sheep, and perhaps pigs, and on the use of stone tools. It was able to diffuse to the drier, open areas of East Africa, which were similar to the environment of the Middle East, but these early farmers were unable to exploit effectively the great forested regions of East Africa and elsewhere. As in Europe, where the early Danubian farmers were able to exploit only a very limited part of the forested areas with their slash and burn agriculture,[37] the advent of metal tools brought the drastic changes that occurred in the heavily forested areas of East Africa. The earliest evidence for Neolithic farming communities in East Africa is from the dry highland area of Kenya and from further north on the Nile River near Khartoum in the Sudan. These early Stone-Bowl Cultures of Kenya had houses similar to the pit houses of the present-day Iraqu who inhabit a very arid region of Central Tanzania.[38] Since the Iraqu speak a Cushitic language, it may be supposed that the Neolithic farmers probably came into Kenya from the Horn area to the northeast where Cushitic languages are spoken today.

The majority of the present populations of East Africa speak Bantu languages, and the linguistic evidence indicates that these peoples spread into East Africa from somewhere in Nigeria. Since Bantu languages are closely related and are spoken over a large area of East and South Africa, the expansion of the Bantu seems to have been quite rapid and recent. The ecological circumstances which gave rise to this veritable explosion of the Bantu people

37. J. G. D. Clark, *Prehistoric Europe: the Economic Basis* (New York, 1952), 97.
38. S. Cole, *The Prehistory of East Africa* (New York, 1963), 313.

out of Nigeria seem to have been the acquisition of tropical root crops and the techniques of ironworking.[39] In East and South Africa, an early, widespread Iron Age culture characterized by dimple-based pottery or channelled ware seems to reflect this early Bantu expansion.[40] Using modifications of the technique of glottochronology, Olmsted has obtained maximum and minimum dates of 3,600 and 2,000 years ago for the separation of several Bantu languages.[41] This would indicate that the Bantu began to spread out from Nigeria sometime in the first millennium B.C.; this accords with radiocarbon dates which place the early Iron Age cultures of East Africa in the first millennium A.D.

The intensive exploitation of the East African environment by these Iron Age agriculturalists began a process of change which is still going on today. Prior to man's alteration of the landscape, most of the southern half of Uganda, northwestern Tanzania, and central Kenya were covered with tropical forests. Since then agricultural usage has converted much of this area to open savanna and woodland. This change has greatly reduced the habitat of some and almost eliminated the habitat of other mammals which previously occupied this area, resulting in a drastic alteration of the mammalian fauna and leaving man and his domesticated animals predominant. Many of the previous occupants were undoubtedly primates. With their reduction or elimination, their parasites had to find a new host, and man's increasing numbers and antigenic similarity made him the obvious choice.

This change in the environment of East Africa from tropical forest to open savanna also made the region inhabitable and exploitable by human cultures with a different economic organiza-

39. Livingstone, "Anthropological Implications," 550; G. P. Murdock, *Africa* (New York, 1959), 273; C. Wrigley, "Speculations on the Economic Prehistory of Africa," *Journal of African History*, I:201 (1960); M. Posnansky, "Dimple Based Pottery from Uganda," *Man*, LXI:168 (1961).

40. J. Hiernaux, "Recent Research at Protohistoric Sites in Ruanda, in the Belgian Congo (Katanga Province), and in Uganda (Kibiro)," *Occasional Paper No. 4 of the Uganda Museum* (1959), 26–30.

41. D. Olmsted, "Three Tests of Glottochronological Theory," *American Anthropologist*, LIX:839–842 (1957).

tion than that of the early Bantu agriculturalists. The Nilotic peoples began to invade East Africa after the Bantu had opened up the country sufficiently for a pastoral culture to exploit it. This phenomenon of the replacement or conquest of agriculturalists by pastoralists is not confined to East Africa but is a general sequence in the culture history of most continents.[42] Pastoralists cannot attack forest and cut it down to provide pasture for their herds but are dependent on the agriculturalists to change the environment to grassland. In Europe, the Teutonic pastoralists moved into Western Europe only after the agriculturalists had opened up the country; and the invasion of agricultural areas by pastoralists in China is an age-old phenomenon.

The removal of a certain amount of forest cover leads to erosion and to a decrease in soil fertility. These changes, in addition to overcultivation, lead to a decrease in the agricultural potential of the land. The Middle East has many areas where Arab sheep, goat, and camel pastoralists have taken over lands which were previously agricultural. In East Africa there are archaeological remains of agricultural settlements in Masailand.[43] (Of course, in most areas there are still favorably situated peoples, such as the desert oasis-dwellers or the riverine Bantu of Somaliland, which continue to have an economy based primarily on agriculture.) In other areas, the fertility of the soil is maintained, and the invading pastoralists are absorbed by the agriculturalists. The resulting economy is based on both agriculture and animal husbandry, although sometimes the pastoralists form an upper caste, as in Rwanda. Many other factors are involved in the culture process, and the preceding generalizations are not meant to be a total explanation of culture history. But hopefully they show the outlines of the history of East Africa which are relevant for the hypothesis of this paper.

Evidence of the invasion of Uganda by pastoralists from the north when this country was occupied by agriculturalists is found

42. T. Dale and V. G. Carter, *Topsoil and Civilization* (Norman, Okla., 1955), *passim*.
43. H. A. Fosbrooke, "Early Iron Age Sites in Tanganyika Relative to Traditional History," *Proceedings of the Third Pan-African Congress on Prehistory* (London, 1957), 318–325.

in both the traditions of the present-day peoples of Uganda and the archaeological record. In some areas, such as the hills of Kigezi in the south, the Bantu were able to stand off the invaders, but on the plains of Uganda between Lake Victoria and Lakes Edward and Albert the pastoralists have been able to conquer the agriculturalists. The rivers in this area flow mostly east and west into either Lake Victoria or the Lakes Albert and Edward watershed. There are many large earthworks along these rivers which consist of trenches and earth ramparts. In most cases the earthworks are situated on the south banks of the rivers and are centered around fords in the rivers. Although considered by some to be bridgeheads built by the invaders from the north, they seem more likely to be defenses erected *against* the pastoral invaders and their cattle.[44] The great lengths of the earthworks and the fact that some were carved out of rock with iron picks indicate that their builders could command a considerable labor supply, which is more characteristic of sedentary agricultural societies.[45] The remains could be called "The Great Wall of Africa," and they show that if their life and livelihood are at stake, a people will go to a great deal of trouble to protect them.

By the time the pastoralists began to penetrate southern Uganda, the country was quite open. Since their arrival, the Bantu agriculturalists had greatly increased in numbers, cleared much of the forest, and started to exterminate much of the original fauna. The practice of annual burning, either for hunting drives or to maintain grass for domesticated animals, greatly hastened this process. Only a few fire-resistant species of trees can survive such burning, and the forest fauna suffers consequent reduction. The competition for the land by the Nilotes and Bantu at a time when the flora and fauna were changing produced conditions of warfare in which famine and disease increased the toll of life.

44. E. C. Lanning, "The Munsa Earthworks," *Uganda Journal*, XIX:179 (1955); R. Oliver, "The Traditional Histories of Buganda, Bunyoro, and Ankole," *Journal of the Royal Anthropological Institute*, LXXXV:111–117 (1955).

45. P. L. Shinnie, "Excavations at Bigo, 1957, "*Uganda Journal,* XXIV:17 (1960).

Since then, the population of Uganda has fluctuated greatly, and woodland or forest have reclaimed much of the land, some of it quite recently. For example, in the late nineteenth century, the kingdom of Karagwe was a fertile, populous state in Northwest Tanzania; with the coming or rinderpest, smallpox, and sleeping sickness, the tsetse fly, wild game, and woodland have taken over much of this region. The British administration's prohibition in this century of late dry season burning has also allowed the tsetse fly, woodland, and wild fauna to overrun much of the rest of East Africa.[46] In other areas, changes wrought by human cultures are still proceeding at a great rate. In the last century, the flora of Rwanda and Burundi has changed from two-thirds forest cover to its present one-sixth. In this last remnant, there are still a few Batwa hunters who are adapted to the forest, but these people are becoming part of the agricultural-pastoral economy as the lower caste of potters and servants. Since contact with the world market economy, the population of East Africa has increased enormously, whereas previously it had been static for many years. For example Buxton estimates the population of Buganda in 1890 before the sleeping sickness epidemic as 300,000.[47] This epidemic killed about 200,000 people, but forty years later the population of this part of Uganda was at least 1,000,000. The enormous change may have resulted in part from immigration, faulty statistics, or perhaps from modern medicine; but it is due even more to the changed ecological niche of the human population and to *Pax Britannica* which was part of that change. This second great change in the human ecology of East Africa has also brought with it changes in the disease pattern. Tuberculosis is now one of the major diseases in Africa, while leprosy is on the decline. Syphilis is also increasing while yaws is declining.

About 2,000 years ago, a similar drastic change in the ecology of human diseases in East Africa must have occurred. The Pygmies and early Bantu were sparsely distributed throughout Central Africa and did not have the diseases which require very

46. P. A. Buxton, *The Natural History of Tsetse Flies* (London School of Hygiene and Tropical Medicine, Memoir 10, 1955), 307–308.
47. *Ibid.*, 658.

large, closely packed populations or at least contact with such groups. Even today many of the isolated Pygmies do not have these contagious diseases, just as they are comparatively absent in other isolated groups such as Eskimos, or the inhabitants of Tristan da Cunha, Spitzbergen, or the Faroe Islands. Virus diseases like measles or the common cold, or protozoans such as falciparum malaria cannot become endemic in such small or migratory populations. Bartlett has shown that in the United States it requires a city the size of Akron, Providence, or Rochester for measles to remain endemic.[48] As the early agriculturalists cut down the forest and thereby changed the environment, while at the same time greatly increasing the human population, *P. reichenowi* of the declining chimpanzee adapted to a new host, man, and became *P. falciparum*. As this parasite began to take a large toll of human life, it became a factor in natural selection. It encountered a peculiar random mutation, the sickle-cell gene, which was rapidly increased in frequency by this selection. Once *P. falciparum* was well established in its new host, it spread rapidly throughout the tropical regions of the Old World, and, where gene flow allowed, this favorable mutant gene spread after it. As was mentioned previously, it takes about 700 years for the sickle-cell gene to approach equilibrium. Although 2,000 years is a very short time in evolutionary terms, it would seem adequate for the sickle-cell gene to increase in East Africa and then spread throughout the Old World to the extent that it has. This gene was carried to the Middle East by the slave trade, to India by the slave trade and the importation of mercenaries, and through Central and South Africa by the Bantu expansion. It was also carried to Madagascar, where it appears to be close to equilibrium in most populations. West Africa is the one region to which the parasite, *P. falciparum,* spread rapidly but to which the sickle-cell gene diffused rather slowly because of the absence of a slave trade or other large scale migration in that direction. Thus, today the only area of Africa which is far from equilibrium for the sickle-cell gene is West Africa, which is inhabited by close relatives of the

48. M. S. Bartlett, *Population Models in Ecology and Epidemiology* (New York, 1960), 67–68.

East Africans and is the area from whence the East Africans came.

On Method

This paper is primarily an attempt to explain some of the genetic variability which exists among the human populations of East Africa. Only a small part of known genetic variability, the human hemoglobin genes, is considered. But the concepts and theoretical approach which apply to this bit of genetic variability apply to all of it, since they are of general validity. This, however, does not mean that all genetic variability will be correlated. Genetic variability is phrased in terms of gene frequencies in populations and can be explained by the factors which control gene frequencies: mutation, natural selection, gene flow, and gene drift. The human hemoglobin genes are somewhat different from most genes because of the overwhelming importance of natural selection; but it should be emphasized that this scheme applies to all genes. The problem of explaining gene frequency differences amounts to estimating the relative importance of these four factors and then attempting to establish the determinants of variability in them.

Since most of the populations of East Africa appear to be close to equilibrium, we assumed that natural selection operating by means of malaria was the major factor determining this genetic variability. Going one step further, we can inquire into the causes of variability in the amount of natural selection. First, variability in certain environmental factors—such as vegetation, rainfall, and altitude—influences the amount of natural selection. Second, one must consider the presence or absence of the various species of human malaria, which in turn are due partly to the history of human malaria parasitization. Third, there is the variability in the cultures of the populations involved which determines to a great extent the epidemiology of malaria.

Although culture as a determinant of genetic variability has been left to the last, one of the assumptions of this reconstruction rests upon the premise that culture is the most important determinant of genetic variability and is in fact a primary cause. If there is anything different about this approach, it is this emphasis on culture as a determinant of genetic variability. Of course, in any particular genetic situation, all three of these factors interact, forcing one to consider all of them.

Culture determines genetic variability directly through differences in cultural practices, such as infanticide or fertility norms. It also effects such things as settlement patterns and population densities. In addition, cultural practices to a great extent determine variability in the first two factors, environment and disease. Man has had little effect on altitude, but in the past 10,000 years his activities have greatly influenced the vegetation and thereby the rainfall, runoff, and erosion of most of the inhabitable earth. In this time, cultural evolution has also altered the patterns of disease in both man and other animals. Although there have been vast changes in both the physical environment and human disease during this period, there seems to be a tendency in historical reconstruction in anthropology to think of them as constant while culture has changed. Africa, as the dark continent, is particularly susceptible to this idea of changelessness. In fact, the cultural backwardness of Africa south of the Sahara has been explained by both environment (either too harsh or the opposite of "no challenge" in Toynbee's terms) and disease. One still reads that Africa's cultural position is the result of sleeping sickness. In addition to being an interpretation of cultural phenomena in terms of biological factors, it fails to recognize that the great spread of sleeping sickness in Africa (particularly that due to *Trypanosoma gambiense*) is a very recent phenomenon and reflects the tendency to consider disease as a constant and, unfortunately, as an explanation.

Although it is frequently stated in anthropological literature that there is no necessary connection between race or biology and culture, the theoretical approach of this paper implies that there are many. Of course, the statement of no relation has been repeated ad infinitum to combat the view that the biological characteristics of human populations determine their cultural capacities, which is exactly the opposite of what is advocated here. As a major determinant of the mortality and fertility of a population and hence of the natural selection operating on this population, the culture of the group precedes and is a determinant of its genes. However, this does not appear to have been the usual conception of the relation between biology and culture. For example, in archaeological reconstruction, many correlations between biology and culture seem to infer a different explanation. The arrival of *Homo sapiens* is correlated with the beginning of blade cultures, and the peculiar biology of the species is considered responsible for this technological development. Conversely, one might better state that blade cultures are responsible for, or caused, *Homo sapiens;* Loring Brace's work on changes in facial morphology resulting from the development of a much more effective and plentiful cutting tool indicates how this may have occurred.[49]

In conclusion, geneticists need to know something about culture and culture history to explain the distribution of genes. In fact, cultural data are the more important items, while information on the distributions of other genes is of little help. In this paper we have dealt with one genetic system and have not even considered the many others for which there are data. This is because, in an equilibrium situation where natural selection is the major determinant of gene frequencies, there will be no correlation between gene frequencies unless the factor of natural selection is similar. For example, in East Africa the distribution of the gene(s) which is responsibile for the deficiency of the enzyme, glucose-6-phosphate dehydrogenase, is correlated with the distribution of the sickle-cell gene since both appear to confer some resistance to malaria. Yet for the most part, the distribution of the ABO blood groups is not correlated with that of the sickle-cell gene. For these reasons, explaining the distribution of the sickle-cell gene does not consist in correlating this distribution with those of other genes or trying to relate it to the races, however defined, of East Africa.

But what can the geneticist do for the cultural anthropologist? Because of the relationships between culture and biology, it is possible that a knowledge of genetic distributions may be helpful

49. C. L. Brace, "Cultural Factors in the Evolution of the Human Dentition," in M. F. Ashley Montagu (ed.), *Culture and the Evolution of Man* (New York, 1962), 343–354.

in reconstructing the culture history of Africa. We have dealt with a genetic system which is close to equilibrium, but there may be other systems which are not and their distributions may reflect recent large scale expansions or migrations of populations. Of course, it would be hazardous to assume that this is the explanation without supporting facts; moreover, one should not depend simply on migration or its counterpart, diffusion, as an explanation for the distribution of cultural phenomena. This may have happened in history, but it does not explain why. Although historical reconstruction is often considered to be simply the collection of facts, one's theory of the "why" of culture process has a very considerable effect on how one reconstructs culture history— one reason being that the data always have great gaps and the kinds of inferences employed to fill these in are grounded in one's theory of the interrelationships of culture. Innumerable pages have been written about human biological and cultural evolution, but we still do not have an explicit, exhaustive statement of the kinds of theoretical assumptions which every historical study makes. The procedures of this paper indicate an ecological approach. This is only a label, but it seems to characterize the present direction of historical studies in the sense of defining what facts and theoretical direction we now feel to be important.

VIII

The Bearings of Botanical Evidence

on African Culture History

Edgar Anderson

Curator of Useful Plants
Missouri Botanical Garden

This paper will summarize the contributions of botany to the cultural histories of Africa. One of the most important areas for study—fossil pollens—is outside my own field. While of great potential significance, such study requires groups of dedicated workers because of the richness and complexities of the African floras and the vast and differentiated areas which must be surveyed.

The oldest contributions of botany and still the most fundamental are those of taxonomy, the science of classification. Fortunately, this scattered literature was reviewed by I. H. Burkill, the most distinguished ethnobotanist of the twentieth century, in his Hooker Lecture before the Linnaean Society in 1951. He was long the director of the Singapore Botanical Garden and was the author of the detailed and comprehensive *Dictionary of the Economic Products of the Malay Peninsula* (London, 1935). Much of the thirty-page Linnaean Society lecture is directly pertinent to the subject of this symposium and has been reprinted so as to be more conveniently available to American scholars.[1]

Burkill's paper is particularly important because he has distilled from J. D. Snowden's excellent but highly technical monograph on the sorghums of the world the chief points which relate to the cultural history of Africa.[2] The sorghums which Africa gave

1. I. H. Burkill, "Habits of Man and the Origins of Cultivated Plants of the Old World," in P. Wagner and M. Mikesell (eds.), *Readings in Cultural Geography* (Chicago, 1962), 248–281.
2. J. D. Snowden, *The Cultivated Races of Sorghum* (London, 1936).

to the world consist of a large and heterogeneous but closely related group of species, races, and subraces which include everything from desert grasses to grain sorghums, syrup sorghums, broomcorns, forage grasses, and weeds. The area where the sorghums were ennobled forms a great backward capital L on the map of Africa (as shown on the map). The long arm of the

Distribution of African Sorghums. The region of the northern sorghums hemmed in by the deserts to the north and the equatorial forests (cross-hatched) to the south is the home of an ancient indigenous agriculture, the most important of whose domesticates made their way to Asia in very early times over the "Sabaean Lane." (Map adapted from I. H. Burkill, *A Dictionary of the Economic Products of the Malay Peninsula* [London, 1935].)

L is a narrow band extending from the west coast of Africa east to the plateaus of Nigeria and Ethiopia. The shorter arm of the L bends southward and eastward, touching the coast at Zanzibar.

Writes Burkill:

> Within the two limbs of the L is the humid equatorial forest area with its own cultigens; and the L-shaped area has cultigens of its own likewise. It is to be observed that the forests nearly cut Africa in two; and it is to be added that east of the end of the forest there lies land desert enough to take a part in the cutting, but leaving a channel in the latitude of the Victoria Nyanza. I have pointed out that J. D. Snowden's excellent taxonomic study of the sorghums suggests that the gap serves as a recasting factory between the northern and the southern sorghums, all the species losing their identity in it. Thus viewed, the gap divides the L into two parts. The races of sorghum which were taken early to Asia (by way of the Sabaean Lane) were those of the eastern end of the northern limb of the L; and they had been evolved by selection in it. The way out was sidewise by the Sabaean Lane.[3]

As early as 1938, Burkill and Sir David Prain pointed out that there have been at least two interchanges of cultivated plants between Africa and India.[4] The first, very early one took place through the Sabaean Lane, a route too dry for such moisture-demanding plants as the greater yam. This was true of other moisture-loving plants as well, "whose coming to Africa from the East was delayed until the Yemenite Arabs had so developed their colonies in Zanzibar as to make a home for them. This they did between the eighth and eleventh centuries A.D."[5] Burkill's Hooker lecture needs to be carefully read and reread by those concerned with African cultural history. Authoritatively and richly documented, it is practically free of European prejudices. It is a remarkably successful attempt to picture as a whole the

3. Burkill, "Habits of Man," 271.
4. D. Prain and I. H. Burkill, "An Account of the Genus *Dioscorea* in the East," *Annals of the Royal Botanical Garden* (Calcutta), XIV:318 (1938).
5. Burkill, "Habits of Man," 271.

development of horticulture and agriculture in Africa, Asia, and the Middle East.

Burkill discusses many African plants. He notes that our common lettuce, *Lactuca sativa,* originated in the Near East from wild lettuce, *Lactuca scariola*. He reports that the latter (which is too bitter for the leaves to be used) is a subordinate oil seed today in parts of Africa, suggesting that it may have come from Africa as an oil seed in its first domestication, and spread into the Near East where it was gradually domesticated as a leafy vegetable. He notes that the related oil seed, upland cress, *Lepidium sativum,* was one of the early African domesticates to reach the Near East. He also mentions sesame, which had spread as far as Sumeria by 2350 B.C. but took several millennia longer to reach northern China.

Burkill believes the cowpea, *Vigna sinensis,* was an early domesticate which spread from Africa over the Sabaean Lane; he credits Schweinfurth with suggesting this as early as 1893. The bulrush (or pearl) millet, *Pennisetum typhoideum,* and the tuberous Coleus are assigned to the same route; Burkill even goes on to suggest that the tamarind may possibly have made the journey. If it is native to India as well as to Africa, then it need not have made the trip, but if it is not really native to India it belongs among the early domesticates which made their way along the ancient lane. Modern taxonomic studies of tamarinds in Africa and in India would make it possible to settle such questions.

In the last fifty years, the development of genetics has brought new techniques and new points of view to the classical problems of taxonomy. In an attempt to study evolution-in-progress, this experimental taxonomy (or "biosystematics," to use another popular designation for the emerging discipline) has begun to turn its attention to the origins and evolutions of cultivated plants.[6] These important new methods, however, are laborious and time consuming; only a fraction of the world's cultivated plants have received attention, even in a tentative way. To the few crops, such as wheat, maize, and cotton, which have been extensively studied,

6. See Jack R. Harlan, "Biosystematics of Cultivated Plants," this volume.

however, they bring a precise and detailed understanding which make the pronouncements of nineteenth-century taxonomists seem naive by comparison. Fortunately for our purposes, cotton has been the most extensively studied of all the world crops. Recently, Sir Joseph Hutchinson, one of the leaders in this international effort, wrote "The History and Relationships of the World's Cottons," a critical summary of the evidence.[7] Although the beginnings of cotton cultivation in the New World are still obscure, there can no longer be any doubt that the Old World cottons began in Africa, probably as oil seeds. Details must remain uncertain until we have a more precise analysis of the increasing desiccation in Africa.

One of the more complex of the newer methods is the analysis of variation through a study of character association. It is possible with these techniques to take a variable population and determine what strains or species contributed to the mixture. For Africa, a pioneer attempt has been made by Hugh Rouk and myself with a sample of thirty-two coffee trees from the old Buda Buna Forest near Jimma in Kaffa province of Ethiopia. With the use of metroglyphs, it was possible to demonstrate graphically that there was a strong association between the characters making up the following two complexes:[8]

short fruit	*versus*	long fruit
long scar		small scar
rounded fruit		tapered fruit
pointed, lanceolate corolla lobes		rounded, obovate corolla lobes
long corolla		short corolla
fruit orange		fruit deep red
bushy trees		tall trees
short wide bean		long narrow bean
round fruit		flat fruit

7. J. B. Hutchinson, "The History and Relationships of the World's Cottons," *Endeavor*, XXI:3–15 (1962); J. B. Hutchinson, *The Application of Genetics to Cotton Improvement* (Cambridge, 1959).

8. E. Anderson, "A Semigraphical Method for the Analysis of Complex Problems," *Proceedings of the National Academy of Science*, XIII:923–927 (1957).

By itself, this analysis merely shows that the ancient Buda Buna trees came from a mixture of two quite different kinds of coffee. Similar analyses made in other parts of Africa and comparisons with the different species of coffee will be necessary before we can discuss its full significance. By itself, it is one precise demonstration that coffee had a long and complex history before it ever left Africa.

For the Darwin–Wallace Centennial in 1959, I reported on several minor crops common to both Africa and India and demonstrated that for each of these it was likely that the crop was derived originally from Africa.[9] For one of these (*Cyamopsis tetragonaloba* [L] Taub. = *C. psoralioides* D.C.), Gillett's 1958 monograph indicates that although the only wild-growing species are native to Africa, they are too different to have served as parents of guar (which, unknown anywhere as a wild plant, is widespread and variable in India).[10] It is therefore likely that it was originally domesticated in India and that its original progenitor has disappeared. For two of the other domesticates, new evidence has increased the likelihood that they were derived from African plants. In 1962, Mr. and Mrs. Hugh Rouk were able to collect the flowers and inflorescences of two species of grains of paradise, *Aframomum sp.;* the collections were made in Africa. For ragee millet, *Eleusine coracana,* Kennedy-O'Byrne has described a closely related species native to Africa with which it hybridizes, and K. L. Mehra has studied character association in one of these hybridizing populations.[11] The new species, *E. africana,* is native to Africa and is not known in India, greatly increasing the likelihood that ragee millet is of African origin.

This same area between the deserts to the north and the humid tropical forests to the south (and which includes the plateaus of

9. E. Anderson, "The Evolution of Domestication," in Sol Tax (ed.), *Evolution after Darwin* (Chicago, 1960), II, 67–84.
10. J. B. Gillett, "Indigofera (*Microcharis*) in Tropical Africa," *Kew Bulletin, Additional Series,* I:1–166 (1958); Burkill, *Dictionary of Economic Products,* 716.
11. J. Kennedy-O'Byrne, "Notes on African Grasses XXIX. A New Species of Eleusine from Tropical and South Africa," *Kew Bulletin,* I:65–72 (1957).

Nigeria, the Sudan, and parts of those in Ethiopia), is also the home of an impressive number of domesticates which have scarcely spread beyond its borders. They include the following: *Digitaria exilis,* fonio, a small-grained cereal; *Voandzeia subterranea,* earth pea, a legume widely distributed in Africa; *Kerstingiella geocarpa,* geocarpa bean, like the preceding legume and similar to the peanut; *Telfairia occidentalis,* fluted pumpkin; *Cucumeropsis edulis, C. mannii,* yergan, a squash-like plant; *Blighia sapida,* akee apple; *Hibiscus cannabinus,* ambary; *Butyrospermum parkii,* shea-butter tree; *Oryza glaberrima,* riverine or African rice.

We conclude that there was an early independent center of agriculture in north central Africa and that there was an early movement of primitive agricultural products through Ethiopia and Yemen and up the seaward edge of the Arabian peninsula and into southern India. Crops included the primitive forms of such major plants as cotton and sorghum, as well as oil seeds, spices, condiments, and a number of minor food plants. The plants were coming from just north of the tropical belt which nearly cuts agricultural Africa in two and were from the interior rather than from coastal Africa. If they were not from the precise area indicated by Murdock from other evidence, they were from not very far away.[12]

The unfortunate feature of this botanical record is that it provides such poor material for the archaeological record. As J. D. Clark wisely points out, aside from the grains they "may not leave any permanent archaeological evidence at all."[13] There is a vast difference between a stone-fruit like a cherry or plum and a soft fruit such as a tomato, whose history can be recovered, if at all, only through laborious microscopic study of coprolites.

The most important part of my discussion has been left to the end, because it is so important and for another rather curious reason. It concerns man's attitudes towards plants, and, because this takes in psychology, a field previously unfamiliar to me, I have moved into this borderland area as slowly as possible. My

12. G. P. Murdock, *Africa: Its Peoples and their Culture History* (New York, 1959), 68–70.
13. See "A Record of Early Agriculture and Metallurgy in Africa from Archaeological Sources," this volume.

only significant papers as yet on the subject are a chapter in a book I wrote for the general public, calling attention to a little paper previously published in *Ceiba;* a series of papers in that wide-ranging quarterly, *Landscape;* and a portion of my contribution to the Darwin–Wallace Centennial.[14] The study of mutual interaction between plants and man is such a fascinating idea and seems basically so easy to execute, that field geographers, anthropologists, and ethnobotanists write me from various parts of the world, frequently from the field, all eager to set to work. In the first chapters of my book, *Plants, Man and Life,* I hinted at the inefficient state into which various taxonomists were leading the science of systematics. They have neglected the study and naming of our commonest, everyday plants—whether cultivated or wild or weedy or generally underfoot. The bulk of the book, however, was a defense of taxonomists for having been intuitively wise enough to neglect these problems. The point was that new experimental methods had appeared in taxonomy, and these and many other problems can now be tackled efficiently. In the decade since the book appeared, the older and narrower approach to botany has gradually been rated as overconservative; various younger people have enthusiastically taken up the technically difficult study of these common plants, made quite possible now by modern taxonomic techniques. The time is now ripe for gathering the necessary data in the study of men's attitudes towards plants. Such deliberately prepared students as J. D. Sauer and Larry Kaplan are already reaping a rich reward in well-earned plaudits.[15]

About twenty years ago, inspired originally by Carl Sauer, I began to realize more vividly certain facts I had half-suspected.

14. E. Anderson, "Dump Heaps and the Origin of Agriculture," in *Plants, Man and Life* (Boston, 1952), 136–150; E. Anderson, "An Indian Garden at Santa Lucia, Guatemala," *Ceiba,* I:97–103 (1950); E. Anderson, "Reflections on Certain Honduran Gardens," *Landscape,* III:21–23 (1954); Anderson, "The Evolution of Domestication."

15. J. D. Sauer, "Recent Migration and Evolution of the Dioecious Amaranths," *Evolution,* IX:11–31 (1957); L. Kaplan and R. S. MacNeish, "Prehistoric Bean Remains from Caves in the Ocampo Region of Tamaulipas, Mexico," *Botanical Museum Leaflets* (Harvard University), 2:33–56 (1960).

Fortunately, I had no training in psychology aside from attending the lectures of the late Oakes Ames of Harvard. Having waited until I was over forty-five before entering the subtropics for the first time, new impressions (in a mind uncluttered by rival and conflicting dogmas) hit me with full force. They went somewhat as follows: agriculture must have originated in the tropics; certain parts of the tropics have various kinds of "traditional" or "primitive" cultures. Why not just look around gradually and find how plants really are grown in the tropics? One of the most common patterns is the use of a plot adjacent to the house in which are grown a variety of plants used for a variety of purposes. In Asia, Africa, and Latin America, such a plot will be protected with a fence or stockade (frequently of living plants), and it will contain trees, shrubs, vines, and annuals. It will be simultaneously an orchard, a vegetable garden, a dump-and-compost heap, and a medicinal garden. Maize and sorghum will frequently be raised there, other cereals rarely if at all. Seldom will plants be grown in straight rows. Planting and harvesting are continuous processes running throughout the year. The plants might be classified as actively discouraged weeds, permitted weeds, encouraged weeds, and cultivated plants. There might be fruits and vegetables, seeds and root staples, and plants with uses other than nourishment: fiber plants (including thatch and plants for brooms); utensil-producers (such as the calabash tree, gourds, etc.); poisons, stimulants, vermifuges, and other drugs; condiments; cosmetics; plants used in brewing to help sterilize utensils; and plants used in ritual.

What are we to call these dump-pile-medicinal-flower-vegetable-compost-heap affairs, consisting mostly of trees and shrubs in some places, nearly always including many vines, sometimes bright with flowers and other ornamentals, nearly always supplied with poison plants (getting rid of people must have been an ancient art)? I can only suggest "dawn gardens." I have photographed, measured, sketched, and studied these in Mexico, Guatemala, Costa Rica, Honduras, and Colombia in the New World. In the Old World, I have made various brief appraisals in Ethiopia among the Galla near Jimma, in the area around Bishaftu, and among Nilotic tribes on the headwaters of the Nile below Gambela on the Sudan border. Help has also come from minds prepared to study such problems. Harold Conklin has shared with me his photographs and experiences in the tiny dawn gardens, found between the frequently photographed rice terraces of Luzon in the Philippines. I also have had a few hours now and then with Ethel Alberts and her notes, photographs, and memories of the Barundi in Central Africa. Best of all, I have read and studied and asked questions about the Atoll Research Projects in the Pacific.

Incidentally, I have read with appreciation Malinowski's works about food plants among the coral islanders.[16] Even he, however, was too much the European. He said nothing about flowers and ornamentals, poisons, or plants used to scrub dishes. He was so enthusiastic about the importance of food plants in the life, ritual, and civic pride of these people that he did not relax and watch their attitudes towards all kinds of plants. If they are like the people on the Pacific atolls, and presumably they must share many attitudes, then even Malinowski must have missed a large segment of the story. Based on what I have learned from the Atoll Research Projects and from discussing atolls with Marston Bates and William Hatheway, it is clear that beautiful plants, flowers, and bright foliage used in ritual and in daily adornment must play a large role in the vital concerns of these people.

If we attempt a global summary of this information, reinforcing it with information derived from the cross-cultural files in the Princeton Library, the world picture proves to be simple in spite of fascinating variations from culture to culture (even when different people are living among each other, as shown by the investigations of Larry and Lucy Kaplan and their associates). Throughout the New World, throughout southeastern Asia and the Near East, and in Polynesia and Micronesia, the dawn gardens have flowers and ornamental plants mixed in with the so-called useful plants, without exception in my experience. In the first dawn garden I investigated in Santa Lucia, Guatemala, I presumed the flowers were there to bolster the family budget, since little nosegays of tea roses and other flowers were offered for sale in nearby markets along with other miscellanies from dawn

16. B. Malinowski, *Coral Gardens and Their Magic* (New York, 1935).

gardens. However, when I got to the back country in Honduras (in the valley of the Rio Yeguare, near Zamorano), I discovered that along the old Guinope Road people living just barely above the level of subsistence were spending considerable percentages of their time tending flowers and ornamentals for which there was no market. In my brief inquiry, I found that some of these plants were used for cures or magic of some kind and that others were a sort of prestige symbol, much as in American garden clubs. A number of people seemed to be growing a lot of flowers simply because it was one of the basic delights of their lives.

The amount of time given to flowers and ornamentals is, for the world as a whole, the largest single variable. Flowers and ornamentals in Africa are proportional to non-African influence. Among Ethiopians, dawn gardens seem to be nearly universal, yet by actual count among the Galla there was not more than one ornamental plant to four huts and associated gardens. Among the Nilotic tribes on the Sudan border, the dawn gardens were very poorly developed, and in a whole village, there were merely various squashes and pumpkins, a number of jatropha trees grown for poison or for use as violent purges, and a few condiments grown by a family who had returned from living among Ethiopians on the plateau above. From reading and from conversations with Africanists, the pattern seems to be clear. Arabs, missionaries, and European administrators have introduced ornamentals into certain areas and they have spread to some degree from these centers. Left to themselves, the Africans are skilled cultivators of food and utensil plants, but without outside contacts flowers and ornamentals are ignored.

If we look at the two ancient cradles of the human race, Africa and southeastern Asia, the contrast is even sharper. In southeastern Asia, we see a whole series of civilizations in which people centered a good deal of their lives and activities around flowers and ornamentals. Dawn gardens there are bright and gay. In Africa, even among the sophisticated agriculturists of Ethiopia, where the soil is rich and people live well above subsistence levels, flowers and ornamentals are lacking or very rare. Here is certainly a major factor in anthropological studies which deserves to be investigated from different points of view and by detailed methods. What kinds of attitudes do various peoples have toward flowers and ornamentals? Why are they so closely woven into the daily lives of many people and yet absent from other cultures? What are the facts concerning who grows them, where they are grown, and in what ways they are used? Here is a whole segment of ethnology which is crying out for investigation.

IX

Biosystematics of Cultivated Plants

Jack R. Harlan

Professor of Agronomy
Oklahoma State University

Since the agricultural revolution, certain crop plants have come to dominate the way of life of many agricultural peoples. Maize dominated the culture of a number of American Indian tribes and provided the foundation for the civilizations of the Maya, the Aztec, and the Inca. Emmer and barley built the civilizations of Egypt and Mesopotamia. Dominant crops for other peoples have been rice, manioc, potatoes, sorghum, tef, enset, sweet potato, and others. While various pulses have often been important in the diet of primitive farmers, it has been the starch crops that have provided most of the energy for agrarian peoples.

An adequate understanding of the origin and spread of some of the ancient staple crop plants would reveal a great deal about the culture history of agricultural peoples. A similar understanding of the lesser plants used as spices, condiments, or ornamentals; for easing fatigue; for medicinal or ceremonial purposes; and for causing visions, revelations, or intoxication might tell us even more. Unfortunately, few people are seriously interested in the origin and spread of cultigens and very little experimental work has been conducted. Admittedly, the task of analyzing any one of our major crops is rather overwhelming; it may be that some of our crops are too complex to be understood by the experimental approach. Nevertheless, some crop plants should lend themselves well to genetic analysis, and certainly plants are easier to investigate than most significant domestic animals.

An effective biosystematic analysis of a major crop plant requires an enormous collection accurately assembled and a prodigious research effort. The heterosis provided by the combination of Edgar Anderson and the Rockefeller Foundation has yielded important results in the study of maize. Dr. Anderson has given us effective methods for analyzing introgressive hybridization and has called our attention to the importance of it.[1] The Rockefeller Foundation, together with the United States Department of Agriculture, began to assemble a world collection of maize a number of years ago. By studying thousands of collections, it was possible to establish which types are "primitive" and to show how the primitive varieties spread from Mexico into South America, how maize evolved in South America and Mexico, and how South American races "returned" to Mexico and introgressed again with local types.[2] It has been possible to reach some understanding of corn-belt maize and its origin from northern flint-southern dent introgression by using Anderson's methods for introgression analysis.[3]

A world collection of sorghum is now being assembled, and we are hopeful of learning something of its migration and evolution since domestication. World barley and wheat collections are available, and a world rice collection is being assembled. Of course, adequate and accurately identified collections are only the first step. These major crops are enormously variable and the story of their migrations and evolution are difficult to unravel. Crops that are not so widely grown might prove more useful in some cases.

So far, no complete biosystematic analysis has been made of

1. E. Anderson, *Introgressive Hybridization* (New York, 1949).
2. L. M. Roberts, U. J. Grant, R. Ramirez, W. H. Hathaway, and D. L. Smith, in collaboration with P. C. Mangelsdorf, *Races of Maize in Colombia* (National Academy of Sciences, National Research Council Publication No. 510, 1957); E. J. Wellhausen, L. M. Roberts, and E. Hernandez X., in collaboration with P. C. Mangelsdorf, *Races of Maize in Mexico* (Bussey Institute, Harvard University, 1952); E. J. Wellhausen, A. Fuentes O., and A. Hernandez C., in collaboration with P. C. Mangelsdorf, *Races of Maize in Central America* (National Academy of Sciences, National Research Council Publication No. 511, 1957).
3. E. Anderson and W. L. Brown, "Origin of Corn Belt Maize and its Genetic Significance," in J. W. Gowen (ed.), *Heterosis* (Ames, Iowa, 1952), 124–148.

a cultivated plant. We have, however, studied several of them well enough to arrive at some basic concepts and to identify some of the causes of complexity which have made interpretation so difficult. Some of these concepts are presented in this paper.

Vavilovian Centers of Origin

Shortly after World War I, when it became evident that the Bolshevik Party would control the remnants of the old Russian Empire, plans were drawn up to establish a new socialist and "scientific" society. Agriculture was to be reorganized on a scientific basis; and a young man, Nikolai Ivanovich Vavilov, was appointed head of the Union-wide Institute of Genetics and Plant Breeding. Vavilov proposed the most ambitious and dazzling program ever conceived by an agronomist. His idea was that the Soviet Union should do no less than to systematically assemble germ plasm from all cultivated plants, and use it as a foundation for a gigantic national plant-breeding program. The party did not permit him to carry out his plan; but early phases of plant exploration and introduction were carried out on a vast scale and permitted him to reach some important theoretical conclusions.

When plant exploration was put on a global basis, it soon became evident that diversity in a crop plant is not uniformly distributed throughout the range of its culture. On the contrary, variation is usually moderate over most of the range of the species, with enormous diversity often concentrated in one, or possibly several, relatively small regions. The small areas of high diversity, Vavilov called centers of origin and specifically stated that such centers represented the geographic area where the crop originated.[4] Since most widespread plants do have centers of diversity, this proved to be a simple criterion and the concept was widely used by biologists, anthropologists, ethnologists, and others.

Unfortunately, it can be shown, rather easily in some cases, that

4. N. I. Vavilov, *Studies on the Origin of Cultivated Plants* (Leningrad, 1926); N. I. Vavilov, "The Origin, Variation, Immunity, and Breeding of Cultivated Plants," translated by K. Starr Chester, *Chronica Botanica,* XIII:1–364 (1951); N. I. Vavilov, *World Resources of Cereals, Leguminous Seed Crops and Flax, and their Utilization in Plant Breeding* (Moscow, 1957).

the centers of diversity cannot possibly be centers of origin, and it has been necessary to abandon the idea that such a center implies the origin of anything except the diverse forms of which it is composed.[5] Still, centers of diversity do exist and are enormously important in helping us to understand the dynamics of crop variation even though they tell us little or nothing about the original cultivation of a crop plant.

But, if centers of diversity are not centers of origin, what are they? Some years ago, I had the opportunity to study a Vavilovian center of diversity in some detail; I concluded that the variability of crops *within* such centers was not distributed uniformly and that still smaller centers of diversity frequently could be delineated.[6] These small regions within a Vavilovian center I called microcenters.

The variation within a microcenter is sometimes astonishing. Areas of only a few dozen square miles may contain more variation than can be seen in thousands of miles of travel and collecting outside of microcenters. Plant populations within microcenters are extremely dynamic and active in an evolutionary sense. Microcenters appear to be centers for originating varieties rather than centers of origin; new and novel forms are continuously being produced.

The genetic basis for these exuberant irruptions of variability seems to be hybridization and introgression between rather widely diverse races or even different species.[7] When I first studied such populations, I could only compare them to artificially produced composite cross-populations in which many diverse varieties are crossed in all possible combinations. Now, with more adequate techniques for introgression analysis, these populations can be

5. See J. R. Harlan, "Anatomy of Gene Centers," *American Naturalist,* LXXXV:97–103 (1951); "Distribution and Utilization of Natural Variability in Cultivated Plants," in *Genetics in Plant Breeding* (Brookhaven Symposia in Biology No. 9, 1956), 191–206; "Geographic Origin of Plants Useful to Agriculture," in *Germ Plasm Resources* (Washington: American Association for the Advancement of Science, 1961), 3–19; "Two Kinds of Gene Centers in *Bothriochloininae,*" *American Naturalist,* XCVII:91–98 (1963).

6. Harlan, "Anatomy of Gene Centers."

7. Harlan, "Two Kinds of Gene Centers."

examined more critically. A. Kamm and D. Zohary have made some studies of crop-weed introgression in barley in Israel, and I have studied similar behavior in wild grasses in Pakistan and India.[8] We are now beginning to understand the dynamics of variability within gene centers and to identify the causes of the extraordinary diversity found in microcenters.

The Principle of Diffuse Origins

Elsewhere, I have suggested that it would be helpful if we thought in terms of diffuse origins.[9] The modern barley crop, for instance, originated with the last harvest. Chinese barleys, as we know them, originated in China; Ethiopian barleys originated in Ethiopia. Mexican maize originated in Mexico, Colombian maize in Colombia, and Burmese maize in Burma. But modern barley and modern maize are very different plants from those that were first harvested by ancient man. Most of the threads of evidence suggest that a barley-like plant was first brought under some degree of cultivation in the Near East, perhaps within the crescent-shaped region running from Palestine through Anatolia to the Zagros of Iraq and Iran; but this barley was a far cry from modern barley. Various threads of evidence suggest that a wild maize might have been domesticated first in Mexico; but this plant was so different from the maize familiar to us that few people would recognize it as progenitor to modern maizes.

Origins are diffuse in time and space. This follows simply from the fact that evolution is a process, not an event. If an original wild *Zea* was first harvested for food in Mexico, we can hardly say that this was maize as we know it. A long and complex process was required to develop modern maize from these beginnings, and part of the process involved transport of germ plasm to different regions where evolution could proceed in relative

8. A. Kamm, "The Discovery of Wild Six-rowed Barley and Wild *Hordeum intermedium* in Israel," *Annals of the Agricultural College of Sweden*, XXI:287–320 (1954); D. Zohary, "Studies on the Origin of Cultivated Barley," *Bulletin of the Research Council of Israel*, IXD:21–42 (1960); Harlan, "Two Kinds of Gene Centers."
9. Harlan, "Geographic Origins of Plants Useful to Agriculture"; and "On the Origin of Barley," (unpubl. MS).

isolation from the original stocks. Thus, the various races of maize have evolved in several places, and we can point to no geographic region and say "maize originated here." Similarly, we can select no period of time and say "this is when maize originated." Maize is evolving wherever it is being grown. As we reach further and further back in time, maize becomes less and less like modern maize. As we reach nearer and nearer to the place where maize of some sort was first grown, we are dealing with a crop less and less famiilar to us.

Other crops, of course, behave in a similar way. Suppose for a moment that we know the geographic region where and the approximate time when barley was first grown. What kind of a plant would we be considering? Certainly it would not be modern barley, but a primitive near-wild barley; certainly not a weed barley, but a primitive near-weed barley. These early near-barleys spread, evolved, changed, and in due time produced the barleys we know today in widely different places far removed from the original center. Thus, centers of origin are diffuse in time and space and the question of a center of origin can never quite be solved.

Crop-Weed Complexes

A remarkable number of crops have companion weed forms. There are weed peppers and weed potatoes, weed barley and weed rice, weed carrots and weed melons. Some crops tend to be weedy and are likely to escape and become naturalized, at least under disturbed conditions.[10] Hemp, *Cannabis sativa,* is a widely distributed weed in North America, and *Citrus spp.* behave as weeds in Southeast Asia and have escaped in South America. More often, however, the weed forms and the crop forms are rather distinct in their habits. The wild oat is a very successful weedy annual in California, but the tame oat must be seeded. Weed barley, *Hordeum spontaneum,* is found everywhere in the Near East within its natural range, but tame barley must be raised under cultivation. Maize cannot reproduce without the aid of man, but teosinte is spontaneous. The cultivated sorghums must be tended,

10. Vavilov, *Studies on the Origin of Cultivated Plants;* Anderson, *Introgressive Hybridization.*

but "chicken corn" is a weed rather extensively naturalized in the Mississippi River system.

The fact that most of the major crop plants have weed forms has led to the rather generally accepted idea that the weed forms are the progenitors of the crops. Some rather elaborate theories have developed based upon this premise. Basically, the argument goes as follows: (1) man disturbs an area; (2) the weeds move into the disturbed area; (3) man finds something useful in the weed to harvest; and (4) in time he learns to purposely disturb (cultivate) the land in order to reap better harvests from the weed, now turned into a crop. The original disturbance may have been due to herding livestock, or to simply living in one place a long time and thus establishing middens, paths, refuse heaps, and soon.

The idea has merit and in some cases may be partly true. But a more sophisticated analysis of crop-weed relationships usually reveals genetic interactions that are basic to an understanding of the biosystematics of crop plants. In some geographic areas, crops tend to cross with their weed forms. Maize crosses with teosinte in Mexico, barley with weed barley in Israel and Afghanistan, rice (*Oryza sativa*) with red rice (*O. sativa* var. *fatua*) in India and African rice (*O. glaberrima*) with wild rice (*O. breviligulata*) in Africa. Cultivated sunflowers cross with the weed sunflowers, tame melons with wild melons, weed peppers with peppers, weed potatoes with cultivated potatoes, and so on.[11]

In most cases, there are distinct barriers to this weed-crop hybridization. Sometimes the barriers are genetic, sometimes ecological, sometimes caused by self-fertilization. The barriers are sufficient to ensure that the crop does not revert to a weed nor the weed become domesticated; yet crossing is frequent enough

11. Zohary, "Studies on the Origin of Cultivated Barley"; R. Freisleben, "Die Gersten der deutschen Hindukusch Expedition 1935," *Kühn-Archiv*, LIV:295–368 (1940); R. Freisleben, "Die Gersten und Weizen der deutschen Hindukusch Expedition 1935," *Angewandte Botanik*, XXII:105–132 (1940); S. Sampath, M. E. B. and N. Rao, "Interrelationships between Species in the Genus *Oryza*," *Indian Journal of Genetics and Plant Breeding*, XI:14–17 (1951); C. B. Heiser, "Variation and Subspeciation in the Common Sunflower, *Helianthus annuus*," *American Midland Naturalist*, LI:287–305 (1954).

so that significant mixing of germ plasm occurs. In some instances, it is precisely in the regions of high diversity that crossing occurs most often. It is more and more clear that the weed forms have played enormously important roles in the evolution of crop plants. It is also likely that selection of crop plants under domestication has had much to do with the evolution and specialization of the weed forms. The weed forms have served as reservoirs of reserve germ plasm and as sources of heterozygosity and heterosis.

With the gradual recognition of the complex interaction between crops and their weed forms, it has become necessary to abandon, in most cases, the idea that the weed forms are the progenitors of the crops. Rather, we must begin to think in terms of the evolution of crop-weed complexes. The original plant from which a crop was derived must also have given rise to the weed form. Such a change in thinking would be a relief on morphological grounds, for in almost no case is the weed form more "primitive" than the crop; in some instances the weed appears to be morphologically even more specialized and derived than the crop.

Mangelsdorf and Reeves presented evidence to suggest that maize was a crop before teosinte existed. Heiser has divided the sunflowers, *Helianthus annuus,* into wild sunflowers, weed sunflowers, and cultivated sunflowers.[12] The weed sunflower can be reconstructed quite well by crossing the wild and the cultivated forms. Nevski has pointed out that weed barley, *Hordeum spontaneum,* is too derived and specialized to have been a progenitor of cultivated barley, and Sampath and Narasinga Rao have expressed the same conviction concerning wild rice.[13] Thus, when

12. P. Mangelsdorf and R. G. Reeves, "The Origin of Corn: Five Papers Commemorating the Darwin Centennial," *Botanical Museum Leaflet* (Harvard University), XVIII:329–440 (1959); Heiser, "Variation and Subspeciation in the Common Sunflower"; C. B. Heiser, "The Origin and Development of the Cultivated Sunflower," *American Biology Teacher,* XVII:162–167 (1955).

13. S. A. Nevski, *Materialen zur Kenntnis der wildwachsenden Gersten in Zusammenhang mit der Frage uber den Ursprung von Hordeum vulgare L. und Hordeum distichum L. (Versuch einer Monographie der Gattung Hordeum L.)* (Academy of Sciences of the U.S.S.R., Flora et Systematica Plantae Vasculares Series 1, fasc. 5, 1941); Sampath and Rao, "Interrelationships between Species in the Genus *Oryza.*"

we look for progenitors of crop plants, we must look for ancestors which could give rise to both the domesticated crops and the weed forms.

The Compilospecies Concept

Ancestral species are conspicuously lacking for some of our most important crops. There is nothing known which could very well have given rise to both maize and teosinte. We can find no species which might logically have given rise to both *Hordeum vulgare* and *H. spontaneum*. Guar, *Cyamopsis tetragonaloba,* seems to have no logical ancestor; other examples come to mind.

A suggested explanation has come out of biosystematic work with grasses.[14] The three genera *Bothriochloa, Dichanthium,* and *Capillipedium* form a closely related group with which we have been working for some years. It has gradually become apparent that the species *B. intermedia* played a unique role in the evolution of the group. First, we received a number of accessions that were obviously interogression products between *B. intermedia* and *D. annulatum*. We later found this to be the only type of *B. intermedia* commonly found on the Gangetic and Punjabi plains of India and Pakistan. Then, we found abundant evidence of introgression between *B. intermedia* and *C. parviflorum* in Australia. A detailed survey showed extensive introgression between *B. intermedia* and *B. ischaemum* in the foothills of north India and west Pakistan. *B. intermedia* × *B. ewartiana* introgression also occurs in Australia, and *B. intermedia* × *B. pertusa* introgression is suspected on morphological grounds in India.[15]

As a matter of fact, in over 200 accessions of *B. intermedia* from all over its range, we have yet to identify a real *B. intermedia*. All we find are hybrids, backcrosses, and so on. This has led us to the concept of the compilospecies—from the Latin *compilo*

14. J. R. Harlan and J. M. J. de Wet, "The Compilospecies Concept," *Evolution*, XVII:497–501 (1963).
15. J. R. Harlan, R. P. Celarier, W. L. Richardson, M. H. Brooks, and K. L. Mehra, *Studies of Old World Bluestems II* (Oklahoma Agricultural Experimental Station Technical Bulletin T-72, 1958); J. R. Harlan, J. M. J. de Wet, W. L. Richardson, and H. R. Chheda, *Studies of Old World Bluestems III* (Oklahoma Agricultural Experimental Station Technical Bulletin T-92, 1961).

meaning to snatch together and carry off, to plunder, to pillage, or to rob. *B. intermedia* was perhaps originally a species of hybrid origin. It has prospered and now has a range from South Africa across India, Malaya, and Indonesia to Australia. As it spread, it has plundered its relatives of their heredities and in the process has completely consumed (genetically) its own ancestral form. At least, we have not been able to find it.

Such species are, perhaps, not uncommon. Our common Kentucky bluegrass, *Poa pratensis,* is one such species, as the extensive studies of Jens Clausen and his associates have shown. *Elymus glaucus* is a compilospecies as Snyder and Stebbins have indicated. Sugar cane is one according to the observations of Parthasarathy and Price. Maize is almost certainly a compilospecies which has genetically plundered the original *Zea* from which maize and teosinte were derived. The crop-weed barley complex is evidently another compilospecies.[16]

Parenthetically, it might be suggested that *Homo sapiens* is a compilospecies, having pillaged Neanderthal man of his heredity and perhaps consuming other heredities as well.

The compilospecies concept is not simply a mental maneuver to account for the conspicuous absence of ancestral forms of some species. In the case of *Bothriochloa intermedia* and *Poa pratensis,* the concept has developed out of solid evidence accumulated at considerable effort over a period of years. There is ample experimental evidence to support the idea of the compilospecies, and the concept should prove useful in understanding the dynamics within some species complexes.

16. J. Clausen, "Introgression Facilitated by Apomixis in Polyploid Peas," *Euphytica,* X:87–94 (1961); L. A. Snyder, "Cytology of Inter-strain Hybrids and the Probable Origin of Variability in *Elymus glaucus,*" *American Journal of Botany,* XXXVIII:195–202 (1951); G. L. Stebbins, "The Hybrid Origin of Microspecies in the *Elymus glaucus* Complex," *Proceedings of the International Genetic Symposium* (supplementary volume to *Cytologia,* 1956), 336–340; N. Parthasarathy, "Some Cytogenetical Aspects of the Origin of Sugarcane," *Indian Journal of Genetics and Plant Breeding,* XI:34–46 (1951); S. Price, "Cytological Studies in *Saccharum* and Allied Genera. II. Geographical Distribution and Chromosome Numbers in *S. robustum,*" *Cytologia,* XXII:40–52 (1957); Harlan, "On the Origin of Barley."

Amphiploid Complexes

Crop plants derived by amphiploidy from wild or weedy species appear, at first glance, to be more straightforward and easier to understand. Wheat, tobacco, oats, and cotton are classical examples. A great deal of cytogenetical work has been done in an attempt to understand the origin and evolution of wheat. In its general features, the story seems to be rather simple. *Triticum aegilopoides* is a wild or somewhat weedy species growing naturally from Iran to the Balkans, northward into the Caucasus, and southward into Lebanon. Einkorn is presumed to be a domesticated form of it. Under natural conditions, *T. aegilopoides* hybridized with *Aegilops speltoides* and produced an allotetraploid called *T. dicoccoides*.[17] The latter species is also spontaneous over parts of the same region as *T. aegilopoides* but is less common and more exacting in its requirements for survival. Emmer is presumed to be a domesticated form of *T. dicoccoides*. Finally, some tetraploid race of wheat crossed with *Aegilops squarrosa* and produced an allohexaploid resembling spelt.[18] The hexaploid forms are so exacting in their requirements that they are not known in the wild. The modern common bread wheats are thought by some to have been derived from spelt or a similar progenitor.

This basic scheme is founded upon solid cytogenetical evidence, but closer examination reveals it to be a tremendous understatement of a vastly complex process.[19] The weed wheats have made their contributions. Other species of *Aegilops*, weed and tame forms of *Secale cereale*, *T. villosum*, and even species of *Agropyron*

---

17. P. Sarkar and G. L. Stebbins, "Morphological Evidence Concerning the Origin of the B Genome in Wheat," *American Journal of Botany*, XLIII:297–304 (1956); R. Riley, J. Unrau, and V. Chapman, "Evidence on the Origin of the B Genome of Wheat," *Journal of Heredity*, XLIX:91–98 (1958).

18. H. Kihara, "Die Entdeckung des D-analysators beim Weizen," *Agriculture and Horticulture (Japan)*, XIX:889–890 (1944); E. R. Sears, "Weizen I: The Systematics, Cytology and Genetics of Wheat," in H. Kappert and W. Rudorf (eds.), *Handbuch der Pflanzenzüchtung* (Berlin, 1959), II, 164–187.

19. D. Zohary and M. Feldman, "Hybridization between Amphidiploids and the Evolution of Polyploids in the Wheat (Aegiops-Triticum) Group," *Evolution*, XVI:44–61 (1962).

have apparently contributed germ plasm ranging from a few genes to substituted chromosomes to entire genomes. Some of the species of *Aegilops* are themselves complex and have absorbed germ plasm from several species before crossing with wheat. Crossing between races of wheat has distributed, diluted, and reorganized the exogenous germ plasm. Cytogenetic studies show that wheat genomes are not necessarily clear-cut and precise in their pairing relationships.[20] Some antosyndesis is commonly encountered and the classic AABBDD genomic scheme can be considered approximate at best. The wheats are among the most complex and "messy" of our cultivated plants, and at the present time we are a long way from a really adequate understanding of their origin and evolution.[21]

It should be pointed out that differences in ploidy level provide barriers to gene exchange but do not necessarily prevent it. Spontaneous field hybrids between cultivated grain sorghum ($2n = 20$) and the naturalized weed sorghum, Johnson grass ($2n = 40$), are commonly encountered in the southern United States, Argentina, South Africa, and elsewhere. The F_1 generation normally has $2n = 30$ and may be highly sterile or somewhat fertile. Succeeding generations revert very quickly to $2n = 40$, and occasional diploids may also be derived from the cross. Even by the F_2 generation, one can find apparently normal tetraploids, although a few genes might have been exchanged in the process.

From the biosystematic point of view, amphiploid complexes have at least one advantage over species at the diploid level. The sequence of major events, at least, can be determined. In amphiploid evolution, the chromosome number increases by steps, and the higher polyploids should be younger than the species at lower ploidy levels.

20. G. L. Stebbins and F. T. Pun, "Artificial and Natural Hybrids in the *Gramineae,* Tribe *Hordeae* VI. Chromosome Pairing in *Secale cereal* × *Agrophyron intermedium* and the Problem of Genome Homologies in the *Triticinae,*" *Genetics,* XXXVIII:600–608 (1953; R. Riley, "Chromosome Pairing and Haploids in Wheat," *Proceedings of the X International Congress of Genetics,* II:234–235 (1958).

21. Zohary and Feldman, "Hybridization between Amphidiploids and the Evolution of Polyploids."

Man-Crop Complexes

The evolution of cultivated plants and their companion weeds has always been profoundly influenced by human activity. This is, in fact, why we are interested in cultigens in culture history studies. The subject is much too large to review here in even the sketchiest way; I only wish to point out that man's attitude toward plants can have profound effects on the genetic systems of the plants involved. Sometimes these attitudes are subtle and easily overlooked by students of both crops and man. Our knowledge of culture history might be greatly enhanced by more complete and accurate observations of human attitudes toward plant species. I shall cite here only three personal observations as examples, and I am sure that all of the other participants of this symposium could cite many more.

The first example is very direct and straightforward. We were watching an Ethiopian farmer select heads of sorghum for his seed stock to be planted the following year. The field was a typically mixed lot, but we noticed he selected only the crook-necked milo types. We asked him why he selected those instead of straight-necked kaffirs or open-panicled types which were also abundant in the field. His answer was that the crook-necked type was easier to hang from the *tukel* roof. The reason is perfectly valid but unexpected.

The second example is somewhat more subtle. At the agronomy farm connected with the Imperial Ethiopian Agricultural College we found it very difficult to persuade Ethiopian students or laborers to chop out any plant that might be used for something. Useless plants they will hoe out readily, but even wild plants that are used for some purpose are always left, even though unsightly and even though they might damage the experimental plots. The same "encouraged" plants are frequently seen about the *tukel* dooryards and village gardens. This attitude is not to be confused with incipient cultivation. The Ethiopian farmer is one of the most skillful in the world. He knows very well what cultivation is, yet he also maintains an almost reverent attitude toward the useful plants that spring up spontaneously about his home or in his fields.

The third example is more sophisticated and represents attitudes and effects on genetic systems that could easily be overlooked. In 1960, I was in Kulu Valley in northwest India at the time of the Hindu harvest festival called Desehra. Kulu Valley is a lovely place tucked between high ridges coming down from the Himalayas. It is a holy valley, and at Desehra pilgrims from all the villages in the valley and from nearby valleys come to Kulu. Each village sends a delegation which carries a shrine containing the village gods; they are accompanied by drummers, horn blowers, flag and standard bearers, and others in procession. Some of the delegations travel for days up over high mountain passes to reach Kulu in time for the religious ceremonies conducted at the beginning of Desehra.

The most important crops in Kulu Valley are maize and grain amaranth. Both are very colorful. Whole fields of amaranth turn crimson in the autumn sunshine and, from a distance, whole villages seem to turn yellow-orange from maize drying on the roofs. The maize is a flint, amazingly uniform and of a special orangey-yellow or yellow-orange color. On dozens of roof tops covered with ears, one can not find a red or purple or white, or even a pure yellow kernel. Both the uniformity and the special shade of color are striking.

Later, I noticed that the red peppers in Kulu Valley are not red. Almost everywhere red peppers are red, but not in Kulu. There the red peppers are orangey-yellow, like the maize. When the delegations from the various villages began to arrive with beating of drums and blasts on the huge trumpets, I noticed that the village gods were reverently decorated with garlands of marigolds. The marigolds were an orangey-yellow of exactly the same shade as the maize and the peppers. In fact, it seemed evident that the marigold had provided the model for the other crops to mimic. Marigolds were everywhere. Garlands were sold on the street, draped from tents, hung over doorways, and worn about the neck. The one restaurant in Kulu is the Marigold Restaurant. The marigold is a sacred flower in Kulu Valley, and varieties of maize and peppers have been bred to match its color.

The most curious and significant feature of this story is the fact that the maize, the pepper, the grain amaranth, and the marigolds are all American plants. We shall not attempt to enlarge on the implications here, but will merely repeat the conviction that the intimate relationships between man and his crops are important to both the student of crop plants and the student of culture history.

Summary

By way of summary, we may say that the domestication and evolution of crop plants is always a complex process; but the mechanisms involved are the same as those found in rapidly evolving wild species. The mechanisms vary in detail, but the net result is a repeated discontinuous mixing of divergent germ plasm. Temporally, there is a divergence under isolation followed by breakdown of isolation and some hybridization between the divergent forms. The alternate divergence and introgression may take place at a subspecific racial level, at the specific level, or even at the generic level.

It is important to point out that freely interbreeding systems tend to be rather stable and conservative and do not lead to rapid evolution. Sewall Wright has pointed out that large, randomly breeding populations are less efficient from an evolutionary point of view than smaller, discrete units in which hybridization only occasionally takes place between units. Edgar Anderson has shown that introgressive hybridization is most effective where the parental types are quite different and where there is only a small amount of crossing. The microcenter patterns found in both wild and cultivated species indicate, in fact, that introgression is not likely to take place over a broad front but is generally confined to small geographic areas.[22]

The crop-weed complex is an especially efficient system. The two populations may grow side by side but are generally rather well isolated. Occasionally and in restricted localized areas (micro-

22. S. Wright, "Evolution in Mendelian Populations," *Genetics,* XVI:97–159 (1931); S. Wright, "The Genetical Structure of Populations," *Annals of Eugenics,* XV:323–354 (1951); Anderson, *Introgressive Hybridization*; Harlan, "Anatomy of Gene Centers"; "Two Kinds of Gene Centers"; Anderson, *Introgressive Hybridization.*

centers) the isolation breaks down, hybrid swarms are produced, and the divergent germ plasm is mixed. Elsewhere, there is little or no crossing, and the two populations may develop separate heredities over long periods of time.

The compilospecies is an even more remarkable genetic system for mixing strange germ plasm. This system operates at the specific or generic level, while the crop-weed system may operate at a subspecific level. The plundering of related species of their heredities is likely to take place primarily in microcenters also.

Amphiploidy may be involved in crop-weed systems or compilospecies or both, but it may also provide effective evolutionary systems on its own. Differences in chromosome number provide isolation, and divergence of heredities becomes feasible. Isolation is frequently not absolute, however, and infiltration of strange germ plasm across ploidy levels can take place occasionally.

The effective systems, then, have a common genetic basis—the *discontinuous* mixing of strange germ plasm. A constant stirring of the genetic system by free interbreeding slows the evolutionary pace, and pure line selection almost stops it. However, the occasional crossing of divergent pure lines can restore evolutionary activity to high levels.

It would seem that the man-crop-weed complex would be the most efficient of all. For reasons not always clear to himself, man often develops relatively uniform populations of his crop plants. He may grow a population under conditions of fairly complete isolation for many generations, but periodically he is likely to move, taking his seeds and crops with him. Contact with other isolated and divergent populations is made. Infusions of strange germ plasm occur, and a new cycle of evolutionary development is started. Thus, the migratory movements of man have profoundly influenced the evolution of cultivated plants. An adequate understanding of the historical evolution of cultivated plants should, therefore, tell us something about the movement and activities of agrarian peoples. The relationships between man and his domesticated and encouraged plants is so intimate that any study of culture history should include a study of plants; any study of cultivated plants must include the culture history of peoples who use them.

X

Murdock's Classification of Tropical African Food Economies

Marvin P. Miracle
Associate Professor of Agricultural Economics
University of Wisconsin

In countries at an early stage of economic development, staple food crops account for the greatest part of the output of what is often labeled the subsistence sector of the economy. Therefore, George Peter Murdock's detailed maps of Africa showing where each of the major foods is "staple" or a "co-staple," "economically important," and present but in "unimportant capacity," are of considerable interest to students and planners of economic development, as well as to those generally interested in the characteristics of tropical African societies and economies.

Murdock ends the article in which he first presented these maps with the following comment:

> The distributions plotted on the maps reflect published ethnographic data only. Unpublished information in the hands of anthropological field workers can certainly amplify these data and doubtless often correct them. However, of potentially even greater scientific interest is the fact that economists and economic geographers have at their disposal, in crop statistics compiled by governments for administrative divisions, a completely independent source of information on the same facts, capable of being mapped in similar fashion. Would the comparison of maps from these two sources show a degree of correspondence reassuring to the practitioners of the several disciplines concerned, or would it reveal discrepancies of such an order as to raise fundamental problems in their reconciliation? [1]

1. George Peter Murdock, "Staple Subsistence Crops of Africa," *The Geographical Review*, L:540 (1960).

I shall argue that for tropical Africa at least, there are considerable data from statistical sources similar to those to which Murdock refers which suggest that his maps are in a large measure incomplete and inaccurate. Moreover, he has presented his data in such a fashion that they are not meaningful; and, as they now stand, they cannot be used even to supplement more reliable sources.

Murdock's Technique

Murdock describes his research technique as follows:

> During the preparation of the author's "Africa: Its Peoples and Their Culture History" data on the incidence and distribution of cultivated plants in Africa were assembled from some two thousand ethnographic sources. Such sources nearly always present precise information on the staple crop or crops in the particular subsistence economy studied and on the plants that hold an economically important place but fall short of the status of staples. Here and there, to be sure, gaps occur in the literature, or a careless ethnographer merely mentions "millets" or "root crops" without supplying enough information to make identification certain. However, only for a few regions are such deficiencies sufficiently prominent to result in possible errors of consequence on the distribution maps. These regions are the Republic of Chad, Ethiopia, northern Mozambique, Southern Rhodesia, and northern, or Arab, Sudan.[2]

Considering the great emphasis on non-economic phenomenon such as kinship, language, and history that is to be found in the ethnographic literature on tropical Africa, it is a little surprising that Murdock is prepared to say ethnographers "nearly always present precise information on the staple crop or crops in the particular subsistence economy studied and on the plants that hold an economically important place but fall short of staples." In order to make precise statements about the importance of crops, one must be able to make a quantitative statement, and ethnographers typically have not the training, time, or inclination to weigh accurately food intake of the villagers they visit. Ethnographers

2. *Ibid.*, 523.

may be able to make a rough ranking of the importance of the major foods in areas they have studied, but this is not precise information even if the people they observe are representative of the whole tribe. Any precise statement of the relative importance of foods in the diet must not only rank foods consumed but must also give some idea of the distance between one food and the next most important on the scale along which they are measured.

It is to some exact position along such a scale that terms like "staple," "co-staple," or "economically important," must refer. Murdock, however, employs these terms without defining them. Does he have in mind the dictionary definition of staple, i.e., chief commodity produced or sold? If so, what is "co-staple"? Logically it would mean that two or more commodities are of exactly the same importance and each is more important than all other commodities of the group. But his usage suggests that he means merely an important food crop by the word "staple." An economic good is generally understood to be any commodity that is useful to man. Murdock, however, means something more than this when he talks of crops that are "economically important." He apparently means that the utility of such crops exceeds some bench mark which he has failed to specify.

Murdock excludes the pulses because he says they "do not attain the level of staples." Consumption data suggest, however, that this is misleading; they appear to be frequently of secondary importance as a group, and in central Rwanda-Burundi, at least, beans alone seem to account for more of the calories consumed than any other foodstuff, as will be shown.

A further imprecision results because Murdock fails to state the period to which his data apply. He almost certainly cannot be referring to the last quinquennium; even if there have been two thousand ethnographical works published on Africa over that period, it is extremely improbable that they would have been well enough distributed geographically to cover the entire continent. Because ethnographers tend to study peoples who have not been studied before—and there are still many in tropical Africa—there is probably at least half a century of spread in the dates which apply to his data. As will be shown, there is evidence that dietary habits change considerably in tropical Africa as well as in western countries over such a time span; hence, maps portraying dietary staples are not meaningful without a time reference.

Comparison of Murdock's Maps and Consumption Data

The most reliable data available on the character of tropical African diets are those obtained through sample surveys of consumption. In such studies an attempt is made to select a representative sample of the consumers in a small area and to record what they say they ate, or to actually weigh amounts eaten. If the sample is in fact representative and of sufficient size, if errors of observation and recording are not large, and if observation covers enough of the year to eliminate the bias imparted by seasonal variation in the composition of the diet, these consumption surveys provide the basis for making reasonably reliable statements about the relative importance of foods consumed.

Many of the surveys carried out to date in tropical Africa have been in urban areas. In these areas the environment is different enough from nearby rural communities—presumably the communities on which ethnographers focus most of their attention —to affect the character of the diet. Therefore, we have not attempted to test Murdock's data with results from urban consumption surveys. The number of rural surveys reliable enough to constitute a valid test of Murdock's maps are few, and for large areas there have been none at all. There are, however, enough to suggest that Murdock's maps may be grossly deficient.

Ivory Coast. Murdock shows yams and bananas each to be staples of co-staples in the Bongouanou area of Ivory Coast; maize, manioc, and taro are listed as economically important. However, a survey of nine villages of the same area for three periods of four months each in 1955 and 1956 suggests that yams contributed 49.5 per cent of ingested calories at that date, and plantains (bananas by Murdock's terminology; he does not distinguish between bananas and plantains) supplied 26.6 per cent.[3]

3. Ivory Coast, Conseil Supérieur des Recherches Sociologiques outre-mer, *Enquête nutrition—Niveau de vie (Subdivision de Bongouanou, 1955–1956)* (Paris, 1958), 84.

Taro was in third place with 5.4 per cent, but the other two economically important crops, by Murdock's classification—maize and manioc—were both less important than rice and peanuts; and manioc was also less important than wheat.

Per cent of total caloric intake

Yams	49.5
Plantains	26.6
Taro	5.4
Rice	1.4
Peanuts	1.0
Maize	0.8
Bread	0.7
Manioc	0.5

Togo. Surveys by J. Périssé provide bases for comparison of Murdock's figures on Togo.[4] In each of five communities, well spaced from the coast to the northern extreme of the country, Périssé selected twenty to thirty-five families which "seemed typical" and measured their food consumption for five to six days at three different times during the year.

Murdock describes an area containing the village of Attigon, located in the southeastern corner of Togo; yams and maize are staples or co-staples, while manioc and bananas are economically important. Périssé's consumption survey records neither bananas nor yams. Other than manioc and maize, in that order, the only significant starchy foods were sweet potatoes. It is also of interest that he found pulses (beans, peas, and peanuts) more important than yams or bananas.

Per cent of total caloric intake

	May	September	January
Manioc and manioc products	59.2	52.7	38.
Maize	20.8	36.1	46.2
Pulses	2.1	1.2	3.6
Sweet potatoes	0	0	1.

4. J. Périssé, *L'Alimentation des Populations Rurales du Togo* (Off. Rech. Scient. et Techn. Outre-Mer, Inst. Rech. Togo, Lomé, n.d.), Table 14.

The zone containing Kouma Adamé, a little over 100 kilometers inland from the coast, is one in which Murdock designates maize and yams as staples or co-staples, with manioc, taro, and bananas listed as economically important. Data from the Périssé consumption survey suggest that yams and maize are neither staples nor co-staples and that they are both less important than manioc and taro. Yams also appear to be less important than rice; and all these appear to be more consumed than bananas which are, by percentage of calories, possibly only very slightly ahead of the pulses.

	Per cent of total caloric intake		
	February	June	October
Manioc and manioc products	18.2	33.3	22.8
Taro	26.3	20.4	22.2
Maize	9.2	31.4	14.7
Rice	17.8	3.8	4.5
Yams	3.1	0.3	12.7
Bananas-plantains	4.7	4.9	3.2
Pulses	4.3	5.9	1.

At Abaka, some 130 kilometers farther north, Murdock indicates yams as the staple and manioc is the only other foodstuff that is economically important. Périssé's consumption data suggest that yams are indeed the major source of calories but not far ahead of millets-sorghums, and that both millets-sorghums and maize are more important than manioc, while pulses are almost as important.

	Per cent of total caloric intake		
	May	September	January
Yams	33.9	46.7	27.3
Millets-sorghums	21.9	9.6	46.3
Maize	3.7	14.4	2.8
Manioc and manioc products	6.3	3.6	3.3
Pulses	3.8	3.8	2.7
Rice	1.7	1.2	4.4

For the area in which the village of Sahoude is found, about 200 kilometers farther inland from Abaka, Murdock designates millets-sorghums as the staple and rice, yams, and fonio as economically important. The Périssé survey shows millets-sorghums to be the major source of calories, but pulses are probably more important than yams; while maize, taro, sweet potatoes, and manioc are more important than rice; all of these are found to be more important than fonio.

Per cent of total caloric intake

	July	November	March
Millets-sorghums	77.0	19.4	59.6
Pulses	11.9	22.2	3.5
Yams	3.3	28.1	9.1
Maize	0.2	6.5	0.4
Taro	0.5	5.5	0.6
Manioc and manioc products	0	2	2.2
Sweet potatoes	0	3.3	0
Rice	0.4	0.7	0.2

Murdock shows the northernmost village, Bambouaka, to be in a zone where millets-sorghums are staples and rice and yams are economically important. The Périssé consumption survey confirms that millets-sorghums are, indeed, the most important source of calories; but pulses appear to be more important than yams and possibly rice, while bananas, sweet potatoes, coleus potatoes, and manioc are close enough to yams to cast doubt on their exclusion by Murdock.

Per cent of total caloric intake

	December	June	October
Millets-sorghums	58.9	63.3	74.9
Pulses	18.6	19.6	9.9
Rice	2.5	0.3	32.8
Manioc and manioc products	0	3.1	0.8
Yams	1.3	0.4	0
Bananas-plantains	0	1	0
Sweet potatoes	1.3	0	0
Coleus potatoes	1.0	0	0

Nigeria. A study of cocoa farmers in southwestern Nigeria conducted by R. Galletti, K. D. S. Baldwin, and I. O. Dina reports food consumption by 187 cocoa farmers in four areas for the year 1951–1952. Murdock characterizes the whole area as one in which yams are the staple, with millets-sorghums, maize, and manioc economically important. In only two of the four areas surveyed by Galletti and his associates were yams the most important source of calories, and in two of the areas there were crops not listed by Murdock as economically important which were more important than millets-sorghums.[5]

	Per cent of total caloric intake			
	Ibadan	Ife-Ilesha	Ondo	Abekouta-Ijebu
Manioc and manioc products	37.2	24.6	11.4	51.3
Yams and yam products	10.5	25.6	38.9	3.1
Maize and maize products	24.6	9.9	4.6	3.9
Other cereals	0.5	5.6	1.5	9.1
Other roots	0.9	0.2	20.5	3.9

Surveys by B. M. Nicol provide food consumption data for thirteen additional rural areas of Nigeria. The earliest of these surveys are three studies that were carried out in Niger Province; the food consumption of three families in each of three villages was measured over four periods of seven days each between March, 1947 and March, 1948, "the periods being distributed throughout the year in accordance with expected seasonal variations in availability of the staple foodstuff."[6] A survey of three villages in Warri Province in 1949 and 1950 and of seven other areas between 1954 and 1957 employed similar techniques.

Nicol's data suggest a different staple crop than shown by

5. R. Galletti, K. D. S. Baldwin, and I. O. Dina, *Nigerian Cocoa Farmers: An Economic Survey of Yoruba Cocoa Farming Families* (London, 1956), 491–492.
6. Cited in B. F. Johnston, *The Staple Food Economies of Western Tropical Africa* (Stanford, 1958), 193.

Murdock's maps in four of the thirteen areas of Nigeria (see Tables 1 and 2). In twelve areas, at least one crop not listed by Murdock contributes more calories than one or more of the crops Murdock classifies as economically important: in nine instances pulses do; in two instances rice does; in two instances maize does; and in two instances sweet potatoes do. There are possibly other disagreements that are obscured because Nicol reports manioc and banana consumption together in seven of his surveys.

Cameroon. A consumption survey of Evodoula village, about sixty-five kilometers northwest of Yaoundé, by R. Masseyeff and A. Cambon in 1954, provides quantitative data on diets in southern Cameroon. All food consumed in each of thirty-one households was measured for periods of six days in February–March, June–July, September, and December. Murdock shows Evodoula in a zone where manioc is the staple with maize, yams, taro, and bananas economically important. Masseyeff and Cambon's data suggest that although manioc is, in fact, the primary supplier of calories, there is wide variation in the importance of the economically important crops. Both taro and plantains appear to be vastly more important than maize or yams.[7]

	Caloric intake per person per day
Manioc	341.4
Plantains	258.2
Taro and "Macabo"	222.1
Yams	77.6
Maize	25.0
Rice	16.7
Wheat	4.8

Former French Equatorial Africa. P. Bascoulergue and J. Bergot provided consumption data for 1956–1958 for five rural areas and Brazzaville in Moyen-Congo, in what was then French Equatorial Africa. In each village studied, the sample of families surveyed was drawn equally from families with two to four, five to eight, and nine or more members. For each family in the sample, food consumption was measured for a week, except at

7. Cited in William O. Jones, *Manioc in Africa* (Stanford, 1959), 143.

Table 1. Comparison of the relative importance of major foodstuffs in the diet of selected areas of Nigeria, according to Murdock.

Area	Millets-sorghums	Maize	Rice	Wheat	Fonio	Manioc and manioc products	Yams	Taro	Sweet potatoes	Bananas-plantains	Pulses
Mbande	—	—	—	—	—	—	Staple/co-staple	Econ. impt.[a]	—	Econ. impt.[a]	—
Warri Province Warri	—	—	—	—	—	Econ. impt.[a]	Staple/co-staple	—	—	Econ. impt.[a]	—
Illu	—	—	—	—	—	Econ. impt.[a]	Staple/co-staple	—	—	Econ. impt.[a]	—
Saragbeni	—	—	—	—	—	Econ. impt.[a]	Staple/co-staple	—	—	Econ. impt.[a]	—
Bero-Okuta	Econ. impt.[a]	Econ. impt.[a]	—	—	—	Econ. impt.[a]	Staple/co-staple	—	—	—	—
Bida	Staple/co-staple	Econ. impt.[a]	—	—	—	—	Econ. impt.[a]	—	—	—	—
Koutagora	Staple/co-staple	Econ. impt.[a]	—	—	—	—	Econ. impt.[a]	—	—	—	—
Zuru	Staple/co-staple	—	Econ. impt.[a]	—	Econ. impt.[a]	—	—	—	—	—	—
Tungan-Madibu	Staple/co-staple	—	Econ. impt.[a]	—	Econ. impt.[a]	—	—	—	—	—	—

Table 1. (Continued)

Area	Millets-sorghums	Maize	Rice	Wheat	Fonio	Manioc and manioc products	Yams	Taro	Sweet potatoes	Bananas-plantains	Pulses
Langai	Econ. impt.[a]	—	—	—	Staple/co-staple	—	—	—	—	—	—
Tangaza	Staple/co-staple	—	—	—	—	—	—	—	—	—	—
Bunga	Staple/co-staple	—	—	—	Econ. impt.[a]	—	—	—	—	—	—
Jarawaji	Staple/co-staple	Econ. impt.[a]	—	—	—	—	—	—	—	—	—

[a] Economically important.

Table 2. Comparison of the relative importance of major foodstuffs in selected areas of Nigeria, according to Nicol's data, 1947–1957 (data given in per cent of total caloric intake).

Area	Millets-sorghums	Maize	Rice	Wheat	Fonio
Mbande					
Males	0	0.2	0.9	0	0
Females	0	0.2	0.4	0	0
Warri Province					
Warri	0	4.1	9.5	8.8	0
Illu	0	2.5	0	0	0
Saragbeni	0	5.5	0	0	0
Bero-Okuta					
Males	13.4	4.1	0	0	0
Females	12	10.1	0	0	0
Bida	73.5	0	0	0	0
Koutagora	85.7	0	0	0	0
Zuru	93.1	0	0	0	0
Tungan-Madibu					
Males	73	0.5	0	0	0
Females	69.2	1.1	0	0	0
Langai					
Males	42.4	0.4	1	0	21.2
Females	41.7	0.1	0.6	0	16.9
Tangaza					
Males	76.4	0	12.3	0	0
Females	94.7	0	6.9	0	0
Bunga					
Males	67.1	11.5	0	0	0
Females	62.5	13	0	0	0
Jarawaji					
Males	81.8	0	0	0	0
Females	80.3	0	0	0	0

Source: From or derived from B. M. Nicol studies cited in B. F. Johnston, *The Stable Food Economies of Western Tropical Africa* (Stanford, 1958), 194–195; and B. M. Nicol, "The Calorie Requirements of Nigerian Peasant Farmers," *British Journal of Nutrition*, XII:297 (1959).

Table 2 (Continued)

Manioc and manioc products[a]	Yams	Taro	Sweet potatoes	Bananas-plantains[a]	Pulses
0–3.4	59.4	0	0.2	0–0.7	6.5
0–4.3	66.5	0	0.1	0–0.9	11.1
25	70.8	0	0	1.4	2.3
48.3	27.2	0	0	0	2.1
54.3	3.4	0.6	1.2	0	0
0–3.4	61.6	0	0	0–0.8	1.5
0–5.2	54.2	0	0	0–1.2	1.2
0	0.3	0	7.2	0	3.7
0	0	0	0.7	0	1.6
0	0	0	0	0	1.4
0	0.2	0	0	0	19
0	0.3	0	0	0	23.6
0–2.2	3.1	0	2.1	0–0.5	6.3
0–1.8	3.3	0	2.3	0–0.4	9.4
0–2.3	0	0	0	0–0.5	3.5
0–5.5	0	0	0	0–1.2	2
0–19.3	0.5	0	0	0–4.2	2.2
0–18.4	1.9	0	0	0–4.6	2.6
0–1.2	0	0	0	0–0.2	3.5
0	0	0	0	0	2

[a] Manioc, gari (a manioc product), and bananas-plantains are given together. Of these, bananas-plantains have the fewest calories per unit and gari the most. The highest [first] figure for bananas-plantains was calculated by assuming that manioc and gari were zero; the [second] highest figure for manioc and manioc products was calculated by assuming that manioc and bananas-plantains were zero.

Table 3. Comparison of the relative importance of major foodstuffs in the diets of selected areas of former French Equatorial Africa, according to Murdock.

Murdock's Classifications	Souanke	Min-douli	Kibou-endé	Mos-sendjo	Madingo-Kayes
Staple or Co-Staple	bananas	manioc	manioc	bananas	bananas manioc
Economically Important	manioc	bananas maize yams	bananas maize yams	manioc	—

Kibouendé where surveyors were in the village fifteen months and every family was surveyed twice, for a week each time. Except to note that 258 families were studied in thirty-five villages, the authors do not give details as to the total size of the sample.

Table 4. Comparison of the relative importance of major foodstuffs in the diets of selected areas of former French Equatorial Africa, according to Bascoulergue and Bergot, 1956–1958 (data given in per cent of total caloric intake).

Food	Souanke	Min-douli	Kibou-endé	Mos-senjo	Madingo-Kayes
Manioc	6.1	48.9	65.2	50.5	43.9
Bananas-plantains	63.2	0.8	0.7	2.1	4.5
Yams	0.4	2.5	0.9	10.1	1.4
Taro	0.8	0.5	0	1.0	1.5
Sweet potatoes	0.5	1.1	1.4	0.8	0.5
Maize	3.5	4.0	3.5	0	0
Pulses	14.4	20.7	0.2	9.9	0.1

Source: P. Bascoulergue and J. Bergot, *L'Alimentation Rurale au Moyen-Congo* (French Equatorial Africa, Service Commun de Lutte Contre les Grandes Endemies, 1959), 29, 31, 34, 40.

In one of the five rural areas, Mossendjo, Murdock's maps show bananas to be the staple but the consumption survey suggests they are much less important than manioc (see Table 4). Murdock portrays the Madingo-Kayes area as one with banana and manioc as the staple or co-staples; but the consumption survey suggests that bananas contribute only about one-tenth as many calories as manioc, a position that hardly justifies calling them co-staples. The considerable contribution of pulses to the diet reported by the consumption surveys in three areas and of yams in another is also not reflected in Murdock's maps.

Sudan. An exceptionally elaborate survey of diets was carried out by G. M. Culwick in Zande district of the southwestern Sudan in 1947–1948. The thirty-seven to forty-seven Taba households surveyed near Yuba Station, which appear to be fairly typical of all the groups studied, obtained by far their largest percentage of calories from manioc.[8]

Per cent of total caloric intake

	August (47 homes)	November (42 homes)	February (40 homes)	May (37 homes)
Manioc and manioc products	72.3	68.7	59.6	81.4
Pulses	10.8	24.0	16.5	13.9
Eleusine (millet)	13.3	5.2	15.5	15.4
Other starchy roots and bananas	1.3	21.9	21.2	0.4
Maize, sorghum, and rice	10.8	3.1	2.8	2.0

Murdock, however, makes no mention of manioc and shows this to be an area where millets-sorghums are the staple and sweet potatoes are economically important.

Ruanda-Urundi. The results of a study in which Philippe Leurquin recorded the daily food consumption of five families in central Ruanda-Urundi for twelve months in 1956 suggest that

8. Cited in *ibid.,* 145.

pulses are the major source of calories, followed by sweet potatoes or manioc (see Table 5). Murdock, however, makes no reference to pulses and classifies this area as one where millets-sorghums, bananas, and maize are staples or co-staples, with sweet potatoes economically important.

Table 5. Relative contribution of major foods to the diet of five rural families in Ruanda-Urundi, 1956 (by per cent of caloric intake).

Food	Family A (Near Astrida)	Family B (Nduga)	Family C (Nduga)	Family D (Nduga)	Family E (Urundi)
Beans	23	48	46	31	8
Sweet potatoes	26	14	19	30	62
Manioc	20	19	17	12	0
Potatoes	4	6	11	9	0
Sorghums and sorghum beer	15	0	0	0	0
Maize	4	0	0	0	13

Source: Data from Philippe Leurquin, "Economie de subsistance et alimentation au Ruanda-Urundi: Quelques cas concrets," cited in William O. Jones, *Manioc in Africa* (Stanford, 1959), 243.

Northern Rhodesia. Data on Northern Rhodesia (now Zambia) are provided by Betty Preston Tompson's survey of three Lala villages from August 1947 to July 1948. In each village records were kept of the total food eaten for six consecutive days out of every twenty-eight. Village size is not specified, but indirect information is provided by a note that the Lala "tend to live in small villages of about 50 people."

According to Murdock this is an area in which millets-sorghums are the staple, with sweet potatoes and maize economically important. The report of the consumption survey does not break down grains; hence, it is impossible to check the importance of maize relative to the millets-sorghums, but it does suggest that, contrary to Murdock, pulses are considerably more important than sweet potatoes.[9]

	Per cent of total caloric intake		
	Village A	Village B	Village C
Flour and grain (calory count based on millets-sorghum)	77.8	82.8	75.9
Pulses (calory count based on peas and beans)	12.1	8.6	15.3
Roots (calory count based on manioc)	5.5	2.7	4.0

Mozambique. Although there has been no consumption survey for southern Mozambique, a sample census of African agriculture is available for 1954–1955. Providing trade in foodstuffs, the use of foodstuffs for feed, and waste are small, or very little from one foodstuff to another, these data should give a good indication of the composition of diets. Murdock shows this area as one where maize is the staple, with millets-sorghums and manioc economically important. The sample census shows considerable variation in production geographically; maize is the greatest producer of calories in only six of the eleven *circunscrições* (counties). Manioc surpasses it in the other five (see Table 6). In ten of the eleven *circunscrições,* at least one foodstuff, other than maize and manioc, was more important than millets-sorghums.

Secular Changes in Diets in Rwanda-Burundi and Uganda

Evidence of the evolution of diet during the colonial period in Rwanda-Burundi and Uganda shows why undated classifications of tropical African food economies cannot be meaningful. It appears that the composition of diets may have changed strikingly

9. Derived from Betty Preston Tompson, *Two Studies in African Nutrition* (Rhodes-Livingstone Papers, No. 24, Manchester, 1954), Appendix III–V.

Table 6. Relative production of the major foodstuffs in circunscriçaoes in the districts of Lourenço Marques and Gaza, Mozambique, 1954–1955 (data in per cent of calories produced).

Food	Ma-puto	Marra-cuene	Ma-nicha	Chi-buto	Bilene	Gaza	Sabie	Ma-gude	Mu-chopes	Guija	Alto Lim-popo
Maize	53.0	42.5	43.5	39.0	50.4	37.5	56.8	78.1	27.7	96.6	69.1
Manioc	19.0	43.4	46.8	55.3	46.5	54.4	26.2	14.1	60.3	2.8	2.3
Beans	8.9	7.0	6.9	4.5	2.8	4.1	3.0	1.0	9.8	0.3	3.9
Sweet potatoes	13.5	1.1	0.3	1.0	0.3	0.9	3.2	3.7	1.6	0.1	0
Rice	1.9	2.8	0	0.1	0	0	9.7	3.1	0.6	0.3	16.1
Millets-sorghums	3.6	3.2	0	0.1	0	0	1.0	0	0	0	8.5
Wheat	0	0	2.4	0	0	3.1	0	0	0	0	0

Source: Data derived from Mozambique, Direcção de Agricultura e Florestas, *Inquérito por Amostragem à Agricultura Indígena, 1954–1955* (Lourenço Marques, 1958), Quadro 16.

in the past four or five decades in these countries. The same may well be true of other areas.

One cannot establish with any certainty what the dominant food crops of Rwanda-Burundi were prior to the advent of Belgian administration at the end of World War I; but it does seem clear that manioc, maize, and sweet potatoes were grown very little, if at all, in most communities.[10]

Beginning in 1922, the Belgian administration, alarmed by food shortages in several parts of the country in nine of the previous twenty-five years, first encouraged, then ordered, Ruanda-Urundi farmers to grow such things as sweet potatoes, Irish potatoes, and manioc because they were relatively drought and locust resistant. The campaign was intensified after a fairly severe famine was experienced in several regions in 1929; compulsory acreages continued to be an important part of policy for the following two decades, at least.[11]

There is some evidence that maize, although not encouraged by the government, became important during the same period. In the parts of Burundi where it is a major foodstuff, the elders are said to claim that it has been established only in the past thirty or forty years.[12]

A similar trend can be found in Uganda with respect to manioc and maize, but sweet potatoes and bananas-plantains appear to have declined in importance since. Estimates of acreages planted to these crops between 1917 and 1959, suggest that both plantain and sweet potato acreages have steadily declined until by the 1951–1955 quinquennium each was roughly half as important as in the 1917–1920 period. Maize and manioc increased from about 1 per cent each to 9 and 13 per cent, respectively. Millets-sorghums registered a gain from 25 to 39 per cent.

These data are undoubtedly far from perfect, but their greatest deficiencies are probably incompleteness and bias; I shall argue

10. Jones, *Manioc in Africa*, 241.
11. Baron Ch. de l'Epine, "Historique des famines et disettes dans l'Urundi," *Bulletin Agricole du Congo Belge* (June, 1929).
12. R. Bruyère, Kizozi, Ruanda-Urundi, communication to the author, May 1959.

Table 7. Acreages of selected food crops in Uganda, 1917–1959 (data given in per cent of total grown).

Year	Average acreage, all six crops (in thousands of acres)	Maize	Manioc	Millets-sorghums	Sweet potatoes	Plantains	Wheat
1917–1920	1,139	1	1	25	24	49	0
1921–1925	1,786	2	2	31	20	43	2
1926–1930	2,202	3	7	36	17	35	2
1931–1935	2,970	2	12	36	17	32	1
1936–1938	3,115	3	11	36	16	33	1
1944–1945	3,602	7	13	39	14	25	2
1945–1950	3,634	8	13	42	14	22	1
1951–1955	4,528	9	13	39	13	26	0
1956–1959	4,786	8	13	39	13	27	0

Source: Data from Uganda Protectorate, *Annual Reports of the Department of Agriculture,* each issue, 1917–1959.

that neither of these deficiencies seem serious in an analysis based on *relative* magnitudes. Incompleteness would be important for our purpose only if unrecorded acreages were unevenly distributed among the major staples, or were a function of time or locality. Although it is likely that recording of crop acreage planted has been more complete with time, there is no good reason for supposing that the accuracy of estimates has changed geographically with time, or that the degree to which the acreage of one crop as related to another was under-reported has changed significantly over the years. Bias in acreage reported, too, is of concern for our purpose only if it varies geographically or with crop over time; this does not seem likely from evidence now available. There is record of change in method of computation in only one or two districts in isolated years.

The impressive gains made by maize and manioc seem undisputably to have resulted in the earlier periods from extension of these crops in areas where they had not been long known; in later periods governmental policy was probably the paramount influence.

Maize. We do not know when or how maize was introduced to Uganda, but there is good evidence that it was not grown earlier than 100 years ago. One of the members of Speke's party which explored Uganda in 1861 and 1862, Captain J. A. Grant, took copious notes of plants found and commented that maize was "very rare as the equator is approached [from the south]; and is quite unknown beyond it northwards to 5°N." [13]

However, when introduced, it was quickly accepted as a vegetable, harvested immature and roasted or boiled. This is perhaps the most obvious method of preparation, and yields a product that seems to be prized throughout tropical Africa. But so long as this is the principal food derived from maize, the acreage is not likely to be large; the immature product must be harvested over a fairly short period—two or three weeks, depending on variety—and once harvested is perishable. Therefore, the acreage appropriate to satisfy demand, but not large enough to create a surplus, is small.

13. J. H. Speke, *Journal of the Discovery of the Source of the Nile* (London, 1864), 651.

In the early period, the role of the government in expanding maize acreage may have been considerable. The Department of Agriculture reported in 1914 that it was growing imported varieties of maize at Kadunguru Plantation "for introduction among the natives"; further details are given in its 1918 report:[14]

> Maize production is being encouraged, and further supplies of seed have been distributed. It is mostly grown as a subsidiary food crop by the natives, although the grain-eating tribes are taking an increased interest in this important crop. Amongst the Buganda maize is chiefly grown for eating green, and as this tribe eats very little grain the extension of maize cultivation is slow in Buganda Province. The other provinces, however, are making fairly rapid strides in maize cultivation.

In addition to direct stimulation of maize production, the government also may have given indirect impetus to the expansion of maize plantings about this time. Migrant laborers working for the government and other employers (mostly as porters and workers for cotton gins or plantations) had been, since the turn of the century, mainly Baganda, whose principal foodstuffs were plantains and sweet potatoes. By 1918, the Baganda had turned from wage labor to the more remunerative production of cotton and coffee, and were themselves hiring labor in order to increase their scale of production, becoming serious competitors for available workers.[15] The government, forced to seek its labor elsewhere, seems to have hired predominantly "grain eaters." (Origin of laborers cannot be determined accurately, but available evidence suggests that the Baganda laborers were largely replaced by men from grain-eating tribes of the north and southwest: the Banyankole, Banyoro, Batoro, and Acholi.)[16] Workers from these tribes probably demanded grain for their ration; and it is reasonable to assume, because of costs, that it was maize they got. Where the government, mining companies, or plantations were employers,

14. Uganda Protectorate, *Annual Report of the Department of Agriculture* (1914), 13; (1918), 13.
15. P. G. Powesland, *Economic Policy and Labour* (East African Studies, No. 10, Kampala, 1957), 25.
16. *Ibid.*, 36.

rations usually had to be imported, and only maize, of the major foodstuffs available, was both cheap and storable.

Besides laborers others have received maize from the government on occasions. In 1928, 1942, 1945, 1948–1951, and 1953, maize or maize meal was issued by the government in several parts of Uganda to relieve food shortages.[17] At such times, the people had no choice but to devise ways of eating maize as a staple.

Even in districts where harvests were not enough below normal to warrant issuance of relief rations, acceptance of maize as a staple was probably linked with poor harvests. With yields of the traditional staple greatly below average, people who found the level of their food bins alarmingly low as planting season approached, probably planted more of their acreage in an early-maturing maize, having learned from experience that they could get an edible product from maize sooner than from any other staple. When weather was favorable, considerably more maize was produced than could be consumed green, providing scope and motivation for consuming a portion of the harvest, not as roasting ears (a vegetable) but as a staple (as maize flour). This was probably one of the principal situations in which dishes made from mature maize were tried.

During and immediately following World War II, expansion of the maize acreage was tremendous and deliberate. Uganda was called upon to produce as much maize as possible as part of her contribution to the war effort and to fill postwar deficits in Kenya and Tanganyika. Prices were guaranteed at high levels, and the Africans' response was immediate and impressive—the acreage appears to have more than tripled before incentives were removed in 1954.[18]

Price guarantees were removed in 1956 and exports to Kenya, Uganda's major market during the war, were prohibited. Maize

---

17. See the Uganda Protectorate, *Annual Report of the Department of Agriculture,* for the various years mentioned.

18. See M. P. Miracle, "An Economic Appraisal of Kenya's Maize Control," *East African Economic Review* (December, 1959), 119, for prices offered and the quantities marketed in Buganda Province, the principal area of commercial maize production during this period.

acreages continued to be high, however, which suggests that domestic consumption had increased.

Manioc. One cannot establish precisely when manioc (cassava) was introduced; it appears, however, to have reached northern districts only after the establishment of European rule.[19] Published estimates of manioc acreages suggest they were of no importance in Uganda in 1917, but increased astonishingly during the next two decades. Government policy was largely responsible for the rise.

Two members of the Uganda Department of Agriculture commented in the late 1930's that: "During the decade following the war period [World War I] natives of . . . grain areas were encouraged to plant cassava on a large scale as reserve against famines . . . The result was that large areas of 'virgin' land were cleared and planted to this crop; the impetus thus given to cassava cultivation still remains to-day in most districts." [20]

It is not possible to ascertain how consistently this policy was followed. In the early period after 1917, there was a belief that years ending in the figure eight were famine years, based apparently on the fact that 1908, 1918, and 1928 were years of particularly bad crops over much of Uganda. There may have been a tendency to intensify the manioc campaign in the two or three years preceding a year of anticipated famine; such a reaction in 1936 and 1937 is recorded.[21]

Between 1942 and 1952, crops failed in one part or another of the country nearly every year, and the manioc campaign was vigorous. Not infrequently, compulsory acreages were imposed. Since 1952, manioc acreages have apparently been voluntary, and the crop appears to have gained a permanent place in the Ugandan diet.

Other Staple Foodstuffs Little can be established concerning the advances made by the millets and sorghums. Since these crops are the mainstay of peoples in the northern and southwestern

19. G. W. Nye and J. W. Jameson, "Cassava," in J. D. Tothill, (ed.), *Agriculture in Uganda* (London, 1940), 135.
20. *Ibid.*
21. Uganda Protectorate, *Annual Report of the Department of Agriculture* (1938), 3.

areas of Uganda, and seldom grown in the south and east, shifts in the population density of these two areas, either by migration or through differentials in birth rates, may be part of the explanation. Unfortunately, available data are too fragmentary and untrustworthy to check this. Government policy has been of some significance; in some areas stores of millet are maintained as insurance against famine.

The decline of sweet potatoes seems largely to reflect a change in preference, for this trend has occurred in spite of continued governmental campaigns to maintain large sweet potato acreages in some areas as famine reserves.

Reasons for the reduction in the importance of plantains have been touched upon in discussion of other crops: increased production of maize and manioc, and a drop in plantain yields over much of the period (caused by the banana weevil and neglect) are mostly responsible.[22] Competition from European-type beer may also have been important, for a sizable portion of plantain production is used in making plantain beer.

Summary

Data from food consumption surveys of twenty-eight rural communities in tropical Africa and from a sample census of African agriculture in southern Mozambique—the most reliable data presently available on rural food consumption in tropical Africa—suggest that George Peter Murdock's classification of the stable food economies of Africa fairly often incorrectly identifies the most important source of calories. His maps sometimes give stable foodstuffs incorrectly and almost always incorrectly identify some of the secondary foods.

It is here argued that his estimates cannot be precise because they depend almost entirely on the conjectures of various observers rather than on actual measurement of food consumption. Moreover, because no time references have been provided, Murdock's maps of staple food crops cannot be meaningful; there is strong evidence that the composition of African diets has changed considerably in some areas—perhaps many—in recent decades.

22. Uganda Protectorate, *Annual Report of the Department of Agriculture* (1950), 26–27, 235.

CODA

Toward an Interdisciplinary Method for African Culture History

Creighton Gabel

Associate Professor of Anthropology
Boston University

From the foregoing papers and the discussions about them, we have derived a number of conclusions regarding individual and combined approaches to the study of African culture history. Some of these are quite specific in application, others are more general, and still others can be voiced only in terms of suggestions for consideration in future work. A few are critical comments by which we hope to stimulate re-evaluation of certain tendencies or attitudes of earlier research. Undoubtedly, other efforts of this kind will produce further contributions to an integrated methodology for delineating culture history in Africa. We feel this modest attempt represents one step in that direction.

Archaeology. Archaeological investigation offers the most direct and systematic means of reconstructing the prehistoric past. While depending heavily upon other sources of information, it takes precedence—in the absence of adequate written records—as the single most important tool of the culture-historian. Its limitations can be summed up in terms of the fact that its range of cultural perspective is relatively narrow, for the hard data are confined exclusively to material culture. On the other hand, improved methods of description and interpretation and their consistent application can result in meaningful inferences about nonmaterial aspects of culture as well. How far such inferences can be carried with any degree of confidence depends upon sound theories of cultural continuity, change, and internal relationships, as supplied primarily by ethnology. These factors and the quality of archaeological work itself will serve to differentiate between the purely speculative and the probable. To attain the goal of making archaeology maximally productive then, there must be increased co-operation with other disciplines in the humanities, social sciences, and natural sciences. Fortunately, there is general recognition of this fact, and although this type of research sometimes fails to achieve reality, one sees some promise of further extensions and improvements.

Archaeology differs from its sister disciplines in that there are few practical restrictions on the time depths that can be considered. These few restrictions relate mostly to dating methods themselves which are subject to constant refinement. By and large, except where historical documents provide exact dates, archaeology is far more capable of establishing reliable absolute and/or relative chronological placement of cultural phenomena than other studies. Ironically, it is probably within Africa's recent past that archaeological dating can be most difficult; this is partly because the chronological requirements are more demanding and partly because the field work has been insufficient and so much of the prehistoric material has come from surface collections. As a result, gross errors in dating may result. Even radiocarbon dating is less useful for very recent periods, since the margins of error may be too great for dates to be meaningful. These difficulties are not so serious, of course, when written documentation can be brought to bear on the material directly or indirectly.

Historic archaeology can be seen to be more dependent upon oral or written sources; even the field work tends to be oriented to a considerable extent by leads from these sources. In a sense then, historic archaeology is the handmaiden of historiography as prehistoric archaeology is subservient to anthropology. A much more intensive and systematic approach to the former, so-called protohistoric archaeology, is long past due in Africa. One obstacle to this has been the well-known fact that the particular archaeological resources of an area strongly influence the kind of work carried on within its boundaries. In Africa, the magnet has been provided by early man and his handiwork, just as ancient civilizations have drawn most archaeologists in the eastern Mediterranean toward the historic end of the spectrum.

Similarly, in Africa as elsewhere, one notes the tendency to concentrate on certain types of sites. This is particularly true with respect to caves or, at later levels, stone ruins and fortifications. Neither of these types of sites will yield a complete cross section of the potential cultural material that might be extracted. With these observations in mind, some archaeologists have suggested that a broader examination of available archaeological sites be implemented. For one thing, the excavation of different types of sites within a limited region should reveal much detailed information about cultural adaptation on seasonal or other bases and about human ecology in general. Furthermore, in some areas at least, selective excavation of individual sites in terms of their preservation qualities should be feasible. Certain climatic or soil conditions tend to promote preservation of organic materials, which are extremely important in identifying subsistence patterns or generally filling in the range of material culture. Some preconceptions of site productivity might be arrived at, for example, with respect to water-saturation, aridity, and soil types identified through surveys and test excavations.

Although constituting a special problem in African studies, the matter of agricultural origins points up rather nicely both the need for interdisciplinary research and the results that might be obtained from co-operative field work. The achievements of Braidwood and his colleagues in Southwest Asia illustrate this very well, for the problem of identifying early agricultural developments is one that requires as much natural-historical as culture-historical evidence.[1] Implicitly at least, it is also recognized that considerable understanding of human behavior and cultural processes is fundamental to the work. Above and beyond these theoretical considerations, it has been found in practice that far more is accomplished when the archaeologist and his co-workers are in the field together where they can follow developments from day to day. Non-archaeologists find it easier to grasp the archaeologist's problems, and he is better able to channel his immediate efforts in useful directions with their help.

Since several members of the symposium have a vested interest in African agricultural origins, quite some time was spent in attempting to sort out the evidence pertaining to this question. The most notable disagreement in the symposium, in fact, arose over the basis of agricultural beginnings in Africa. Professors Murdock and Anderson, arguing primarily from botanical and ethnological evidence, express the opinion that certain plants were initially

1. R. J. Braidwood and B. Howe, *Prehistoric Investigations in Iraqi Kurdistan* (The Oriental Institute of the University of Chicago. Studies in Ancient Oriental Civilization, No. 31, 1960).

cultivated in tropical Africa without external influence. Desmond Clark, while acknowledging the African origin of some cultigens, appears convinced that the concept of plant domestication was introduced from outside Africa and adapted to local plants more suitable to a tropical environment. The essence of the argument, then, really centers about the question of cultural innovation and not so much about the geographical source of the plants (although many details remain to be worked out in this aspect of the problem). Clark maintains that the Sudanese setting for this presumed series of independent experiments with cultivation is one of the least well-known in Africa, archaeologically speaking, and that more substantive proof in the way of chronology, cultural details, and prehistoric botanical evidence is required. Dr. Miracle demonstrates how unreliable plant distributions may be for historical purposes.

There seems little possibility of settling this debate prior to more intensive archaeological exploration in the Sudan. Even then, it may be that no conclusive cultural evidence will appear (cf. the Natufian problem in Southwest Asia) and that only the acquisition of botanical specimens will serve as proof. On the other hand, careful excavation may well produce something in the way of preserved plants, pollen, carbonized matter, or vegetation impressions on ceramics. This likelihood might be increased through the use of specialized techniques such as flotation or, as Harlan has suggested, crushing potshards to locate bits of vegetation unintentionally incorporated into the clay. Clearly, more botanical work on the possibly African cultigens themselves and better dating of their occurrence outside Africa are also necessary.

There are those who contend that prehistorians frequently display a strong conservatism based on negative archaeological evidence; this is perhaps the result of seeing too many intricately-devised non-archaeological explanations of historical events disintegrate in the face of subsequent spadework. Archaeology is far from infallible as a culture-historical method, but more than any source (other than extensive written documentation), it puts the proof in the pudding.

Historiography. Rather little needs to be said of historical and archival data, but a few observations about them were made in connection with other sources. The value of written records, alone or in conjunction with other materials, is self-evident. From the point of chronological detail alone, their utility is immense. While the distribution and quality of historical documentation in Africa is spotty, there is a wealth of more or less untouched material. Without any doubt, a great deal of it is completely unknown, still tucked away in archives or private papers. Thus, it can scarcely be said that the historian has little with which to work. Of course, a good deal of material is inadequately published and therefore generally unavailable.

One very important use of historical and archival data is to provide background information for the anthropologist working in any given area. Certainly, to ignore these sources is inadmissible, even if many of them are open to criticism as being inaccurate, slanted, or incomplete. The fact remains that some of this material can be most enlightening, if only in terms of what the reader can see between the lines or extract as fragments here and there. Historiographers themselves, of course, have devised their own techniques of judging these materials in order to separate the wheat from the chaff. All culture-historians, and even specialists who are not particularly historically inclined, should take advantage of local historical data; they cannot afford to do otherwise.

A question which inevitably arises has to do with the position of historiography among other culture-historical disciplines in terms of relative accuracy and coverage. It seems to be a common belief that historiography is more "true" than other means of observation. One can only say in response to this belief that the most extensive documentation can leave room for differing interpretation about historical events and processes, as any historian would be the first to admit. Possibly it would be more to the point to say that written records have their blind spots just as other approaches do. In Africa especially, there is a notable lack of time depth for most areas which also must be taken into account. Many of these records are biased or ethnocentric, reflecting the particular interests or prejudices of the observers. Unfortunately, almost all of the historic accounts were written by outsiders, and these Arab or European writers usually describe the Africans from an Arab or European viewpoint; of course, some were more observant, sympathetic, or knowledgeable than others. From the culture-historian's standpoint, these accounts can be tantalizingly uninformative with respect to the peoples and cultures under observation, so that in this sense historical data are neither fully reliable nor sufficiently broad in coverage.

Ethnology. Cultural anthropology offers two primary methods of reconstructing culture history. The first of these is in the area of distribution studies which may establish or suggest culture contact and population movements. The degree of probability in any specific instance can be controlled to some extent by the application of methodological procedures defined essentially on the basis of the nature, complexity, and quantity of cultural traits compared and the geographical and chronological settings in which they occur. It goes without saying that supplementary evidence from independent sources greatly enhances the probability of conclusions reached. Some concept of relative chronology can be attained through the application of the corollary age-area hypothesis, although this badly needs reassessment (which might be accomplished by detailed studies of historically documented distributions, as represented by Margaret Hodgen's *Change and History*.) [2] It is worth emphasizing, in light of the many wide-ranging theories of diffusion and migration which involve American Indians in Polynesia, Indonesians in Mexico, Japanese in Ecuador, or Phoenicians in South Africa, that all of the evidence must carefully be reviewed before decisions are reached. This includes recognizing and weighing the negative evidence revealed by unconformable cultural elements, chronological discrepancies, or physical impediments.

The second major approach to historical problems is, in many ways, fraught with even more difficulties. This is the inferential reconstruction of past cultures by analogy with behavioral patterns among living peoples—projecting our knowledge of culture process into prehistoric settings, using material culture as the base

2. M. Hodgen, *Change and History* (New York: Viking Fund Publication No. 18, 1952).

line for comparison. This is a complex matter which is highly subject to uncertainties and fallacious reasoning. The range of interpretation runs the gamut from explanations of prehistoric tool manufacture to assessments of prehistoric social or political structures. Two complementary approaches are involved in this: the accumulation of ethnographic data bearing on the interrelationships of specific material and behavioral traits in existing cultures, and the formulation of acceptable theses concerning the identification and explanation of cultural mechanisms—such as diffusion or innovation—given certain constants and variables.

With respect to the first approach, most modern ethnographers tend to ignore some key subjects of interest to the culture-historian, including material culture, settlement patterns, and etnobotany. What can be done to overcome this problem is not immediately apparent. One possibility is that archaeologists or botanists themselves look into these matters, although this seems an inefficient way of obtaining the necessary data. It would be preferable to stimulate the interest of ethnographers. On the suspicion that their reticence results in part from a lack of sufficient professional rewards for such research, it was suggested that ways be found to provide recognized outlets for publication of these "less popular" materials. The ethnologists present also felt that greater cooperation might be gained by simply making ethnographers more aware of the need for such materials, so that they could either gather some of it while in the field or make their notes on the subject available to interested parties.

With regard to the more theoretical side of reconstruction, through ethnological inference, the obstacles are fundamentally more imposing. Even if we ignore the fact that anthropological work in Africa has so often been carried out by nonhistorical, sometimes even ahistorical, workers, we still must reckon with conflicting ideas about the ways in which cultures function and change. Here it is not so much a matter of finding relevant material as it is selecting the right methodological approaches. Barring a radical convergence of individual anthropologists toward a universally acceptable theory of culture, the culture-historian will be left to choose most of his own devices for interpretation.

His only guidelines at present can be an awareness of the all-pervasive nature of culture in human affairs, a good grasp of the facts pertaining to his particular problem, and familiarity with culture theory.

Oral Tradition. Among historians using narrative as a source of documentation, there is a greater sense of urgency than among those relying upon written records or archaeology, for the raw data are dependent upon human memory. This very facet of the subject also has led to a certain amount of skepticism regarding the reliability—and, therefore, the usefulness—of the historical evidence oral tradition is likely to furnish. Similar apprehensions are expressed, too, about the chronological depth achieved through the collection of traditions. Vansina meets these criticisms effectively with his carefully reasoned methodology; it is designed to (1) factor out uncertainties and errors, (2) define the precise range of information covered by oral tradition, (3) demonstrate the variations in reliability by subject matter and relative time depth, and (4) illustrate the use of oral traditions in relation to other historical approaches. Perhaps most importantly, oral tradition is treated in proper cultural perspective and its functions for the people studied are given full recognition.

We learn that the chronological scope of oral tradition extends over a period of at least a few centuries, making it particularly significant for the African interior. However, at such remote time depths one is more likely to learn of such things as population movements, political structures, technology, economy, or religion than of the arts, ceremonial life, or social structure. Considerably more precision, even for the latter items, can be achieved for the past century or so. Especially important is the demonstration of the complementary, rather than repetitive, nature of written and oral sources. Oral tradition is frequently more informative and detailed on certain subjects than contemporary written accounts, which are naturally not as vitally concerned with the events in question since they were written mostly by non-Africans.

While the subject is not dealt with in any detail, it is worth citing, in this vein, the potential value of oral literature. Its significance as an unconscious expression of cultural attitudes has long been perceived, but it should also be remembered that some historical information may be identifiable, either as explicit or implicit elements. The most obvious source of data is analysis of comparability in characters, plots, and themes in folklore, which can be profitably employed in distribution studies.[3] These same criteria may aid in establishing relative dates as well. It is of course necessary to utilize this literature with the same caution one would use in other forms of reconstruction. Popular clichés, for example, undoubtedly account for some broad similarities in folklore motifs, just as in oral tradition.

Art. The role of African art in historical reconstruction is subject to some limitations that do not always apply as rigidly in other areas of the world. There is, at this time anyway, a relative shortage of architectural and sculptural material which has an appreciable antiquity. Some exceptions, such as the Nok terra cottas or southern African stone building complexes, exist, but no such chronological depth can be assigned the woodcarving traditions which dominate West and Central African art. Whether any substantive evidence regarding their background can ever be obtained is highly questionable; the nature of the material makes it unlikely. But firmer ties may be ultimately established with sculpture in less perishable media, such as the Nok terra cottas. Otherwise, the art historian will be forced to rely primarily upon distributional data.

We are told that art offers four distinct means of probing culture history. Archaeologists in Africa already have made great use of the first, ethnographic content, because of the prolific rock art executed by Later Stone Age hunters. Neither style nor symbolism has been exploited as much (excepting some attempts to establish local dating sequences on stylistic grounds), probably because they require more sophisticated techniques of evaluation. Furthermore, symbolism cannot be objectively and confidently utilized without the support of historical documentation. In the

3. M. J. Herskovits, "The Study of African Oral Art," *Journal of American Folklore,* LXXIV:451–456 (1961), noted the occurrence of almost identical folktales among Africans as far apart as the Guinea Coast and Zambia.

analysis of African art styles, where the size of collections of any age is likely to be restricted, one probably has to reckon with an idiosyncratic factor of some importance. In general, this may be more true of the plastic and graphic arts than of most aspects of culture. It is emphasized that art reflects the culture producing it and that any significant alteration in style leads one to suspect marked changes in culture as a cause. Sieber's distinction between art styles and art types, with the accompanying comments on temporal and spatial extensions of people versus the spread of concepts, seems to have particularly significant implications for the study of culture history.

Distribution studies are badly needed in this area too, for historical purposes; these should include analysis of raw materials and manufacturing processes as well as analysis of the art forms as such. Art therefore is ideally to be compared on the basis of variation in subject matter, symbolism (where relevant), style, type, possible idiosyncrasies, and production techniques, in order to insure accuracy and full exploitation of the historical potential. Gross parallels alone are not sufficient unless there is incontrovertible evidence of other kinds to demonstrate contact or origins; this is an especially appropriate maxim in Africa where numerous wild misinterpretations have resulted from poorly conceived notions of art history.

Musicology. In the broadest sense, musicology contributes to culture history in two primary ways: through the description of instrument distribution and the analysis of music structure. The former, as a part of traditional trait-distribution studies, requires no additional comment beyond that advanced in Merriam's paper. Music structure, on the other hand, appears to provide a unique method within the arts of establishing cultural relationships on the basis of the qualitative and quantitative precision with which it can be described.[4] There is also the advantage that music can be exactly reproduced by standardized notation or recording, feature it shares with linguistics. Merriam pursues the analogy

4. Murdock also stressed the importance of Lomax's "cantometric" analyses (A. Lomax, "Song Structure and Social Structure," *Ethnology*, I:425–451 (1962), although these appear to be more behaviorally than historically oriented and also less quantitatively precise than Merriam's method.

with linguistics still further, suggesting it may be possible to work out a sort of "musicochronology," analogous to glottochronology and based on historically documented rates of change in European music. The largely subliminal nature of music style places music on a par with language in yet another respect. Along this line, Merriam has indicated elsewhere that song texts may reveal cultural attitudes not ordinarily expressed in conventional speech.[5]

Linguistics. The paper on historical linguistics in this collection sets out clearly a number of significant methodological considerations for the analysis and classification of languages. In discussion, it was particularly stressed that linguistic change is asymmetrical; that, first of all, certain types of vocabulary items change rapidly while others do not show nearly the same amount of flux. Secondly, it would seem that grammatical and vocabulary elements are not necessarily subject to the same rate of change in a given language; it would be interesting to look into this from the viewpoint that grammar can be considered the more subliminal element of language. One difficulty for the historical use of syntactic change is the problem of quantification. Secondly, syntax appears to change cyclically whereas there is no tendency for vocabulary change to repeat itself. Thirdly, one may find differing rates of change with respect to segmental (consonant, vowel) features on the one hand and tone or tempo on the other. Clearly, then, language cannot be taken as a single, homogeneous unit in studying historical relationships; and we can extend this observation to include other aspects of culture as well.

Another factor that enters into the matter of linguistic relationships is that of continuous variability or intergradation, wherein close analysis of languages sometimes shows that two supposedly unrelated groups do merge with intermediate languages in a manner prohibiting the establishment of a sharp boundary between them. Such a situation appears to arise, for example, between the Kwa and Central (Benue-Congo) languages in West Africa. Apparently the linguists have a problem here somewhat analogous to the biological one of racial classification.

The subject of glottochronology was considered briefly, the con-

5. A. P. Merriam, "A Prologue to the Study of the African Arts," Founders Day Lecture No. 7, Antioch College (Antioch, 1962), 28–31.

clusion being reached that it should be neither accepted at face value nor rejected outright. Lexicostatistics in general does serve to establish degrees of relationship between languages and may, at the same time, give an idea of relative time relationships. But employed alone as an absolute chronological device, glottochronology may be subject to too many variables to be wholly reliable. However, Greenberg's estimated timing of the outward spread of Bantu-speaking peoples from the Benue region into southern and Central Africa seems tenable on the basis of corroborative evidence from ethnology, archaeology, and radiocarbon dating. The question arose as to how one is to know whether this was caused by population movements or just the diffusion of language, inasmuch as language can spread without population dispersals. In this case, the answer appears to be fairly simple since this spread was so wide and appears to have been associated with other, archaeologically-identifiable culture traits (metallurgy, agriculture, Dimple-based and Channelled-Ware pottery) and probably a Negroid physical type.[6]

Physical Anthropology. Only one aspect of physical anthropology—human genetics—has received attention here. Studies of the sickling gene in Africa, in which Frank Livingston has played so prominent a role, constitute the best demonstration we have at present of the intimate relationship between genetics, culture, and environment. For better understanding of these complex interrelationships, much more detailed information is required on population densities, cultural factors, and natural selection in terms of their effects on genetic systems. Gene distributions and gene frequencies, taken alone, will tell us little in the long run. More factual evidence on gene flow, for example, is needed, and the existing ethnographic literature seems relatively uninformative in this respect. The ethnographer could make a contribution through the collection of precise quantitative description of social systems, with special attention given the effects of endogamy and exogamy on mating patterns, the recording of biologically accurate genealogies, and so on.

Perhaps most significant from a methodological viewpoint is the radical change in opinion regarding the place of human genet-

6. M. Posnansky, "Bantu Genesis," *Uganda Journal*, XXV:86–92 (1961).

ics in culture history which has transpired since W. C. Boyd published his *Genetics and the Races of Man* in 1950.[7] During the past decade, new data relating to the selective processes acting upon the ABO and other blood groups, as well as advances in knowledge concerning the abnormal hemoglobins, have introduced a new dynamism into genetic anthropology. The adaptability of human genetic systems (rather than their changelessness) and their dependence upon cultural and environmental factors have led us to realize that genetics seldom can be a very reliable historical tool in itself; instead, the geneticist is forced to depend upon the culture-historian in order to reconstruct the histories of specific genes.

Intensive research into African demography, ecology, and epidemiology—to which the anthropologist certainly can contribute —appears long overdue. Too much emphasis has been accorded the influence of disease and environment in the determination of African cultural change and development. Some of these "facts" do not stand up to examination now, and probably fewer still would do so in the light of careful scientific appraisal. What applies to genetics also applies to these—cultural patterns may well be the cause rather than the result.

Ethnobotany. It is heartening to find that our colleagues in botany likewise insist upon an evaluation of cultural factors in discussing the origin, uses, and diffusion of plants. Apart from the obvious fact that cultural determinants control the spread of different crops, we are shown that they may even alter plant genetics appreciably. Man's intrusions and activities can stimulate or retard the viability of plants and cause the formation of new varieties and species. The history of cultivated plants must be related to culture history, and, conversely, the development and dispersal of crops can tell us something of population movements and culture contact.

It is now generally recognized that Africa may have been the source of origin for a number of cultigens, even though the exact processes of domestication and diffusion are but vaguely understood. Vavilov's concept of centers of diversity suffers a reversal at the hands of Dr. Harlan, who feels that diversity may be en-

7. W. C. Boyd, *Genetics and the Races of Man* (Boston, 1950).

hanced by certain environmental or cultural circumstances more than by the passage of time. Since the linguist or ethnologist usually views diversity as a function of age, this seems to be a point worth noting in regard to the uncritical application of cultural techniques to biological problems, and vice versa.

Searching for plant ancestors may be more difficult than most realize also. Harlan's "compilospecies," in which modern crop-weed complexes absorbed their ancestors, and his insistence that weed forms are not necessarily the ancestors of crop forms will not make the culture-historian's task easy with respect to tracing agricultural origins and dispersals.

Harlan, solicited for comments on the practical difficulties faced by botanists and zoologists in historical reconstruction, indicated that pollen analysis, genetics, and cytology at present offer better approaches for the botanist than plant anatomy, which is often utilized but is not yet well enough developed as a subject. Zoologists, on the other hand, have been able to employ genetics less effectively and rely primarily upon comparative anatomy.[8] In both disciplines, there is a serious shortage of personnel who are interested in and trained for these historical problems. As a result, most of the work is done as spare time research by self-trained individuals.

As far as pollen analysis is concerned, much of the work in Africa has been carried out by Professor E. M. van Zinderen Bakker at the University of the Orange Free State. (The results of African palynological research are published periodically by that university as reports entitled *Palynology in Africa*.) One of the greatest practical problems arises in trying to build up a pollen bank for comparison of the many African floras. Up to the present, most of the work has been done with montane or savanna-type floras rather than with those of the lowland forests, but some correlations with Pleistocene and post-Pleistocene climatic fluctuations are beginning to emerge in the former areas.[9]

8. But see R. Singer and H. Lehmann, "The Haemoglobins of Africander Cattle," *Occasional Paper No. 18 of the Royal Anthropological Institute*, 1963.

9. E. M. van Zinderen Bakker, "Carbon-14 Dates," *Current Anthropology*, III:218 (1962); E. M. van Zinderen Bakker and J. D. Clark, "Pleistocene Climates and Cultures in North-eastern Angola," *Nature*, CXCVI:

We may now turn to a consideration of certain central issues that appear to crosscut several of these fields or to infiltrate the whole area of culture-historical research.

In the first place, there are some peculiar circumstances which have tended to flavor the interpretation of culture history in Africa. One of these is the relatively shallow time depth for adequate written documentation, coupled with the fact that both linguistic and archaeological classifications are more newly developed there than in many parts of the world. Ethnographic work, as already indicated, frequently has been carried out by investigators with very little sense of, or interest in, historiocity. Especially in archaeology and ethnology, it is hoped that techniques found useful elsewhere will be adapted to the African field. A positive contribution for use in both these fields was advocated for a long time by M. J. Herskovits.[10] This has to do with the methodological approach to ethnohistory established by North American anthropologists in tracing the background of Indian tribal groupings. In the Southeast and Southwest United States particularly, very substantial returns have been gained from this direct historical approach; it would seem that the methods devised by Sapir and his successors in the United States could be applied to Africa with profit.

African culture history has suffered to some extent, too, from certain well-ingrained biases that seem not to have affected any other region so severely. Apart from the attitude of earlier European observers that Africans had no history until the colonial period, there is the idea that Africans have been particularly backward in cultural development or even that most of them have been culturally stagnant. The anthropologist is impressed with neither of these arguments, for he can readily discern the complexities of

---

639–642 (1962); D. A. Livingstone, "Age of Deglaciation in the Ruwenzori Range, Uganda," *Nature,* CXCIV:859–860 (1962); J. D. Clark and E. M. van Zinderen Bakker, "Prehistoric Cultures and Pleistocene Vegetation at the Kalambo Falls, Northern Rhodesia," *Nature,* CCI:971–975 (1964).

10. M. J. Herskovits, "Anthropology and Africa—A Wider Perspective," *Africa,* XXIX:225–238 (1959). For a specific application, see C. Fuller, "Ethnohistory in the Study of Culture Change in Southeast Africa," in W. R. Bascom and M. J. Herskovits (eds.), *Continuity and Change in African Cultures* (Chicago, 1959), 113–129.

African life and, in at least some instances, can show how these have altered through time. A further belief, to which even some anthropologists pay homage, is that Africa has been a "closed area," not subject to influences from the outside world. Closer examination of this hypothesis shows Africa to be a part of an Old World culture area and that as such it has given as well as received.

As Lewis indicates, the imprudent confusion of race, language, and culture in Africa—something that seems to occur much less often any longer in other areas—still detracts from meaningful interpretations of Africa's past. Constant reminders of this infraction of scientific method are seen in the variable usage of terms such as "Hamitic."

It was generally agreed that in dealing with African culture history, as well as that of any other region, little is to be gained from attempts to dichotomize different kinds of historical approach into "genuine" and "inferential" types. All forms of historical inquiry are inferential to some degree; furthermore, there is variation within each of the individual approaches, depending on the data with which one has to work. A more reasonable attitude would be to subject all materials to rigorous examination and to define methods for so doing. In doing so, we need to create more interest in crucial linkages of an interdisciplinary nature, as we have already mentioned. No single field can provide all the evidence; even on a full-scale interdisciplinary basis we can only hope to improve the level of probability.

All the authors demonstrate and stress the omnipresence of cultural factors in treating their materials—this appears to have been the salient outlook of the symposium. Most of the queries pertaining to consideration of the cultural element lead sooner or later to questions of defining culture contact and cultural change. There is, for one thing, the problem of differentiating migration and diffusion which has long plagued the culture-historian. Migration in particular appears to have been overworked as an explanatory device for cultural change in Africa, as in the Hamitic question. The core of the problem, if it is recognized as a problem, is the identification of past population movements. Archaeologically, such movements can be most easily confirmed when the change is marked by a sharp and rapid break in previous traditions as reflected in material culture. One can identify the first farmers in central Europe or southern Africa as immigrants because technology, subsistence, and settlement patterns suddenly undergo radical alteration in the archaeological record. In each of these cases, this assumption is strengthened by geographical and chronological considerations. Ethnographic distributions may provide some evidence of population movements as opposed to diffusion but, as with oral tradition, such evidence is more convincing when substantiated by linguistic similarities.

The question of the *speed* of migration over large areas was raised also, since some migrations seem almost unbelievable as actual events in terms of the distances involved. While one certainly must subject these to careful scrutiny, we may be too prone to scoff at the possibility of very widespread movements of people, who in fact sometimes travel great distances for seemingly trivial purposes. Also, ecological considerations are important here. In a zone of similar environment, it is conceivable that culturally well-adapted groups would fill it up rapidly and thus effect marked changes over a large area in a short space of time.

Distinguishing both migration and diffusion from innovation as agents of cultural change and differences is another headache encountered by the culture-historian. Again, however, there are some guiding criteria: geographical and ecological probabilities, trait complexities, the total cultural context of the traits concerned, and chronological considerations. There are also behavioral problems to be considered with respect to either change through contact or change through innovation. We must ask ourselves what circumstances are likely to promote inventiveness in relation to particular changes; what actually happens when different peoples come into contact. Can "six men and a very active boy" from an alien culture effect any real change in a densely settled area with its own cultural traditions? What is the probability of multiple independent developments of agriculture or iron metallurgy?

Thus, in examining the possibility of agricultural origins in Africa, we must consider the behavioral mechanisms theoretically involved in such an innovation, the ecological and cultural context in which it is supposed to have taken place, the geographical and chronological position with respect to currently known areas of agricultural origin, and the relative chronology of the presumed African cultigens inside and outside of Africa. Murdock, looking at these criteria, is convinced that the plants were initially and independently cultivated in Africa and does not believe stimulus diffusion will serve as an explanation; he questions the likelihood of hunter-gatherers, in contact with farmers, accepting the process of cultivation but not the plants themselves.

In addition to these problems, there is the matter of acculturative and internal variations in cultural change. In viewing different aspects of culture, the question of differential change arose several times. It appears almost certain that there are distinct levels of change, stability, and transfer within or between different aspects of culture, although rather little has been done to define them properly. Much might be learned of this through case studies of subliminal cultural factors, such as linguistic syntax, music structure, art styles, folklore motifs, or kinship systems; technology, iconography, political institutions, vocabulary, and other elements seem to operate on a level of greater consciousness. In any studies involving acculturation, it is highly desirable that we investigate more examples that do not include Western influences.

Lack of sufficient distributional data in almost all fields contributing to African culture history is a serious shortcoming; but we also have the problem of defining just what kinds of studies it is that we need. Some balance must be achieved, at least in relation to particular problems, between over-generalized and over-detailed studies that lead nowhere. Likewise, we require reassessments of historical reconstruction via distributions, including an up-to-date appraisal of the age-area hypothesis and its utility in this light.

Clearly, many of these problems are interdisciplinary in scope and can only be overcome by a joint frontal attack, if for no other reason than that no single means of investigation can stand alone. No single culture-historical question, in fact, can be fully answered solely within the perimeters of one disciplinary approach.

DATE DUE	
MR 7 '73	